The Rise, Fall, and Rebirth of Chicago: The History and Legacy of America's Third Largest City
By Charles River Editors

A monument at the site of the Battle of Fort Dearborn

About Charles River Editors

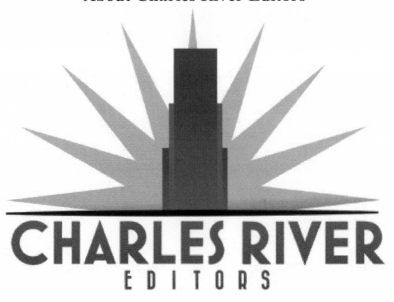

Charles River Editors is a boutique digital publishing company, specializing in bringing history back to life with educational and engaging books on a wide range of topics. Keep up to date with our new and free offerings with this 5 second sign up on our weekly mailing list, and visit Our Kindle Author Page to see other recently published Kindle titles.

We make these books for you and always want to know our readers' opinions, so we encourage you to leave reviews and look forward to publishing new and exciting titles each week.

Introduction

Harper's Weekly **illustration of the Great Chicago Fire**

The Making of Chicago

"We had marched half a mile, when we were attacked by 600 Kickapoo and Wynbago Indians. In the moment of trial our Confute savages joined the savage enemy, Our contest lasted ten minutes, when every man, woman and child was killed except 15. Thanks be to God I was one of those who escaped. First they shot the feather of my cap, next the epaulet from my shoulder, and then the handle from my sword. I then surrenered to four savage rascals. The Confute chief, taking me by the hand, and speaking English said, 'Jordan, I know you, you gave me tobacco at Fort Wayne. We wont kill you, but come and see what we will do with your captain;' so leading me to where Wells lay, they cut off his head and put it on a long pole, while another took out his heart and divided it among the chiefs, and eat it up raw. Then they scalped the slain and stripped the prisoners, and gathered in a ring with us fifteen poor wretches in the middle. They had nearly fell out about the divide, but my old chief the White Racoon, holding me fast…they made the divide and departed to their towns." – Walter K. Jordan, one of the men present at the Battle of Dearborn

The area that became Chicago caught the eye of European settlers as far back as the 17th century, when the French explorers Marquette and Jolliet found that waterways in the area connected the Mississippi River to the Great Lakes. The area became an outpost for the fur trade long before it was settled, and Fort Dearborn was built there in 1803.

Throughout the 19th century, American settlers pushing across the Western frontier came into contact with diverse American tribes, producing a series of conflicts ranging from the Great

Plains to the Southwest, from the Trail of Tears to the Pacific Northwest. Indian leaders like Geronimo became feared and dreaded men in America, and Sitting Bull's victory over George Custer's 7th Cavalry at Little Bighorn was one of the nation's most traumatic military endeavors.

The ongoing fighting between white settlers, militias, Army units, and Native Americans not only bled into the War of 1812 but was one of the main causes of it. Many Americans chaffed at the fact that along the Northwestern frontier, the British in Canada were supporting Indian resistance to American settlement. So-called "War Hawks" from that region in Congress pushed for a declaration of war, and many hoped that a war would not only stop Indian depredations but evict the British from Canada and lead to completion of some unfinished business from the American Revolution, namely Canada joining the U.S.

Although there had been treaties and seemingly cordial trading between the Native Americans and the new settlers in that area, recent fighting in nearby areas like the Battle of Tippecanoe less than a year earlier kept all sides on edge, and the British aim to maintain a barrier between America and Canada by propping up Native American tribes led to a controversial battle in the Illinois Territory at Fort Dearborn, a fort built along the Chicago River, shortly after the War of 1812 broke out. When the war came, the close proximity of British forces compelled American military officers in the area to attempt to evacuate the garrison at Fort Dearborn, but misunderstandings and a lack of time resulted in Potawatomi warriors ambushing the soldiers and several civilians before they could retreat back to Fort Wayne, Indiana. In the wake of cutting down dozens of whites, the Potawatomi laid waste to Fort Dearborn itself, and though the fighting was technically a battle, in America the Battle of Fort Dearborn was known colloquially as the Fort Dearborn Massacre.

Thus, even as the conflict was relatively minor in scale, it had far-reaching implications. Although Americans wouldn't be able to rebuild the fort until after the war ended, the memory of what occurred there increased the hostility towards Native Americans and helped ensure policies of removing the area's natives were popular among settlers. The most noteworthy result was the way in which events there culminated in the Treaty of Chicago, which would allow the creation of one of America's biggest cities and the westward movement of the region's native inhabitants.

Though it started as a 300 person settlement in 1832, Chicago's location near the Great Lakes and its access to the Mississippi River turned it into a major trading city overnight. The city became even more important when railroads were constructed to connect the country, making it the first major city in the "West" during the mid-19th century. By 1871, the original 300 person settlement was now home to about 300,000 people, and Chicago had become the first major city built by Americans rather than European colonial powers

Thus, it had taken less than 40 years for the new settlement of 300 to become a city of nearly 300,000, but it only took two days in 1871 for much of it to be destroyed. On the night of October 8, 1871, a blaze in the southwestern section of Chicago began to burn out of control. The popular legend is that a cow in Mrs. Catherine O'Leary's barn had kicked over a lantern and started a fire. The story blaming the cow was a colorful fabrication, but the fire itself was very real, lasting almost two whole days and devouring several square miles of the city. The fire was so powerful that firefighters could not put it out, due to dry conditions, stiff winds, and the fact the city was mostly made of wood.

Walking around Chicago today, it's easy to forget about its past as a rural frontier. That's due in no small part to the way Chicago responded to the Great Fire of 1871. Immediately after the fire, Chicago encouraged inhabitants and architects to build over the ruins, spurring creative architecture with elaborate designs. Architects descended upon the city for the opportunity to rebuild the area, and over the next few decades they had rebuilt Chicago with the country's most modern architecture and monuments.

Chicago recovered well enough within 20 years to win the right to host the World's Fair in 1893, which was commemorating the 400th anniversary of Columbus' discovery of the New World. Covering nearly two square miles, the Fair's grounds created a city within a city, and Daniel Burnham was in the middle of it all. With several other noteworthy architects, including Louis Sullivan, Burnham designed the layout of the grounds and the construction of the buildings on the ground. During the late 19th century, "neoclassicism" was in vogue, and American architects designed buildings incorporating ancient Greek and Roman architecture.

With its white colored buildings, the Fair stood out from the rest of Chicago, earning it the label "White City." Throughout 1893, it attracted millions of visitors, allowing Chicago to introduce itself to foreign visitors and reintroduce itself as a major American city.

As the 19th century gave way to the 20th, it became apparent that Chicago's prominence had ended, and it moved ahead with the rest of the nation, a city among many. The 20th century brought new problems, not just for Chicago but for the entire nation. Labor, crime, and race relations rose to the forefront as major issues faced by cities throughout the nation, and how Chicago handled these issues shaped the city throughout the century, transforming the Windy City permanently.

The Making of Chicago: The History of the Windy City in the 19th Century

Note

The spellings of Native American tribes used in this are compliant with current spellings preferred by the tribes, with the exception of quotes where the spellings sometimes differed.

The Northwest Territory

The site of Fort Dearborn was across the river from where French explorer Père Jacques Marquette reportedly spent the winter of 1674, near Chicago. René-Robert Cavelier, sieur de La Salle, commonly referred to as LaSalle, proclaimed the entire Mississippi River Valley for France, and called it Louisiana. LaSalle was in Chicago as late as the summer of 1683, as he was busy making the rounds between the forts he had established and his supply base in Montreal.[1]

Marquette

---

[1] Currey, J S. *The Story of Old Fort Dearborn*. Chicago: A.C. McClurg, 1912. Print.

LaSalle

Over the next century, North American lands were transferred from Native Americans to the United States, Britain, and France at a dizzying rate. Then there were tribal lands, land tracts that specific tribes considered their own, further confusing the matter. It did not help that these tribes spoke their own languages and had their own customs and attitudes toward land use.

The area that served as the location for Fort Dearborn became part of the Northwest Territory in 1783, when land was ceded to the United States by the British Empire, France and Ireland according the terms of the 1783 Treaty of Paris.[2] The territory included parts of modern day Ohio, Indiana, Michigan, Wisconsin, Minnesota, and Illinois.

---

[2] "Treaty of Paris." West's Encyclopedia of American Law. 2005. *Encyclopedia.com.* 17 Mar. 2016<http://www.encyclopedia.com>.

Northwest Territory (1787)

Remainder of MN added via 1818 Convention & Louisiana Purchase

Great Lakes

Mississippi River

Ohio: 1803
Indiana: 1816
Illinois: 1818
Michigan: 1837
Wisconsin: 1848
Minnesota: 1858

Ohio River

The Northwest Territory

That 1783 treaty accomplished a number of other significant things. In addition to freeing the original 13 colonies from Britain, the treaty guaranteed fishing rights to the inhabitants of the United States, regardless of whether or not they were Native American residents. The signees of that treaty agreed that the Mississippi River would, from that time on, be free and open to subjects of Great Britain as well as the United States.

The treaty also settled debts. All prisoners of war were to be freed on both sides, provided it did not cause destruction of property. The treaty included the phrase "or carrying away any Negroes or other property," very much reflecting the attitudes of the European immigrants who claimed ownership of both places and people. Moreover, the document guaranteed freedom of travel to anyone who had not taken up arms against the United States. It promised a "firm and perpetual peace" between the Britannic Majesty and the United States.

Nonetheless, peace remained out of their reach. One of the reasons for this was that the treaty overlooked the original owners and inhabitants of the lands in question. Within two years, the decade-long Northwest Indian War started, beginning in 1790 when Miami chief Michikinikwa led the Miami, Wyandot, Delaware, Potawatomi, Shawnee, Chippewa and Ottawa tribes in war against the U.S. in an effort to drive the white settlers' arrivals back east of the Ohio River.

A lithograph of Michikinikwa, also known as Little Turtle

On September 30, 1790, General Hamer and the tribesmen clashed at the Miami Village, in Ohio. The U.S. military burned 300 wigwams and killed 120 Native Americans. By comparison, the U.S. military suffered worse, with 183 dead soldiers and 31 more wounded,[3] but it nevertheless served to arouse a sense of anger and indignation in most Native Americans against all whites. In that sense, these hostilities also set the tone for the eventual massacre at Fort Dearborn.

Both sides regrouped and clashed again on November 4, 1791, at the Miami Village. Determined to annihilate the native population, the military arrived with 1,400 soldiers led by Gen. St. Clair. Again, the military failed. While the 1,500 Miami Indians suffered perhaps no loss, there were 631 U.S. deaths.[4]

Nearly three years later, on August 20, 1794, General "Mad Anthony" Wayne's soldiers attacked the Miami Village once more, during which 900 Americans fought unsuccessfully against some 2,000 Indians. The Indians, with an unknown number of losses, were overwhelmed,

---

[3] Strait, N A. *Alphabetical List of Battles, 1754-1900: War of the Rebellion, Spanish-American War, Philippine Insurrection, and All Old Wars with Dates; Summary of Events of the War of the Rebellion, 1860-1865, Spanish-American War, Philippine Insurrection, 1898-1900, Troubles in China, 1900, with Other Valuable Information in Regard to the Various Wars*. Detroit, [Michigan: Gale Research Co, 1968. Print.

[4] *Ibid.*

and there were 107 American soldiers killed or wounded. In the annals of history, this event became known as the Battle of Fallen Timbers, which was a reference to Wayne's military style.

Wayne

After that campaign, Little Turtle, Blue Jacket and a whole host of other allied chiefs and warriors from the Wyandots, Delawares, Shawnees, Ottawas, Chippewas, Potawatomis, Miamis, Piankeshaws, Weas, Kickapoos, and Kaskaskias agreed to cease hostilities and sign a humiliating treaty dictated by Wayne. Under the Treaty of Greenville's terms, a boundary line between the Native Americans and whites was drawn on the map, with the Indians being pushed back well north of their former Ohio River villages and hunting grounds. What was left to the

Indians to live on was only northwestern Ohio, and not even all of that area, as certain specified enclaves were reserved for whites at strategic geographical locations and around military posts and with the guarantee of white transit through Indian lands or along waterways. The Indians were forced to pay with their ceded lands for the injuries and expenses incurred by the U.S. in warring against them. The only thing tangible they received in return was a lump sum of goods delivered at Greenville, along with an annuity of trade goods in perpetuity, part of which was to come in the form of livestock, tools and compensation for teaching them the art of farming in the white manner. Furthermore, pursuant to the Jay Treaty in 1795, Great Britain gave up its forts at Detroit and elsewhere in the Northwest Territory that it had held since the Revolution, making it harder for the natives to continue to resist the Americans.

Although many Native American leaders signed the Treaty of Greenville and thought it was the right thing to do in order to save at least some of their land and sovereignty, not all of the Indians present were willing to sign onto such an arrangement. One who refused to sign was a Shawnee warrior named Tecumseh.

19th century depiction of Tecumseh

Ongoing Friction

The first set of laws for the Indiana Territory was published on January 12, 1801,[5] and that same year, Major Gen. William Henry Harrison was appointed as the first governor of the Indiana Territory. Harrison would later become president after being in command of the forces at the Battle of Tippecanoe in November 1811, but at that time, there were only a few American

---

[5] *The Laws of the Indiana Territory: 1801-1806, Inclusive.* Paoli, Ind: Throop & Clark, 1886. Print.

settlements in Indiana Territory. One was Clark's Grant in what is now Ohio; another was Vincennes, Indiana; and the third was a tract along the Mississippi River in southern Illinois. There were about 5,000 residents between the three settlements. The remains of the vast area to the north and northwest were either inhabited by, or in possession of, various Indian tribes.

Harrison

According to one source, British agents, remaining after the independence of the new country from the commonwealth, continued to incite hostility among the Native Americans against the United States.[6] This same source asserts that it was the British who established forts and factories beyond the agreed-upon boundaries of the United States in 1783, which helped the British retain a monopoly on the fur trade. To further the British cause, they spread rumors that the Americans were only interested in taking the land away from the Native Americans.

At the same time, the U.S. government attempted to "civilize" the Native Americans in place with the hope they would become farmers. The government reportedly intended to purchase all land that became U.S. soil and was "endeavoring to introduce among the Indians the arts of civilized life instead of exterminating them by the sword." The British convinced the Native

---

[6] DAWSON, Moses. *A Historical Narrative of the Civil and Military Service of Major-General William H. Harrison, and a Vindication of His Character and Conduct As a Statesman, a Citizen, and a Soldier. with a Detail of His Negotiations and Wars with the Indians, Until the Final Overthrow of the Celebrated Chief Tecumseh, and His Brother the Prophet.* M. Dawson: Cincinnati, 1824. Print.

Americans that the government was being duplicitous in hopes the Native Americans would abandon arms, making them an easier conquest. The British also supplied liquor to the Native Americans; King George III made sure they were well-supplied with rum.

Shortly after Harrison was appointed, the chiefs of most of the nations inhabiting the region visited him to express injustices committed by the white people against them. "They said their people had been killed, their lands settled upon, their game wantonly destroyed, their young men made drunk, and cheated of the peltry which were the means of procuring for them the necessary articles of clothing, arms, and ammunition to hunt with."[7]

For his part, Harrison was hesitant about enforcing the law for a practical reason. The region was so large that the precise boundaries of the Territory, or of the United States, were not certain. He proposed that the land be surveyed immediately in order to create fixed boundaries. "If the obvious construction of the treaty of Greenville is to be taken as the ground upon which our claim to land in this country is to be supported, I believe it will be found to be much more extensive than is generally imagined."[8]

There were additional issues, such as the fact that the deed to one tract of land by the Indians to Monsieur De Vincennes (Vincennes, IN) was lost. Protecting Vincennes was a high priority, and four companies of the Kentucky militia were called into service whenever necessary to do just that.

Even in 1801, there was no record proving that either the French or the United States had paid the Indians for the land. Harrison was aware that the plan was for the U.S. to take the entire, fairly large, tract of land, even though a promise had been made in 1793 that the U.S. claim would not be very extensive. The natives said "it had been often foretold to them that the period would arrive when their country would entirely be usurped by the white people, making any land discussion a source of contention."

Harrison did advocate that, where there was a clear boundary, whites who violated the treaties should be punished. He understood that the influx of Europeans was decimating wildlife, and that "[m]any parts of the country which had abounded with game at the conclusion of the general peace of 1795, scarcely contained as many as would subsist a few Indians that would pass through them." Kentucky settlers were especially known for killing deer, bear and buffalo for their skins, and abandoning the meat.

Then there was the cultural aspect in regards to land ownership. When a salt spring was being considered for sale to the U.S. government, the chiefs could not agree on whether to sell such a sacred site or whether it should be given as a gift. An agreement to the terms of exchange was a sticking point, and in the end, the chiefs agreed that the United States could use the salt spring for as long as the Great Spirit produced water there.

---

[7] *Ibid*

[8] DAWSON, Moses. *A Historical Narrative of the Civil and Military Service of Major-General William H. Harrison, and a Vindication of His Character and Conduct As a Statesman, a Citizen, and a Soldier. with a Detail of His Negotiations and Wars with the Indians, Until the Final Overthrow of the Celebrated Chief Tecumseh, and His Brother the Prophet.* M. Dawson: Cincinnati, 1824. Print.

As this suggests, land ownership and land use was at the heart of the issues of the day. The boundaries were unclear, so the compensation might be a sale or an annuity for use of the land or a spring, or the exchange could be in the form of a gift. Then the U.S. government would reconsider; for example, after that salt lick site was leased to the U.S. by treaty, the government later decided to purchase the land. In September 1802, another treaty was signed stipulating that the U.S. would relinquish all claim to lands in the neighborhood of Vincennes, save for one tract. The same treaty signed over the salt lick on the Saline River to the United States "for ever."[9]

Throughout this time, Harrison respected the Native Americans' patience. "All these injuries, the Indians have hitherto borne with astonishing patience. But though they discover no disposition to make war upon the United States at present, I am confident that most of the tribes would eagerly seize any favorable opportunity for that purpose. And should the United States be at war with any of the European nations, who are known to the Indians, there would probably be a combination of more than nine-tenths of the northern tribes against us, unless some means are made use of to conciliate them."[10] It was a premonition that came to fruition in the form of the War of 1812, one which would come about with the Fort Dearborn Massacre.

On July 15, 1801, Harrison saw another phenomenon when the local tribes, known as the Piankashaw, the Weas, and the Eel River Miami, merged themselves into a single tribe. They would become intoxicated frequently, with as many as 30 or 40 drunks stabbing everyone they met, breaking into houses, killing cattle and hogs, and breaking down fences. Worse yet, they killed each other without mercy, and without repercussion from their own people. Perhaps worst of all for the tribes, they tended to murder their own chiefs, especially those who were in communication with Harrison and the U.S. government, and they eventually killed all of the Piankashaw and Wea chiefs who agreed to the Treaty of Greenville.

In response to these actions, Harrison ordered the militia to reestablish the peace, and on a more positive note, Harrison observed that the Delaware tribe was attempting to become farmers, settling on the White River branch of the Wabash River. The Delaware chiefs asked for farm equipment, cows, and hogs. Similar requests came from the Kaskaskia, Piankishaws and the Pottawattami.

In a lesser known event, Chief Sun of the Potawatomi, asked for a "coat and hat of the uniform of the United States" for himself and other chiefs of his nation, and Harrison requested that the Secretary of War meet that request. Ongoing government annuities were being paid to the tribes, based on population. Harrison kept an inventory and warned that the Kickapoo, "a strong warlike nation," were not receiving their proper proportion allowed. In fact, the Kickapoo of the Prairie had never received compensation at all. In response to this, they became horse thieves.

The Sacs, a large nation living on the banks of the Illinois River, had not signed any treaty with the U.S. They maintained that they had mistaken the time, and did not attend the treaty signing.

---

[9] DAWSON, Moses. *A Historical Narrative of the Civil and Military Service of Major-General William H. Harrison, and a Vindication of His Character and Conduct As a Statesman, a Citizen, and a Soldier. with a Detail of His Negotiations and Wars with the Indians, Until the Final Overthrow of the Celebrated Chief Tecumseh, and His Brother the Prophet.* M. Dawson: Cincinnati, 1824. Print.

[10] *Ibid.*

They refused to return stolen horses or prisoners until they were put on equal footing with the rest of the tribal nations. Harrison advised that the Sacs should be included in the treaty because they reportedly held white and Negro people as prisoners and, without the Greenville Treaty, the U.S. government had no recourse for rescuing them. American law did not apply to the Sacs' lands if they were not included in the treaty as a result.

Harrison, more than anyone, was aware of the chaos and anarchy in the Indiana Territory. Courts were slow to assemble, so if a crime was committed beyond the Indiana Territory, the perpetrator could not be charged by U.S. law. This became more of an issue as whites settled farther and farther west. No one was really sure whether an Indian could be punished by U.S. law for a murder committed on their native lands, or on a road leading through their country.

Again, cultural perceptions came into play. whites were known to kill Indians under the delusion that it was not murder and therefore did not merit punishment. To the new arrivals, anyone who was not white was less than human and did not warrant humane treatment. The criminal system was inconsistent, and even murderers were given various treatment ranging from execution to release. During one murder case, a judge was told that he had the power to try a man, and condemn him to death if he was inclined, but pardoning was uniquely the power of the government. All matters of legal justice were further muddied by the unclear designation of boundaries, and under whose reign the jurisdiction fell.

Harrison was determined to change things. He arranged for superintendents on behalf of the U.S. government, to reside among the tribal nations in order to report on the adherence to law. The superintendents were required to report on all circumstances relating to the Indians every three months.

On this matter, President Thomas Jefferson, was torn. He sincerely, if naively, believed he was being magnanimous in his acculturation solutions. On February 27, 1803, Jefferson wrote, "Our system is to live in perpetual peace with the Indians."[11] He also said that, "When they withdraw themselves to the culture of a small piece of land, they will perceive how useless to them are extensive forests." Suffice it to say, even Jefferson sincerely believed in the efforts of the U.S. government to nudge the Native Americans toward an agricultural life. He never suggested that European immigration be slowed or in some other way controlled. He clearly advocated European settlement of what is now the lower 48 states of the United States of America.

Like many Europeans, Jefferson acknowledged that Native Americans were different from whites. But rather than embrace or honor the differences, Jefferson and Harrison both set about to change Native American culture. In addition, all that pristine wilderness, stretching farther than either of them would ever venture, was just too tempting to ignore.

In April, 1803, Harrison set out to visit all the Indian villages on the Wabash River. He had issued precise instructions, and was surely expecting to see them carried out, maintaining fairness and justice in every respect. When Harrison arrived at Fort Wayne, he discovered the agents there had made no preparations for providing edibles for the treaty meeting. Goods he had sent to the fort had failed to arrive. Some of the supplies that formed part of the annuity

---

[11] *Ibid.*

payments—payments made on a regular basis, serving as rent for Indian lands– arrived so damaged they were virtually unusable. Harrison continued to visit American forts, discovering that such issues were rife throughout the territory.

At the same time, there was conflict between the tribes, primarily sparked by an Indian with the name of The Owl, who was urging the tribes not to meet with Harrison. He also managed to divide Miami chiefs Little Turtle and his nephew, Jean Baptiste de Richardville, from their own tribes, even though they had been the recognized leaders. After much struggle, Harrison and the other tribes agreed to sign yet another treaty.

By the end of April 1803, all of Louisiana had been ceded to the United States by France, for 60 million francs. Louisiana was then annexed to the Indiana Territory, placing it under the oversight of Gov. Harrison. The governor was determined to prevent the British agents, who had caused so much friction with their lies, from moving into Louisiana. In spite of the treaties that were in place, the British continued to indirectly attack the U.S., inciting Native Americans with lies, and plying them with liquor, in spite of U.S. law.

Part of the challenge for the U.S. was that it was difficult to keep all of the tribes and their alliances straight, which was imperative in order to stipulate who owned which lands and when. In an attempt to resolve the confusion over what was a tribe and what was a related tribe, the Treaty of Grouseland declared, with or without their consent, that the Miami, Eel River and Weas tribes were a single nation. One reason this was important was that the tribes traded lands between themselves. Article 5 of the Treaty of Grouseland dictates, "The Putawatimies [sic], Miami, Eel River, and Wea tribes, explicitly acknowledge the right of the Delawares to sell the tract of land conveyed to the United States by the treaty of the eighteenth day of August, eighteen hundred and four, which tract was given by the Piankashaws to the Delawares, about thirty-seven years ago."[12] Harrison was, among other things, trying to solve a 37-year-old land dispute.

In June 1803, a number of Indians, primarily Potawatomi, attacked the Kaskaskia tribe. Those who attacked were not included in any treaties, and presumably were exempt from all the peace efforts of those legal efforts.

Harrison also discovered that Europeans living among the tribes often intentionally mistranslated messages, speeches and treaties. There was also talk of a British agent who had caused mischief when he had visited the various tribes, telling them they no longer owned their land, when they rightfully did, according to American law. He went as far to tell them that he was there to take possession of their land, on behalf of the United States. That agent singlehandedly sparked an Indian revolt. A group of Potawatomi, led by Turkey Foot, chased him down the Mississippi River with the intent of killing him. When he escaped, they killed a Frenchman instead.

Harrison, not knowing quite what to do about the matter, and hoping to end it, called for the militia from Kentucky to be ready for a clash. In the meantime, Turkey Foot was taking scalps,

---

[12] Kappler, Charles J. *Indian Affairs: Laws and Treaties.* , 1904. Print.

not for himself, but for a British agent who was collecting scalps taken by the Potawatomi and other tribes.

To convince everyone, especially when they were so dispersed, to follow a single law and to honor white morals and ethics, was seemingly impossible. Indians continued to murder individual whites in areas that might or might not be American-owned land, and even if the land had been ceded to the U.S., law enforcement was virtually missing from the vast remote areas of the country to follow through.

All the while, Harrison's men continued marking the boundaries of the Vincennes tract and the rest of the territory. Lines needed to be drawn, as there were laws and treaties to be honored and enforced. It was time there was a fort in Chicago.

Building a Fort

According to the 1795 Treaty of Greenville, a tract, six miles square at the mouth of the Chicago River, was ceded by Native Americans to the United States, and in early summer 1803, Gen. Henry Dearborn, the Secretary of War at the time, ordered construction of a fort at the mouth of the Chicago River. It was one of many to be constructed in remote areas, and staffed with the military. In what was perhaps a touch of irony, Dearborn had fought against the Six Nations in 1779, and three years before the massacre at Fort Dearborn, he had been involved in the plan to remove the Indians beyond the Mississippi.[13] The coming events around the fort bearing his name would make it obvious that implementing such removal plans would not be a simple matter, and the early efforts at Fort Dearborn soon proved disastrous.

---

[13] *U.S. Army Center of Military History*. U.S. Army Center of Military History, 2013. Internet resource.

Dearborn

The Fort Dearborn site was as remote as any fort; there were no roads to the area, but since it was located at the mouth of the Chicago River where it entered Lake Michigan, water transportation was an option. Thus, a U.S. government transport vessel brought building materials and supplies from Detroit to the fort.[14] The vessel, the schooner *Tracy*, was small, but the commanding officer, Captain John Whistler, sailed aboard the *Tracy* with his wife and their two children. Their eldest, Lieutenant William Whistler, had recently been married, and his wife accompanied them onboard as well. The captain's younger son, George Washington Whistler, was about two-years-old at the time.[15] 66 men and three commissioned officers departed from Detroit as well, but on foot.

Capt. Whistler was an Irish immigrant who had come to the New World to fight on the side of the British during the Revolutionary War, but he remained in the U.S. after the war, and participated in U.S. Army campaigns against the Indians in the West. Now, he was charged with building and staffing the first fort at the site that would eventually become the bustling city of Chicago.

---

[14] Currey, J S. *The Story of Old Fort Dearborn*. Chicago: A.C. McClurg, 1912. Print.
[15] *Ibid.*

Despite its small size, the *Tracy* was a sight to behold. An estimated 2,000 Indians visited the site while the *Tracy* was there, calling her 'a big canoe with wings.' Five days later, the *Tracy* departed.

Evidence of earlier forts, probably built by the French, have been found on the site of Fort Dearborn. The six square miles were never surveyed and did not even show up on all maps. Reportedly, the Indian tribes refused to permit construction of another fort on Lake Michigan. As one writer commented, "We conclude that had the fort been built at St. Joseph there would have been no Chicago."[16]

There was a house across the river from the site of the fort, built sometime prior to 1779, by Jean Baptiste Point du Sable. Originally from Haiti, Du Sable is considered by some to be the original founder of the settlement that became Chicago. Du Sable married a Potawatomi woman and was loyal to the French and the Americans. In 1779, the British arrested him and took him to Fort Mackinac. The Du Sable house had become important in the fur and grain trade. Du Sable sold his house to another fur trader, Monsieur Le Mai, and Du Sable and his wife returned to his wife's people by the time Fort Dearborn's construction began.

---

[16] Currey, J S. *The Story of Old Fort Dearborn*. Chicago: A.C. McClurg, 1912. Print.

Du Sable

The intention was for the fort to be occupied by 1798. Instead, it stood empty for five more years, and when the fort was complete it was named Fort Dearborn, in honor of the Secretary of War. At first, Winnebagoes, Miami, Ottawas and Chippewa were all known to pass through the area, but the principal tribe residing near Fort Dearborn in 1803 was the Potawatomi. They continued to live there until their final removal to the reservations in 1835.

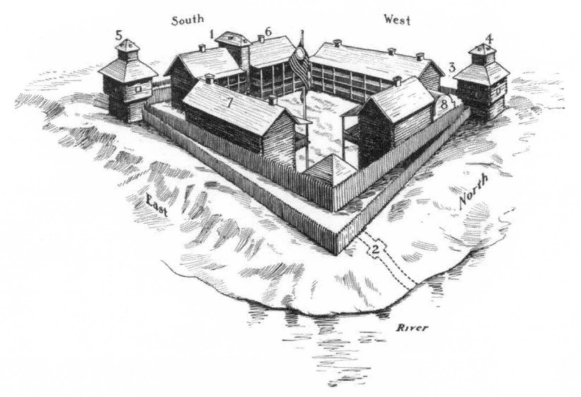

A rendition of the original Fort Dearborn

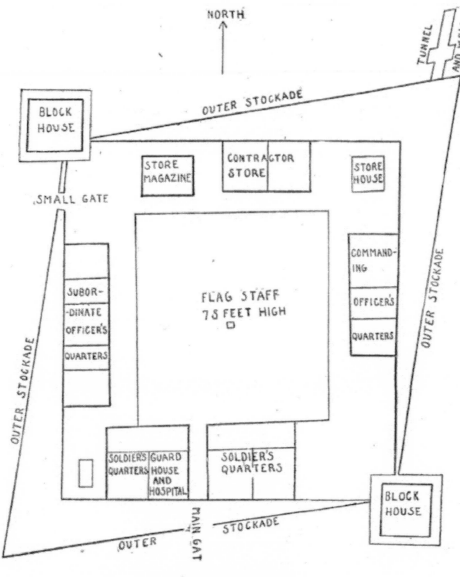

A model diagram of the fort

In 1804, after the fort was garrisoned, Le Mai sold the Du Sable home to John Kinzie when he and his family arrived from Detroit that fall. Mrs. Kinzie had been kidnapped as a child and adopted as a sister by a chief of the Seneca tribe, but after four years, she was returned to her parents, and the family moved to Detroit. Later in life, Mrs. Kinzie wrote a book, *Wau-Bun*,[17] containing a firsthand history of the occupation and destruction of the first Fort Dearborn.

Kinzie renovated the house, landscaping the slope that faced the river. The "Kinzie Mansion" was a familiar object in many early Chicago portraits. The Kinzies lived there until 1828, save for the war years between 1812 and 1816.

---

[17] Kinzie, Mrs. John H. *Wau-bun: The "early Day" in the North-West*. Chicago: Lakeside Press, 1932. Print.

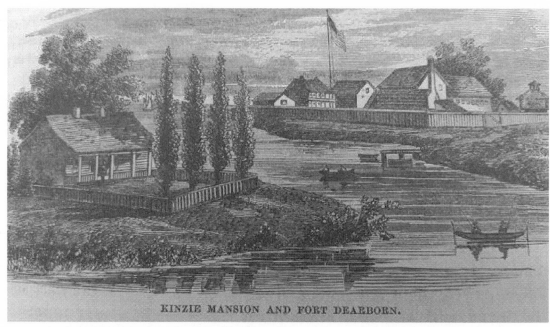
KINZIE MANSION AND FORT DEARBORN.

A sketch depicting the Kinzie Mansion with the fort in the background

Kinzie was familiar with the new frontier. He learned to speak the native languages and was respected as a fair and reliable dealer. He moved to the Du Sable house with the intention of increasing his business holdings. It was because of his business dealings with the tribes that he and his family were spared a few years later when the massacre occurred.

Antoine Ouilmette, a Frenchman with a Potawatomi wife, lived in a cabin near the building site beginning around 1790. Ouilmette's wife received a tract of land some 14 miles from the mouth of the Chigago River as the result of a treaty. Today, that site is the Village of Wilmette.

Another cabin outside the fort was owned by a Mr. Pettell. A trader named Guarie had conducted a trading house there since 1778, and the North Branch of the Chicago River was known colloquially as the River Guarie in his honor.

Outside the fort and to the west, American soldiers built a double log house, composed of two log houses connected by a single roof, with a walkway between them. This became the Agency House, also known as the United States Factory. It was used as a storage facility for goods to be sold to Indians under government regulations, often in exchange for furs. Government employees, who served as blacksmiths or laborers, lived in residential cabins nearby.[18] The Agency protected the Indians from unethical traders. Among them were traders who sold liquor to Indians, in violation of strict U.S. laws on the matter. According to the laws of the Indiana Territory, violation of this law could result in a $100 fine per offense, which was a large sum of money at the time.

The John Burns family lived a bit farther away on the north bank of the Chicago River, and four miles southwest of the fort was Hardscrabble, or "Lee's Place," owned by Charles Lee. He and his wife and two children were among the first farmers in the Chicago area to break the prairie and turn the sod into cropland.

---

[18] *Ibid*

A farmhand, Liberty White, and a discharged French soldier named Debou, assisted Mr. Lee and his 12-year-old son to keep the farm afloat. The Lee family used the nearby river for transporting their crops and other goods to market. The canoe was also their only means of communication.

The new fort was destined to bring numerous people to an area where only a handful of non-Indians had taken up residence, but the construction at Fort Dearborn was no easy task. The *Tracy* had to anchor half a mile from shore due to a sandbar, so cargo was moved ashore by loading it onto smaller boats. Once ashore, provisions were stored in tents until the buildings could be constructed.

Soldiers cut timber, but there were no horses or oxen available to haul them. The soldiers dragged the logs with ropes and floated them down river. There were some trees very close by, but to the south was the Grand Prairie of Illinois, extending hundreds of miles. It has been said that this spot was the only place where the Grand Prairie bordered Lake Michigan.

By the end of the first summer, the soldiers had built two blockhouses at opposite corners of a stockade enclosure, with a second row of pickets surrounding the fort. There was an underground passage leading from the parade ground to the river bank on the north side of the fort. The passage was used to obtain water, in addition to the well inside the garrison.

Acquiring More Land and New Enemies

On August 13, 1803, Kaskaskia chiefs signed yet another treaty. The Kaskaskia, who had been all but ignored in previous treaties, now ceded to the United States the entire area formerly possessed by all the tribes of the Illinois Indians, with the exception of the Peorias. With the stroke of a pen, 8 million acres of land was transferred from its native inhabitants to the United States.[19]

The question of the leasing of the salt spring on the Saline River was no longer a sticking point. The Kaskaskia sold it to the U.S. government, along with most of what is now the State of Illinois. Altogether, the Kaskaskia sold these vast lands for $896.66. Given inflation, the amount would have been a little more than $14,000 in today's currency; throughout Illinois today, that represents the cost of about a half an acre.

The Kaskaskia was a highly civilized tribe, having embraced European customs. Most of the tribe had been baptized and received into the Catholic Church. Along with this latest treaty, the U.S. promised to build a house for the chief on a 100-acre lot, and to pay $100 a year toward the support of a Catholic priest for the tribe, to perform as both priest and schoolteacher. The government gave $300 toward the construction of a Catholic church.[20]

By 1804, the renegade Piankishaws signed a treaty acknowledging the right of the Kaskaskias to sell the Illinois lands to the U.S. government. That year, three Europeans were murdered by

[19] DAWSON, Moses. *A Historical Narrative of the Civil and Military Service of Major-General William H. Harrison, and a Vindication of His Character and Conduct As a Statesman, a Citizen, and a Soldier. with a Detail of His Negotiations and Wars with the Indians, Until the Final Overthrow of the Celebrated Chief Tecumseh, and His Brother the Prophet.* M. Dawson: Cincinnati, 1824. Print.

[20] *Ibid.*

the Sack tribe. There were also contentions between the Sack and Fox tribes and the United States.

Harrison negotiated yet another treaty, transferring the largest tract of land, delineated by a single treaty, since the settlement of North America. The treaty effectively turned 51 million acres of fertile soil--largely Illinois lands--into U.S. property. The price was less than $3,000, with $600 being paid to the Sacs, and $400 to the Foxes.

The treaty also promised the protection of tribes on U.S. land, provided the tribes agreed not to sell any land to any other entity. The law was intended to treat Indians and Europeans alike. The Sacs and Foxes were guaranteed the right to continue to hunt on the ceded property, and if they no longer wanted unlicensed traders to live among them, they had the right to have them removed.

There was also a provision in the treaty for the U.S. to build a fort on a two-mile square tract of land. The U.S. planned to build a factory or a trading house where goods were to be sold at lower prices than the private traders were charging.

Things seemed fine until August 1804, when Little Turtle incited the Potawatomi, the Miami, and the Eel River Indians over the Illinois lands treaty, and they questioned who had the right to cede land to the U.S. This was doubly important because when the population of the Indiana Territory had reached 5,000 free male inhabitants of voting age, the territory was to be split in two. According to law, this would mark the beginning of government by representation in these new lands. The requirement for being a representative in territory government stipulated that the representative needed to be a resident citizen of the United States for at least three years. In addition, he had to be a resident in the district for three years. Plus, he was required to own at least 200 acres within the district. Voters were required to be citizens and residents for only two years. Only men, specifically white men, were allowed to be elected.

Elsewhere across the territory, fortifications were being built. Fort Mackinac had been constructed in 1781, prior to the Treaty of Greenville, which subsequently averred that the fort was within the boundaries of the United States. Although the British did not accept this and refused to withdraw their troops, two companies of U.S. troops arrived and took possession of the fort in 1796.

One of the most important events in the region took place in 1805 with the rise of Tecumseh's Confederacy. As Native Americans continued to struggle as more whites arrived, and answers for their plight were widely sought but hard to come by, accusations of witchcraft flew among the Indians. This was a situation ripe for what anthropologists call "revitalization movements." In times of severe social and cultural distress and unwelcome transition imposed by outsiders, some people may conclude that the fault is their own, and that they must return resolutely to the old ways, which would somehow make everything better. Among Native Americans having to confront the white invasion from colonial times into the 19th century, there were a number of such cases, the most famous of them being the Ghost Dance that took hold among the Great Plains Indians during the 1880s and contributed to the massacre of more than 200 Lakota followers by the 7th Cavalry at Wounded Knee in 1890.

The genesis of a major revitalization movement among Indians in the region occurred one day in April 1805 when an often-drunken and not so highly-regarded 37-year-old Shawnee healer named Lalawethika fell into a profound death-like state. Ironically, Tecumseh would become one of the most famous Native Americans in history, but it came about only because his influence increased when he started advocating a rising religious movement led by his brother Lalawethika. Lalawethika (One Who Makes a Great Noise), Tecumseh's younger brother, was born after his father Puckshinwa's death at the Battle of Point Pleasant (1794), Lalawethika was also soon abandoned by his mother, leaving him an orphan. He never learned the vital warrior skills of hunting and fighting and also lost an eye in a hunting accident. Quickly becoming a wayward soul lost in the cracks of his tribal society, Lalawethika was prone to heavy drinking and was known by other Native Americans as a braggart, with his poor looks and behavior resulting in him growing up as an outsider.

One night, while heavily under the influence of alcohol, he fell into a fire and was thought to have died, but he unexpectedly awoke and told of a vision he'd received from the *Master of Life*, the Algonquin title for "god" (the Shawnee shared the Algonquin language group and likely their foundational religious beliefs). After this vision, Lalawethika changed his name to Tenskwatawa (the Open Door or One with Open Mouth) and began preaching. He declared he would never again drink any whiskey. Other Indians should also reject the white man's firewater. He called for a return to traditional Indian habits and dress, denounced the practice of witchcraft (and launched a witch hunt that led to several executions), and advocated a sort of communism of property. Indian women should stop marrying with white men, and young people should respect and care for their elders. As a sign of converts' acceptance of his spiritual message, Tenskwatawa ordered Indians to throw away their old medicine pouches.

Charles Bird King's portrait of Tenskwatawa

While mainly a nativist movement, several aspects of this new spiritual movement seem to have come from Catholicism, most notably the use of prayer beads and the use of a confessional. The traditional practice of men taking multiple wives was banned in favor of monogamy. At the same time, however, Tenskwatawa's movement, unlike some other nativist movements, did not advocate that followers give up their firearms and return to chipping flints for spears and arrows.

With his popularity and following growing, Tenskwatawa founded a settlement for his small group of followers near present-day Greenville, Ohio, where he preached that the white settlers were the spawn of the "Great Serpent", which according to Algonquin tradition came from the sea and stood for evil powers. The Prophet, as Tenskwatawa became known, was a follower of Delaware holy men who had died years early but had predicted that the white men would be overthrown by supernatural powers. This apocalyptic theology was a precursor for the Ghost Dance movement that would rise among Native Americans of the Great Plains and Southwest near the end of the nineteenth century. When the Delaware (Lenape) chief Buckongahelas died of either influenza or small pox during 1805, Tenskwatawa declared it an act of witchcraft and began a witch-hunt, which resulted in the deaths of several Delaware "witches."

By this time, Tecumseh had already participated in many of the battles to try to stem the white tide since the Revolutionary War. He had refused to sign the Treaty of Greenville in 1795 when respected older chiefs like the Shawnee Chief Blue Jacket had given up resistance and signed. At first, Tenskwatawa denied having any political goals, but in the skillful hands of Tecumseh, the spiritual and cultural movement begun by Tenskwatawa was reworked into a renewed effort at pan-Indian unity to confront white encroachments on Indian lands. As such, the spiritual and political aspects of their joint brotherly movement were mutually reinforcing, and it would cause substantial problems for the U.S. in the coming years.

Tenskwatawa, the Shawnee Prophet, established a base for himself and his followers at the symbolically-charged site of Greenville, Ohio, where the 1795 treaty giving up all the Indian lands in southern Ohio had been signed. At this settlement, the Prophet's fame spread, and the number of his followers increased when, due to a tip from some white surveyors, he was able to give a dramatic display of his spiritual prowess by successfully predicting the day and the hour of a total solar eclipse that occurred on June 16, 1806. The Greenville village consisted at its peak of 60 dwellings and a large frame council house where the Prophet preached his message and the assembled Indians danced and prayed. Hundreds of pilgrims came from as far away as the Potawatomis in Michigan and the Chippewas on Lake Superior.

Meanwhile, the Shawnee, many of whom still remembered Tenskwatawa as the old Lalawethika, and some of whom were trying to follow a path of assimilation, were sharply divided. The important chief Black Hoof, who led a band of Shawnee in an enclave in Wapakoneta, Ohio (where they were practicing white-style farming and seeking peaceful coexistence), was particularly antagonistic to the separatist renewal message. However, the highly-respected Shawnee war chief from the 1790s, Blue Jacket, threw his support behind the movement and spent time at Greenville. The powerful Potawatomi shaman, Main Poc (Crippled Hand), also lent them his support.

In the spring of 1808, to move further away from whites and closer to his now numerous western followers, the Prophet and his followers headed west to a new base. A site was chosen in northwestern Indiana on bluffs above the west bank of the Wabash River near the mouth of its tributary, the Tippecanoe River. This location was already important as a confluence of trails from the days when the French had operated a nearby fort and trading post. This new spiritual village became known as "Prophetstown," and at its peak, Prophetstown became the largest multi-tribal gathering of Native Americans ever assembled in the Midwest and Great Lakes region, boasting as many as 3,000 inhabitants. Along with a council house as had existed at Greenville, Prophetstown provided a "House of the Stranger" to accommodate the large stream of visitors, some of whom decided to stick around the area and set up their own villages nearby. According to a white observer who found the sight menacing, the men at Prophetstown combined spirituality with the practice of military sports, using war clubs, bows and arrows and other traditional Indian weaponry.

As Shawnees, the two brothers were well-positioned to be the organizers and leaders of a pan-Indian movement. Since the invasion of North America by Europeans in the 17th century, the Shawnee had broken into fragments and moved around considerably, with some of them spending time in Pennsylvania and others living as far south as Alabama before trying to reunite again in the Ohio region. Due to these splits, the Shawnee had made contact and entered into relations with many other tribes, and Tenskwatawa and Tecumseh seem to have had relatives among the southern Creek tribe, probably through their paternal grandfather and quite possibly through their mother. The Shawnee, who had no dominant chiefs for their nation as a whole, also had a lot of experience with practicing consensus-building within their own tribal structures.

Upon learning of the Shawnee Prophet, Governor Harrison investigated and denounced his teachings as totally fraudulent. He urged the Indians to stop the horrific practice of burning accused witches, demand proof of the Prophet's supposed powers, and cast him out of their midst. The greatest fear of Americans was that the British in Canada, with war clouds growing between the U.S. and Great Britain in 1807 over issues related to neutrality on the high seas, would encourage the Indians to rise up. Harrison suspected a sinister British hand lay behind the Prophet and his message of Indian renewal and unity, and there is evidence that British agents were indeed being active again in the region. Writing directly to the chiefs and headmen of the Shawnee in August 1807, Harrison told them they were receiving "bad advice" from the white people beyond the lakes and reminded them of their previous betrayals by the British. He warned them about being deceived by a "fool [the Prophet] who speaks not the words of the Great Spirit but those of the devil, and the British agents."

The Prophet responded that he was sorry Harrison had been listening to "bad birds." He denied having spoken with the British, or that he had sent for distant Indians to come to his place, insisting that the latter had come of their own accord "to listen and hear the words of the Great Spirit." In June 1808, the Prophet again wrote to Harrison, calling him "My Father" and saying that he had been misrepresented. He denied any hostile intentions towards Americans and offered to visit Harrison to reassure him once the new village was finished. He asserted it was against the Great Spirit for him ever to lie, and he ended by asking for material assistance -- some corn for the women and children until the harvest arrived. In reply, Harrison wrote that it was true that he had heard some bad reports: "But the solemn assurance which you now give me that you have no other object but that of making your people happy and live in peace with all mankind have in a great measure removed my prejudices and if your subsequent content agrees with your present profession you may rest satisfied that you will continue to enjoy the favor and protection of the 17 fires." At the same time, Harrison issued a stern warning not to have anything to do with the British or there would be unwelcome consequences.

In the summer of 1809, Tecumseh took the message of unity to the Indians in Ohio, the first of what would be a series of outreach travels covering thousands of miles. Tecumseh traveled around the lower Great Lakes region that year, visiting Native American leaders and using his considerable rhetorical and oratorical skills to urge them to stop cooperating with invading Americans and threatening to kill those leaders who continued to do so. As his best biographer,

John Sugden, put it, the Treaty of Fort Wayne on September 30, 1809 was "a treaty too far" for Tecumseh. Signed by chiefs of the Delaware, Potawatomi, Miami and Eel River tribes, the treaty ceded a large territory north of Vincennes to the U.S. government. When some of the Miamis were reluctant at first to sign, Harrison put aside his previously avowed scruples about mixing up Indians with liquor and served some of it to them on this occasion. Tecumseh was outraged that the chiefs, including the former Miami resistance leader Little Turtle, had been bribed into giving up 3,000,000 more acres of land. Tecumseh now felt that all the treaties made since the Treaty of Greenville were invalid, and that the natives should refuse the annuities. If older chiefs had become corrupted by annuities, then younger warriors should push them aside and take over power. In fact, after the signing of the Treaty of Fort Wayne in 1809, Tecumseh warned Native American leaders who had signed the treaty that those who attempted to carry out the terms would be killed.

The real goal for Tecumseh was to convince Native Americans to unite in a multi-tribal confederacy strong enough to halt westward expansion by settlers. Numerous tribal leaders agreed to join Tecumseh's confederacy, but even those who did not lost warriors and families to the Prophetstown settlement. It's believed that in 1808, Tecumseh had about 5,000 warriors at his disposal, scattered about the region in villages or at Prophetstown, and that same year the British in Canada approached the leader hoping to form an alliance. The British and U.S. had seen their own tensions rise over issues like trade and the British impressments of American sailors, and they would fight the War of 1812 a few years later. At this time, however, Tecumseh refused the offer and gradually grew to become the leader of the confederacy, much of which was built upon the religious appeal of his brother's purification movement.

One of the seminal and most legendary moments of the era took place in 1810 when Tecumseh and about 400 warriors marched to Governor Harrison's house to meet with Harrison, where they demanded that the Treaty of Fort Wayne be rescinded and that American settlers should not try to begin settling the newly acquired territory. With his warriors dressed up and wearing war paint, Tecumseh and the group unnerved the townspeople at Vincennes, but Harrison kept calm, even as the situation seemed about to deteriorate. Harrison denied any need to nullify the Fort Wayne treaty and dismissed Tecumseh's ideas regarding Native American land ownership, insisting that the United States could deal with tribes individually and that if the Indians were truly one nation they'd all speak one language. In response, Tecumseh became more agitated and said to the governor, "You have the liberty to return to your own country ... you wish to prevent the Indians from doing as we wish them, to unite and let them consider their lands as common property of the whole ... You never see an Indian endeavor to make the white people do this ... Sell a country! Why not sell the air, the great sea, as well as the earth? Did not the Great Spirit make them all for the use of his children? How can we have confidence in the white people?"

Grouseland (Harrison's house)

Since Tecumseh was speaking a language Harrison was unable to understand, at this point one Shawnee working with Harrison and the settlers signaled that Tecumseh appeared to be whipping up his group and possibly intended to kill Harrison. As that Shawnee cocked his pistol, Harrison pulled out his sword, and the garrison defending the town added to the stand-off. Seeking to ensure cooler heads prevailed, Potawatomi Chief Winnemac urged Tecumseh and the warriors to leave peacefully, and as they left Tecumseh told Harrison he would ally with the British unless the Treaty of Fort Wayne was rescinded.

A depiction of the famous encounter between Tecumseh and Harrison

Tecumseh met again with Harrison in August 1811 at the latter's home in Vincennes after Harrison summoned him to answer for the murder of some settlers. Tecumseh assured the governor that he and his Native American brothers at Prophetstown intended to maintain peace with the United States, but that there were still differences between the two sides that had to be bridged. With nothing being settled at the meeting in 1811, both sides could sense war was looming on the horizon.

Tecumseh was now convinced "the only way to stop this evil is for the red man to unite in claiming a common and equal right in the land, as it was first, and should be now, for it was never divided." Thus, after his August meeting with Harrison, Tecumseh left his brother Tenskwatawa in command of his confederate allies and traveled south, eventually meeting with each of the "Five Civilized Tribes". The Cherokee, Choctaw, Muscogee, Chickasaw, and Seminole were so-named because European American settlers considered them civilized as a result of the fact they had largely adopted colonial ways.

After consulting with the Secretary of War in Washington, Governor Harrison decided that a show of military force was needed. Word had come to him that Tecumseh was away and would not be back for some time, so this seemed liked a good opportunity, he told Secretary Eustis, for breaking up the Indian confederacy. The original plan Harrison proposed was to go with a sufficiently-sized force, which the Indians would not feel they were able to attack, to the top of the new purchase of land under the Treaty of Fort Wayne and to build a fort there. This would show that the land was now irrevocably under U.S. control. If that show of force was not effective in dispersing the Prophet's party by demonstrating to them that the Prophet was unable to defend them, Harrison proposed proceeding farther northward to Prophetstown itself in order to seize some hostages to enforce compliance with his demands.

Ironically, Tecumseh was not present for the most famous battle of the war against his confederacy, the Battle of Tippecanoe. Along with a hand-picked delegation of six Shawnees, six Kickapoos and six Potawatomis, the Shawnee leader was still on an extended six-month trip through the South visiting with the Creeks, Choctaws, Cherokees and other tribes to try to gain their support for his plan of a greater pan-Indian confederacy. On his way back north, Tecumseh also visited tribes in Missouri where he was present for the great earthquakes. According to some accounts, when he returned to Indiana in January 1812, he was exceedingly angry with his brother for having launched a war before he felt their plans were sufficiently matured.

After the Battle of Tippecanoe, the natives had precipitously abandoned Prophetstown and left behind all kinds of supplies in the form of corn, hogs, poultry, numerous brass cooking kettles. A few guns, some of which were apparently gifts from the British, were still in their original coverings and had never been used. The herd of cattle brought along by the soldiers for meat had been driven off by the Indians, so the soldiers had to subsist on horse meat or whatever they were able to plunder from the village. Harrison had his men burn the town and its contents and then marched his troops back to Vincennes, stopping at the blockhouse on the Vermillion River to put his wounded men into canoes. From his headquarters near Prophetstown on November 8th, Harrison had already sent a dispatch to the Secretary of War claiming the battle was a "complete and decisive victory."

The Start of the War of 1812

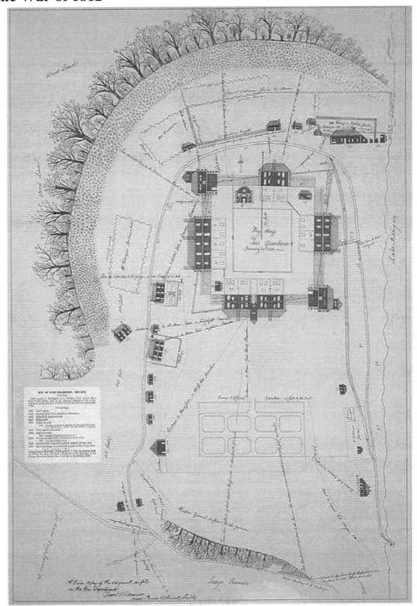

John Whistler's map of Fort Dearborn made in the 1800s

In 1810, while Harrison had his hands full with Tecumseh, Capt. John Whistler was ordered to another post. He was replaced by Capt. Nathan Heald, a much younger man who did not seem to relish the post. The fort was remote, and the 35-year-old bachelor found himself surrounded by still younger officers. Within days of arriving at Fort Dearborn, he wrote to Detroit requesting a reassignment, but it was not granted. He later married to a young woman he had briefly met two years earlier. Conversely, Mrs. Heald loved the wildness of the place and the people.

Capt. Heald had a reputation for being a stickler about detail, and he insisted on instant and implicit obedience. Even without taking that into account, life was always a challenge at Fort Dearborn. In early 1812, John Lalime, an interpreter at the fort, attacked John Kinzie, and while grappling for Lalime's knife, Kinzie and Lalime were both wounded. Finally, Kinzie took hold of the knife and used it to kill Lalime. Kinzie was charged with justifiable homicide as a result.

Meanwhile, the local tribes and the white immigrants had remained amiable until 1811, when things started to heat up between the Americans and Tecumseh's Confederacy. At the time, the Indians near Fort Dearborn seemed peaceable and congenial toward their white neighbors, and they continued to migrate seasonally and camp in wigwams along the Chicago River without disruption. The main interest whites had in the Indians was in their competition to sell them supplies in exchange for furs or 25 lb. packages of maple sugar. This trade situation allowed whites to overlook the seemingly odd behavior of the Indians. For example, native men, women and children would wander aimlessly about, peering into the windows of any white house. If they wanted to enter a house, they did not knock; instead, they walked in, uninvited, and squatted on the floor.

On June 18, 1812, Congress voted to declare war against Great Britain. It was formally proclaimed by President Madison the next day, but as Porter Hanks, Lieutenant of Artillery, would soon point out, the war was hardly being fought by the British. Native Americans and Canadians were fighting on their behalf, or at their bequest. Altogether, around Fort Mackinac in Michigan, there were only 46 British troops, and four of them were officers. The British troops were aided by 260 Canadians, but the bulk of them were Native Americans. A few dozen Sioux, Winnebagoes, and Menomonees went into battle alongside 572 Chippewas and Ottawas. Thus, there were 1,021 British, Canadian and Native American troops fighting against just 306 Americans.

Madison

By July, Little Turtle died, but Fort Mackinac and Mackinac Island were lost after Hanks surrendered the fort on July 17, 1812. He was killed a month later by a shot from the Canadian side at Fort Detroit.[21]

That same summer, trouble came to Fort Dearborn. On one of the hot summer days, seven soldiers obtained leave to go fishing. They canoed past Lee's Place and greeted Lee and the farmhands. Afterward, perhaps a dozen Indians entered the house and squatted, in their usual way, but the residents were wary because something seemed suspicious about these squatting men, particularly the fact they were not wearing the familiar clothing and tribal paint of the Potawatomi.

The soldiers fished until dark, when they paddled back toward the fort, but as they neared, they heard cannon fire. Lee's Place was silent by the time the concerned soldiers went ashore to the darkened house, where they found a grisly scene.

Unbeknownst to them, hours earlier Charles Lee and his young son had made their way toward their waiting canoes after the squatting natives appeared. Pretending to gather hay from haystacks across the river, the men made their way toward safety. They disappeared behind the haystacks, ran for the woods, and made their way to the fort, but they heard two gunshots before they arrived. The Indians who had been squatting at Lee's Palace had fired at Liberty White and Frenchman Deboou.

[21] Kelton, Dwight H. *Annals of Fort Mackinac*. Chicago: Fergus Print Co, 1882. Print.

The Lee men continued past the home of John Burns. It happened that Mrs. John Kinzie was there, delivering Mrs. Burns's baby. They warned the women of the impending danger. Mrs. Kinzie ran as fast as she could back to her own home, just outside the fort, and the rest of her family joined her, quickly paddling canoes across the river and dashing inside the walls of the fort. Mrs. Burns and her newborn had been left alone and defenseless by Mrs. Kinzie. Half a dozen young soldiers went up the river to the Burns's home, picked up the mattress with mother and child still on it, and put them in the small boat. Soon the new mother and newborn were safe inside the fort as well.

The next morning, soldiers and civilians alike went up the river to Lee's Place to find that Liberty White had been shot twice and Frenchman Debou had been stabbed 11 times. Their bodies were removed and buried near the fort. The attackers were Winnebagos who had come into the fort with the intention of massacring all the men at Lee's Place and then killing every white man they could find outside the fort. When the soldiers fired the cannon's warning shot, the Winnebagos quickly returned to their villages along the Rock River.

Later on that summer, two Indians from an unidentified tribe reportedly were visiting inside the fort. Mrs. Heald and Mrs. Helm were playing a game outdoors on the parade ground and overheard one of the Indians apparently say to an interpreter, "The white chiefs' wives are amusing themselves very much; it will not be long before they are hoeing in our cornfields!" This warning signaled that what had happened at the fort was merely a precursor of what was to come.

When the United States declared war against Great Britain, it took 50 days for Fort Dearborn to learn the news. It was August 7, 1812. Fort Detroit had known for nearly a month, but they failed to send a messenger to Fort Dearborn informing them that the country was at war. It has been speculated that had Detroit notified Fort Dearborn immediately, the disaster that occurred at Dearborn could have been avoided.

Once everyone in the area knew the War of 1812 had broken out, the tribes sided with the British for a very simple reason: the British gave the more generous gifts. Fort Dearborn was vulnerable, having only four commanding officers in charge of 66 enlisted men (54 regulars and 12 militia). In addition, the fort was home to 9 women and 18 children.

Ironically, Capt. Heald learned about the existence of the war from Winnemeg, a chief of the Potawatomi tribe who was friendly to the Americans. Winnemeg brought with him a letter from General William Hull, with very specific instructions for Heald to destroy all arms and ammunition. He was directed to give goods from the Factory to any friendly Indians willing to escort the soldiers safely to Fort Wayne (since Mackinac and the Island of St. Joseph's had already been surrendered by that time).

Hull

Despite the orders, Heald realized that evacuating the fort would not be a simple matter. He was responsible for nearly 100 people, and they were surrounded by Native Americans in league with Great Britain, America's enemy. Winnemeg himself advised Mr. Kinzie that evacuation would be dangerous, and he argued that the garrison was well-supplied with provisions and arms enough to protect the fort until reinforcements could come to their aid. Later, an inventory showed that the fort was in possession of 200 stands of arms, 4 pieces of artillery, 6,000 pounds of powder, and a healthy supply of shot and lead. There was Indian corn and other provisions enough to last three months. This did not even take into account a herd of 200 cattle and 27 barrels of salt.

Winnemeg further advised that, if they were going to evacuate, they should do it as quickly as possible, before the local tribes became aware of the war situation.

The Battle of Fort Dearborn

Capt. Heald was a stickler for detail. Not one to make quick decisions or act in a rash manner, Heald was determined to follow the instructions he'd been given to the letter. Heald held onto the letter until the following morning, when he read it aloud to the troops while on parade. Even then, he did not act quickly. He continued to delay for five more days while he called a council of Indians to notify them that the dozens of men, women and children within the fort were going to evacuate, and that he was requesting an escort to Fort Wayne.

In doing this, Heald made an extreme error in judgment. As a result, some Indians defied the guards and entered the fort, visited the officers' quarters, and threatened the soldiers. Undeterred, Heald took Mr. Kinzie with him to the Indian council and scoffed at the notion that the young braves might murder them. That said, he had cannons aimed toward the council meeting while he explained that the fort was being evacuated and all goods were being distributed. He asked the Potawatomi to serve as escorts, promising generous rewards upon their safe arrival at Fort Wayne, but Mr. Kinzie remained skeptical and eventually convinced Heald of the danger in trusting the Potawatomi.

On August 13, blankets, calicoes, paints and other goods were freely distributed among the Indians in the neighborhood. The vast supplies of arms and ammunition were tossed into the well, and all liquor was poured into the Chicago River. The Indians anticipated that the ammunition and liquor was to have been distributed, along with the other goods. When it wasn't, they crept up on the fort in the dark.

8 days had passed since Capt. Heald had received news that America was at war and that the fort was to be evacuated. Given that it would be a slow march with the large number of women and children who would be making the journey, his officers were convinced they would never reach Fort Wayne safely. The troops unanimously advised Heald to remain at the fort, prepare to defend themselves, and wait out whatever the natives might be planning.

As they stayed inside the fort, everyone lived in fear, and by the two week mark, any hope of a rapid evacuation was long gone. So were the munitions. One good sign was that Capt. William Wells arrived from Fort Wayne with about 30 friendly Miami. Wells was known as the "perfect master of everything pertaining to Indian life both in peace and war and withal a stranger to personal fear." Wells had been kidnapped by the Miami when he was a young boy. He was later rescued, only to return to the Miami, whom he preferred. Not only was he a friend of the Miami, he married a Miami woman and became a Miami chief.[22]

---

[22] Helm, Linai T, and Nelly K. Gordon. *The Fort Dearborn Massacre*. Chicago: Rand, McNally & Co, 1912. Print.

Wells

As it turned out, when the evacuation order was sent to Capt. Heald, a copy was also sent to Maj. Stickney, an Indian agent at Fort Wayne, along with a request for him to do everything in his power to assist in implementing Heald's orders. Unlike Heald, Stickney acted immediately by sending Capt. Wells with Miami warriors to rescue Fort Dearborn.

Wells arrived with every intention of holding the fort, regardless of Capt. Heald's orders, in the belief that certain destruction was in store if the fort were abandoned. He was further convinced that the whites would be slaughtered before they could make the 150 mile march to Fort Wayne. However, Wells also believed that it was too late; Heald had reacted slowly and methodically to destroy the last hope for saving the fort and the people inside. He had followed the orders to the letter, but he took far too long to react to the impending danger posed by the Indians.

After Wells' arrival, yet another council was held with the Indians, who were clearly angry. They considered the destruction of arms and liquor to be an act of bad faith, and the younger men were ready to immediately attack. Black Partridge, a prominent Potawatomi chief, appeared in person at the fort. Around his neck, he wore a medal that he gave to Heald, explaining that it had been given to him by the Americans and that he had worn it for a long time as a token of mutual friendship. "I will not wear a token of peace while I am compelled to act as an enemy," Black Partridge explained. It was apparent an attack was coming.

Even the most reliable firsthand and secondhand accounts of the impending battle are suspect since they were recorded after the event, in some cases years later. One contemporary letter was written by Walter K. Jordan, who wrote, "Captain Wells, myself, and an hundred friendly Indians, left Fort Wayne on the first of August to escort captain Heald from fort Chicauga, as he was in danger of being captured by the British, Orders had been given to abandon that fort, and retreat to Fort Wayne, a distance of 150 miles. We reached fort Chicauga on the 10th of August, and on the 15th we prepared for an immediate march, burning all that we could not fetch with us."

In essence, the story of the battle/massacre began at 9:00 a.m. on August 15, 1812 as Capt. Wells took the lead on horseback after Capt. Kinzie received a message warning him that the Potawatomi would definitely attack the column. Capt. Wells' face was blackened, according to the Indian custom "in token of his impending fate," indicating that Wells himself had given up hope.

If the accounts are accurate, half of the Miami warriors rode behind Wells. Behind them were musicians playing the Death March, and behind them were soldiers carrying 25 pounds of ammunition each. Following the soldiers was a train of wagons carrying camping equipment and provisions. Nine women and their children rode in the army wagons, with the exception of Mrs. Heald and Mrs. Helm, who rode on horseback. The remaining Miami warriors brought up the rear of the procession.

Missing was the Kinzie family. Mr. Kinzie put his wife and four of their children into a boat and sent them on their way while he joined the troops, along with their oldest daughter, Margaret. Their eldest son, who was only 9 years old at the time, joined his mother in the boat. Their youngest was a two-and-a-half-year old toddler. They were accompanied by the Kinzie family's nurse, a French-Ottawa half-breed named Josette La Framboise. He sent a clerk who worked for him, Chandonnais, two more servants, a boatman, and the two Indians who had brought Heald the message that the U.S. was at war. Altogether, there were a dozen people in the boat.

Antoine Ouilmette and his family knew the Potawatomi considered him one of their own, so the Ouilmette family did not worry about remaining in their home.

As soon as the fort was evacuated, the Indians began to plunder anything that was not nailed down. The soldiers had left a herd of cattle, which they allowed to run loose as they left, and the Indians chased and shot them for sport. None of the carcasses were saved for meat.

Traveling on land in the area was extremely challenging. There were boats on Lake Michigan, but not enough to have transported such a large group of people. Even had there been boats, the Indians likely would not have allowed them to board. As it was, the beginning of the route was on a sandy beach; there were no roads at the time, and the wagons had to make their way as best they could, even as the terrain became more and more difficult to navigate.

Some of the Potawatomi began the journey as escorts of the soldiers and the Miami, but soon they veered off from the group they were escorting. As both groups passed near sandy hills and sand banks, the Potawatomi slowly disappeared. Capt. Wells was the first to realize the soldiers, men, women, children and Miami were surrounded by warriors, so he turned his horse and rode back toward the marching men, but there were nowhere near enough to defend the column. The Potawatomi escort had now started attacking party, choosing to murder the whites they were escorting, rather than join the others who were looting the fort.

As the Potawatomi rushed toward their intended victims and fired at them; the Miami fired back. The Potawatomi scattered in opposite directions before surrounding the marching line, and at this point, the Miami abandoned the march and disappeared, to be seen no more.

As the Potawatomi continued firing, a few of their number attacked with tomahawks and scalping knives. When Sergeant Holt was shot in the neck, he handed his sword to his wife, who was on horseback, to defend herself. The Potawatomi wanted her horse, but they didn't want to harm her, preferring instead to take her as a captive, as they were wont to do. She resisted, but she was eventually dragged from her horse. She became a prisoner and was held captive in Illinois River country, but she was treated well and was eventually ransomed.

When a young Indian attempted to attack Mrs. Helm with a tomahawk, she grabbed him around the neck. She tried to snatch his scalping knife, but she, too, was dragged away. Her captor took her into the waters of Lake Michigan and appeared to be drowning her at first, but it turned out that this native was Black Partridge, the chief who had surrendered his peace medal the evening before. He allowed Mrs. Helm to make her way ashore. Walking across the sand was difficult, so she removed her shoes, and no sooner had she done this than a squaw stole them. By the time Mrs. Helm reached the prairie's edge, she had met Mr. Kinzie, who reported that her husband was wounded but safe.

Captain Wells reportedly killed at least seven Potawatomi before he was shot through the lung. If that's true, he almost certainly killed more warriors than any other soldier on that day. His horse was also shot and fell on him, pinning him down. Mrs. Heald was forced to helplessly watch as a Potawatomi shot him in the head. Wells was loved by so many of the Native Americans that one of the warriors traveled the 150 miles to Fort Wayne afterward to tell Mrs. Wells (who was none other than the daughter of Chief Little Turtle) that her husband was dead.

In the meantime, Mrs. Helm was taken to the Indian encampment on the banks of the Chicago River, where someone attempted to put her on a horse bareback. She fell off, only to be supported by Black Partridge and Pesotum, another Indian, who carried Capt. Wells' scalp in his hand. Mrs. Helm made her way to a chief's wigwam, where his wife took pity on her and gave her sugar water to drink.

Throughout the fighting, the soldiers continued to fire, but they inevitably fell, and the prairie was soon scattered with both the wounded and the dead. In short order, half the soldiers were dead or dying. Soon the warriors began attacking the wagons loaded with women and children. The troops were so isolated in their marching column that there was nothing they could do to protect the helpless victims in the wagons.

Among the soldiers was Dr. Van Voorhis, a military surgeon, who asked Mrs. Helm if there wasn't a way to barter with the Potawatomi for their very lives. She responded, "Our fate is inevitable." The 22-year-old doctor, who had seen more than his share of death up close and in person in his short life, feared death, perhaps more than anyone out on the field that day. Shortly thereafter, a Potawatomi killed him with a tomahawk.

Another 22-year-old, Ensign George Ronan, was a recent graduate of West Point, but all of his military training proved insufficient against the larger contingent of Potawatomi warriors.

The surgeon's mate, John Cooper, was but a little older. He was married, and his wife and two young daughters lived at Fort Dearborn with him. Cooper died in battle, and a warrior attempted to nab his wife and daughters. His eldest daughter, Isabella, fought back, and the warrior began to scalp her in retaliation. Remarkably, Isabella survived the scalping when an elderly squaw who knew the Cooper family stepped in to save her life. She took Mrs. Cooper and the girls to her wigwam and nursed them back to health. The Coopers endured two years of captivity before they were finally ransomed, and went to Detroit.

The slaughter continued unchecked. One Corporal Simmons was married and the father of two children. He was on horseback, but the rest of his family was in an army wagon. A warrior attacked the wagon and killed their older boy. Mrs. Simmons hid their youngest, an infant girl, in a shawl, saving her life, but Corporal Simmons was not so fortunate, and ended up dying on the battlefield. Mrs. Simmons and the baby would be forced to walk from Fort Dearborn to Green Bay as prisoners. There, the women were beaten, but she and her infant survived. A friendly squaw helped care for Mrs. Simmons and her baby. It is unclear how Mrs. Simmons and her daughter made their way to a frontier post in Ohio a year later, but they were finally redeemed.

During the fighting, some Potawatomi were able to catch the attention of Capt. Heald, and Chief Blackbird spoke with Heald through an interpreter. There is more than one version of what was said in that conversation. According to one version, Heald was asked to surrender in exchange for sparing the lives of all the prisoners the Potawatomi had captured from among the dozens of people he was hoping to lead to Fort Wayne.[23] Lieut. Linai T. Helm's version claims that Capt. Heald offered $100 for every surviving male.[24] Whatever the case, there was some discussion among the Potawatomi, followed by another chat with Heald, during which they agreed that Heald and the Potawatomi would meet halfway, shake hands, and the white people would be returned to the fort.

Helm later claimed that Heald had asked his opinion three times about whether to surrender. Helm insisted he had no idea of surrender. The interpreter then shouted to Heald and Helm, "Don't surrender for if you do they will kill you all, for there has been no general council held with them yet." After more discussion, the interpreter changed his mind and agreed that surrender would not be fatal.[25]

---

[23] DAWSON, Moses. *A Historical Narrative of the Civil and Military Service of Major-General William H. Harrison, and a Vindication of His Character and Conduct As a Statesman, a Citizen, and a Soldier. with a Detail of His Negotiations and Wars with the Indians, Until the Final Overthrow of the Celebrated Chief Tecumseh, and His Brother the Prophet.* M. Dawson: Cincinnati, 1824. Print.

[24] Helm, Linai T, and Nelly K. Gordon. *The Fort Dearborn Massacre.* Chicago: Rand, McNally & Co, 1912. Print.

Heald had no choice but to surrender, which he did. It was reported that fighting ceased immediately. The Potawatomi shouted about their victory, even as moans were heard from those who lay wounded on the battlefield. The saddest of all was the cries from the mothers whose children had just been killed.

The massacre was over in about 15 minutes. By the end, virtually all the women and children were now prisoners. Lieutenant Helm was wounded and counted among the captives, but he was later taken to live with the Peoria tribe.

In spite of the vast acreage of the Indian Territory, the whites, as well as the Native Americans, seemed to form a sort of small, distantly-related family, which made it possible to free prisoners. Mr. Kinzie's half-brother, an Indian agent, made Helm's liberation possible, sending him from Peoria country to St. Louis for safety. After seven months and one week, he joined Mrs. Helm in Detroit.[26] Two years later, Helm wrote one of several accounts of the Fort Dearborn massacre.[27]

The soldiers relinquished their arms, and then were taken to the Potawatomi encampment near the decimated Fort Dearborn. Perhaps for the first time, Capt. Heald saw that they were facing perhaps as many as 500 warriors, mostly Potawatomi. The Potawatomi claimed they had lost only 15 warriors. When Capt. Heald inventoried the loss on the American side, he learned that at least 60 whites had been slain. The dead lay on the prairie, and their bones would be washed white with the passing of the seasons for four years until U.S. soldiers could finally return to bury the dead and rebuild the fort.

When the Potawatomi promised the lives of the survivors would be spared, they actually meant only the prisoners who had survived--they never promised to spare the wounded still on the battlefield. Five soldiers were tortured to death. Most were tomahawked. According to Helm, the sandy beach was littered with men, women and children lying naked and beheaded.

When they reached the fort, Helm was relieved to find his wife was there in the company of the squaws, and she was allowed to wash and dress her husband's wound. Then the Potawatomi brought some of the other soldier prisoners to see Helm, and proceeded to kill one with a tomahawk while the rest of them watched.[28]

In the meantime, the Kinzie family's boat was following shoreline trek with the rest of the whites. From the water, Mrs. Kinzie, her children, and the other passengers saw the annihilation. The Kinzie's boat was heading toward the fray of the massacre. They were close enough to recognize their friends who were under attack.

Mrs. Kinzie saw Mrs. Heald on horseback, led by a Potawatomi. She was wounded, and some squaws had attempted to strip her of her shoes and socks. Realizing the Potawatomi would probably kill Mrs. Heald, Mrs. Kinzie told Chandonnais to alight and offer a mule, tied to a nearby tree, to the Indian in exchange for Mrs. Heald's freedom. The Potawatomi was already

[25] *Ibid.*
[26] Helm, Linai T, and Nelly K. Gordon. *The Fort Dearborn Massacre*. Chicago: Rand, McNally & Co, 1912. Print.
[27] *Ibid.*
[28] *Ibid.*

attempting to snatch Mrs. Heald's bonnet from her head, probably intent on scalping her, when Chandonnais surprised him with the mule.

The Potawatomi negotiated for Mrs. Heald's exchange, demanding an additional two bottles of whiskey, as soon as they reached a destination where Chandonnais could fulfill this demand. He callously argued with Chandonnais that Mrs. Heald was badly wounded, and not likely to survive. He was willing to trade the wounded and frightened woman, provided Chandonnais guarantee the two bottles of whiskey, whether she survived or not. Sealing the deal, Chandonnais transported Mrs. Heald to Mrs. Kinzie's boat. As Mrs. Heald was moaning in pain from her wounds, Mrs. Kinzie and her crew concluded they had no other alternative but to return to the Kinzie house, located just outside the plundered fort, near the Potawatomi village.

Miraculously, Mrs. Kinzie, 11 passengers, and Mrs. Heald, made their way ashore and safely to the Kinzie home. Mr. Kinzie, who had survived unscathed, was reported to have been there as well, though it is unclear how they arranged for that to happen. Friendly Indians joined them as well, ready to help the Kinzie company reach safety at St. Joseph. Among them was Black Partridge, who had rescued Mrs. Helm from the Potawatomi village and brought her back to the Kinzie house.

Mrs. Burns, who was giving birth when the massacre had started, was also at the Kinzie house and had a more harrowing experience than the others, even though she was not wounded. Mrs. Burns and her newborn were taken to the Potawatomi village, along with other women and children, where she was brought to one of the chief's wigwam, and he treated her kindly. Unfortunately, his wife grew jealous, and threw a tomahawk at the newborn with the intention of killing her. The baby survived, but was permanently scarred with the imprint of the tomahawk on her forehead.

It is unclear how, but Mrs. Burns and her baby eventually made their way to the Kinzie house. Charles Lee and their eldest son had been killed during the battle, but Mrs. Lee and their 12-year-old daughter and an infant had been captured and found themselves held captive by Black Partridge. During the early part of their march, Mrs. Lee's 12-year-old daughter was tied to the back of a horse to prevent her from falling off. In the ongoing battle, she was seriously wounded by a musket ball. Her startled horse ran off, leaving the girl dangling from her horse and bleeding. It was obvious she was mortally wounded and would die soon, in great agony. Black Partridge killed the girl with his tomahawk in order to put her out of her suffering.

Black Partridge delivered Mrs. Lee and her infant to his village. When the infant became ill, Black Partridge returned to Chicago for medical assistance from Monsieur du Pin, a French trader who was living there, who paid the ransom to free Mrs. Lee and her infant.

In the end, Mrs. Heald and Mrs. Helm were the only two white women who survived unscathed. Two other women were slain on the battlefield, and the rest were taken captive by Potawatomi warriors. They survived the massacre, but not all survived the difficult life in the Potawatomi village. There were 18 white children on the field that day, 12 of which were killed.

After an initially slow response, a British agent eventually tracked down the white captives in the wake of the massacre. As 10-year-old John Kinzie confirmed, the soldiers who survived spent a miserable winter in the Potawatomi village, where they had inadequate shelter. Though the Kinzie family and their houseguests were practically prisoners in the Kinzie house, they survived due to their accommodations. Black Partridge and some of his fellow tribesmen had taken up residence on the front porch of the Kinzie house, serving as sentinels.

From inside the Kinzie house, the inhabitants could see the Potawatomi celebrating as they plundered Fort Dearborn, decked out in women's hats, shawls and ribbons. The day after the massacre, the warriors set fire to the fort and the agency house. The fire must have been massive given the size of the fort and the double log house.

Hearing rumors of the military dispensing food and other supplies from the fort, Indians arrived from other locations, hoping to be on the receiving end of their generosity. They were disappointed to discover they had missed the handouts and the massacre.

Shortly after the battle, Black Partridge disguised Mrs. Helm and sent her to Ouilmette's house. He was a Frenchman and his wife was Indian. They were unlikely targets, but while she was there, the visitors let themselves into the house. Ouilmette's wife hid Mrs. Helm beneath a feather bed and sat on it while the Indians searched the entire house. Luckily, they steered clear of the bed.

Not finding anything, the Indians visited the Kinzie house next, and even Black Partridge himself believed all was lost. In an instance of truly miraculous timing, Sauganash, a half-breed Potawatomi chief greatly respected by the Potawatomi, arrived. If anyone could save the residents of the Kinzie house, it was Sauganash. He went there and made it clear to the Wabash intruders that the white people there were friends who had never refused the Potawatomi, or anyone else, anything in their time of need. Perhaps to save face, the Wabash explained their uninvited presence by saying they were there in search of cloth to wrap the bodies of the Potawatomi dead before placing them in graves.

Like that one, there was an array of incredible stories of survival. Allegedly, early on in the march, the horses hauling the surgeons' equipment and medicines strayed off. Quartermaster Sergeant William Griffith left the parade column, setting off to find the straying horses, and was captured by Topenebe, who was friendly to whites. Topenebe took Griffith across the river in a canoe and hid him. The next day, Griffith also made his way to Ouilmette's house. The Ouilmettes disguised him as a Frenchman, complete with a pipe, and he strode over to the Kinzie house to join their household.

A handful of people in the column managed to evade the Potawatomi, at least for a time. One of them was Walter K. Jordan, who was eventually captured but unharmed. He noted, "They tied me hard and fast that night, and placed a guard over me. – I lay down and slept soundly until morning for I was tired—in the morning they untied me and set me parching corn, at which I worked attentively until night. They said that if I would stay and not runaway, that they would make a chief of me, but if I would attempt to runaway they would catch me and burn me alive. I amused them with a fine story in order to gain their confidence; and fortunately made my escape from them on the 19th of August, and took one of their best horses to carry me, being seven days in the wilderness. I was joyfully received on the 26th at Wayne. On the 28th they attacked the fort, and blockaded us until the 16th of September, when we were relieved by Gen. Harrison."

Meanwhile, Heald was taken prisoner by the Kankakee tribe, where he was eventually joined by Mrs. Heald. Together, they made their way to Mackinac, where the captain surrendered himself to the British as a prisoner of war. He was treated very well, and the wound he'd received during the massacre had healed as well as it ever would. Heald was eventually freed, but he suffered from his wound for the rest of his life.

Eventually the surviving captured soldiers were taken to Detroit and became prisoners of war. A dozen soldiers were never accounted for after the massacre, and it is unknown whether they deserted, died, or were captured.[29]

[29] Helm, Linai T, and Nelly K. Gordon. *The Fort Dearborn Massacre*. Chicago: Rand, McNally & Co, 1912. Print.

An engraving of a tree believed to mark the site where the massacre started

Rebuilding

Since they had burned down the Agency House, which had served as the local trading post, there was little reason for the Potawatomi to remain around Fort Dearborn and the settlement that eventually became Chicago. Instead, they chose to go elsewhere, including places like Detroit, to trade furs. Their elders had warned this would happen, but the younger warriors had forged ahead without thought to the future. Even as they began leaving the Chicago area, the Potawatomi were beginning to realize the British were not their friends, and that only the American government had the authority to make treaties regarding their lands and claims of territorial ownership.

While details remain sketchy, the handful of residents who had made the Kinzie house their temporary abode boarded a boat and left the fort and its nightmarish memories behind 18 days after the massacre. They left Ouilmette and his family as the sole remaining inhabitants of Chicago.

The Kinzie family was placed under the protection of Chief Topenebe until November, and they were subsequently escorted to Detroit and given over to the British as prisoners of war. John Kinzie was paroled, only to be taken into custody again, and was finally released when the War of 1812 concluded.

In spite of the massacre and the immense loss of life on both sides, Kinzie did the unthinkable by returning to Chicago in 1816, just four years later, when the second Fort Dearborn had been built and was again occupied by American troops. The first school teacher, William Cox, also arrived in 1816 and taught in what was left of the bake-house at the former Fort Dearborn. In 1832, Capt. John Whistler's son, Major William Whistler, returned to Fort Dearborn. He was the second generation of that family to be stationed there.

FORT DEARBORN, IN 1830.

U. S. Marine Hospital. Big Locust Tree.
Storehouse, Magazine. Block-house.
Soldier's Barracks. Officer's Quarters. Light-house.
Stables, Artillery. Commandant's Quarters. Light-keeper's House.
         Ferry Slip.

FORT DEARBORN IN 1850.

Engravings of the second Fort Dearborn

During that time, peace was achieved between tribal nations, and treaties of peace and friendship were forged with various tribes. Years later, a Potawatomi named Chief Shavehead accompanied some hunters into Michigan without realizing that one man in the party had been a soldier at Fort Dearborn prior to the massacre. After listening to Shavehead recount that bloody day with bravado, the soldier followed him into the woods and shot him with a rifle.

While most of the local tribesmen left the Chicago area following the massacre and the destruction of the trading post, a few residents still remained, and slowly the population grew. The goal remained the same as it ever was: the settlement of previously Native American lands. In 1832, Col. Thomas Joseph Vincent Owen became Indian agent at Fort Dearborn. He negotiated the final Indian treaty at Chicago, the Treaty with the Potawatomi in 1832, which was unpopular with many natives but defended by Potawatomi Chief Metea:

"We meet you here to-day, because we had promised it, to tell you our minds, and what we have agreed upon among ourselves. You will listen to us with a good mind, and believe what we say. You know that we first came to this country, a long time ago, and when we sat ourselves down upon it, we met with a great many hardships and difficulties. Our country was then very large; but it has dwindled away to a small spot, and you wish to purchase that! This has caused us to reflect much upon what you have told us; and we have, therefore, brought all the chiefs and warriors, and the young men and women and children of our tribe, that one part may not do what others object to, and that all may be witnesses of what is going forward. You know your children. Since you first came among them, they have listened to your words with an attentive ear, and have always hearkened to your counsels. Whenever you have had a proposal to make to us, whenever you have had a favor to ask of us, we have always lent a favorable ear, and our invariable answer has been 'yes.' This you know! A long time has passed since we first came upon our lands, and our old people have all sunk into their graves. They had sense. We are all young and foolish, and do not wish to do anything that they would not approve, were they living. We are fearful we shall offend their spirits, if we sell our lands; and we are fearful we shall offend you, if we do not sell them. This has caused us great perplexity of thought, because we have counselled among ourselves, and do not know how we can part with the land. Our country was given to us by the Great Spirit, who gave it to us to hunt upon, to make our cornfields upon, to live upon, and to make down our beds upon when we die. And he would never forgive us, should we bargain it away. When you first spoke to us for lands at St. Mary's, we said we had a little, and agreed to sell you a piece of it; but we told you we could spare no more. Now you ask us again. You are never satisfied! We have sold you a great tract of land already; but it is not enough! We sold it to you for the benefit of your children, to farm and to live upon. We have now but little left. We shall want it all for ourselves. We know not how long we may live, and we wish to have some lands for our children to hunt upon. You are gradually taking away our hunting-grounds. Your children are driving us before them. We are growing uneasy. What lands you have, you may retain forever; but we shall sell no more. You think, perhaps, that I speak in passion; but my heart is good towards you. I speak like one of your own children. I am an Indian, a red-skin, and live by hunting and fishing, but my country is already too small; and I do not know how to bring up my children, if I give it all away. We sold you a fine tract of land at St. Mary's. We said to you then, it was enough to satisfy your children, and the last we should sell: and we thought it would be the last you would ask for. We have now told you what we had to say. It is what was determined on, in a council among ourselves; and what I have spoken, is the voice of my nation. On this account, all our people have come here to listen to me; but do not think we have a bad opinion of you. Where should we get a bad opinion of you? We speak to you with a good heart, and the feelings of a friend. You are acquainted with this piece of land— the country we live in. Shall we give it up? Take notice, it is a small piece of land, and if we give it away, what will become of us? The Great Spirit, who has provided it for our use, allows us to keep it, to bring up our young men and support our families. We should incur his anger, if we bartered it away. If we had more land, you should get more; but our land has been wasting away ever since the white people became our neighbors, and we have now hardly enough left to cover the bones of our tribe. You are in the midst of your red children. What is due to us in money, we wish, and will receive at this place; and we want nothing more. We all shake hands with you. Behold our warriors, our women, and children. Take pity on us and on our words."

In the end, the Indians were poorly compensated for their Illinois possessions, although a dozen or more tracts were reserved for certain Native Americans. Eventually, all the Potawatomi and the other remaining Native Americans were removed to a reservation in Kansas.[30] There were also reserves for those tribes that had remained faithful allies to the United States, namely

---

[30] *Illinois Catholic Historical Review*. Chicago: Illinois Catholic Historical Society, 1918. Print.

the Sacs and Foxes, who were permitted to continuing fishing and hunting on the lands ceded at that time, along with government land on the Wabash and Sangamon Rivers, for as long as those lands remained the property of the United States.[31]

Although Fort Dearborn was located within what is now Chicago's Loop, people have by and large forgotten the massacre at Fort Dearborn, if they ever heard an account of it at all, but it remained a hotly contested topic of debate in Chicago as late as the mid-20th century. A century after the debacle, the *Illinois Catholic Historical Review* wrote, "It seems necessary in order to keep the history of this bloody tragedy straight to say that General Hull who ordered the evacuation of the several forts including Fort Dearborn, was court-martialed for cowardice, found guilty but pardoned by the President; and though opinion be somewhat divided most of the investigators of the history of the surrender of Fort Dearborn, have arrived at the conclusion that the Commander Captain Heald was a coward." Naturally, the story of the Americans was considered the important factor, not the response by the Native Americans.

Eventually, a memorial tablet reciting the facts of the massacre was designed and attached to a building on Rush Street,[32] and today, the name Dearborn is most frequently associated with Chicago's Dearborn Street. The sculpture depicting the massacre and commissioned by George Pullman was initially installed near his home, the presumed site of the conflict. It had been placed under a tree on the Pullman property, but it began to deteriorate due to the effects of smoke and weather. At the time, it was described as a "group of relief statuary, 100 feet east of the famous cottonwood massacre tree," and was unveiled on June 22, 1893.[33] In the same article, the location of several historic sites were listed along with a reason as to why they, too, should be marked and commemorated. The list included the Kinzie Mansion and Charles Lee's Hardscrabble farm (now known as the Bridgeport area). In 1931, the Pullman monument was moved to the lobby of the Chicago Historical Society, along with a portion of the tree, where it remained for more than a decade.

In 1943, H. A. Musham, a naval architect and chairman of the Fort Dearborn Memorial Commission, challenged the memory of the massacre. He wrote an article for the *Journal of the Illinois Historical Society*, insisting that the "Fort Dearborn action" should not be called the Battle of Chicago, the Fort Dearborn Massacre, or the Chicago Massacre. He explained in his article that there was no massacre, because a massacre is an indiscriminate killing, whereas "[t]hose who perished were killed in the fighting or soon afterward in accordance with Indian customs, or died because of the privations of their captivity. It was in fact, a minor engagement, a physical struggle between opposing forces, American and Indian. While it did take place at Chicago, it did not occur at Fort Dearborn. It is therefore correct to call it the battle of Chicago."[34] He contended that the battle would have taken place at what is now Michigan Avenue and 12th Street.

[31] Kappler, Charles J. *Indian Affairs: Laws and Treaties.* , 1904. Print.

[32] *Illinois Catholic Historical Review*. Chicago: Illinois Catholic Historical Society, 1918. Print.

[33] "To Mark Famous Sites." *The Reporter: the first and only journal published exclusively in the interest of the Granite and Marble Monument Trade*. Chicago, Ill. Nov. 1909. Print.

[34] "No 'massacre,' Fort Dearborn Historian Says." *Chicago Tribune*. Chicago, Ill: Tribune Co, July 6, 1843. Print.

A plaque on Michigan Ave. in Chicago indicating the southern perimeter of Fort Dearborn

In response to protests in the 1960s by Native American groups that the monument falsely represented their people, the monument was moved to the corner of 18th Street and Prairie Avenue, very close to its original site. Ultimately, the Chicago Department of Cultural Affairs' Office of Public Art put the statue in storage. It is now kept off-view, safely stored, for conservation reasons. As the Chicago Historical Society concluded, "The significance of the monument now may lie as much in its own history as in the historical events it purports to represent."[35]

---

[35] Grossman, James R, Ann D. Keating, and Janice L. Reiff. *Electronic Encyclopedia of Chicago*. Chicago: Chicago Historical Society, Newberry Library, 2005. Internet resource.

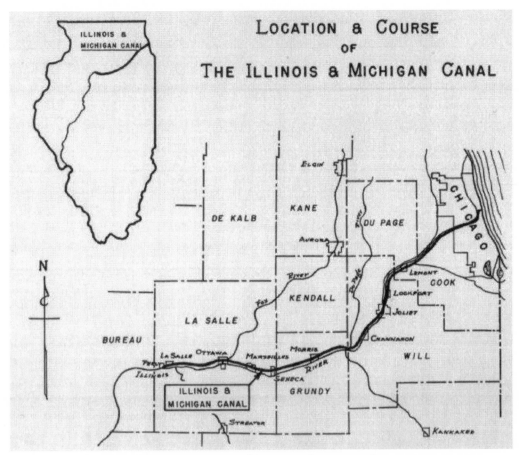

The location of the previous canal

At the groundbreaking, the Chicago Canal was called the Chicago Divide, in reference to a small split of land that actually did divide the Illinois River from the Great Lakes.[36] For years, an especially polluted section has gone by the well-deserved, if unflattering, name of Bubbling Creek. Some Chicagoans call it Chicago's "second shoreline." Some have called it the "Stinking River." Most people call it the Chicago Canal, but the full name is the Chicago Drainage Canal. No one wants to call it what it really is, a sewage channel.

The canal was built to redirect sewage so that it "relieves Lake Michigan of the burden of filth which now flows into it and pollutes the drinking water of this great city."[37] As a result, it was also needed in order to reduce the concentration of sewage flowing from the residents of the city of Chicago far out into the midst of Lake Michigan and beyond.

In essence, the first part of the canal project involved cutting a pass between one small strip of land that prevented vessels from sailing from Lake Michigan through the Chicago River then down the Illinois River to the Mississippi River all the way to the Gulf of Mexico. It was known as the Chicago Divide, because it divided the river in two parts.

If cutting an opening into the Chicago Divide, joining the two sections of the Chicago River,

---

[36] Seeger, E. (1893). *Chicago, the wonder city*. Chicago: G. Gregory Print. Co.

[37] Chicago and Alton Railroad Company. (1895). *A guide to the Chicago Drainage Canal with geological and historical notes to accompany the tourist via the Chicago & Alton Railroad*. Chicago: Chicago and Alton Railroad Co.

sounded like an achievement, it was just the beginning. Canals had been dug before. What was different about the Chicago Canal was that engineers planned to stop pollution from emptying into Lake Michigan by actually reversing the direction of the Chicago River. No one had ever done that before, not even Mother Nature.

Illinois Railroads

The Illinois state legislature had passed an act on Jan. 28, 1831, to survey St. Clair County, Ill., and to create a route for either a canal or a railroad. St. Clair County initially included most of the state of Illinois. The state was divided up into more counties and, by 1831, St. Clair County became a smaller county directly across the Mississippi River from St. Louis and included the city of East St. Louis. Most migrants entered Illinois from St. Louis, or at least the southern point of Illinois – not from Chicago or other places east.

But, there was optimism that Lake Michigan could be a profitable route for transportation, making it possible to travel from points east to Chicago. The Baltimore & Ohio offered the promise of an inland route that would reach from the Great Lakes, down the Illinois River, all the way to the Mississippi River and down to the Gulf of Mexico. Whether the railroad would become a reality or not, the legislature was open to the idea of a railroad system but they committed first to creating the Illinois & Michigan Canal, which exists today.

Illinois was a very different place in the 1830s.[38] Prior to Dec. 9, 1778, Illinois was merely a far-flung county of Virginia. In 1790, Virginia ceded the Illinois lands and they became part of the Northwest Territory. St. Clair County represented about one-third of the acreage known as Illinois. The eastern half of the state, bordering the entire state of Indiana, was Knox County.

In 1795, the state legislature divided St. Clair into two counties. About two-thirds of St. Clair remained intact while the southern third became Randolph County and both were still part of the Northwest Territory. About half of the remaining portion of Illinois became Knox County.

By 1801, Illinois became part of the new Indiana Territory. Randolph County became a bit larger. Knox County was reduced to a sliver and St. Clair County represented the vast majority of the state of Illinois and some of what is now Indiana. More Europeans were moving to Illinois and the smaller counties meant closer representation for those residents. County seats meant business and business needed transportation.

On March 1, 1809, the entire state of Illinois became two counties. Randolph County was the land at the very southern tip. All the remaining lands between Indiana and Missouri, all the way north to Wisconsin, were then designated as St. Clair County.

In 1812, most of St. Clair County became Madison County. Knox County disappeared. Randolph County was divvied up into the three counties of Randolph, Gallatin and Johnson. St. Clair remained as a tiny sliver near St. Louis. St. Clair remains a county to this day and has always played a role in transportation.

Other county revisions continued until 1818, when St. Clair became an even smaller county, one of 15 named counties. By the end of 1818, Illinois became a state and, over the next decade,

---

[38] *"Illinois County Boundaries 1790 – Present." IL GenWeb Project., & US GenWeb Project. (1996). Illinois genealogy & history. Illinois: s.n.* Retrieved from http://www.ilstatehouse.com/past_capitols.html

the population grew sizably. While the state divided up land into more and more counties it is obvious that the greater population areas were in the far southern tip of the state. Chicago's home, Cook County, did not even appear on the map until 1831, more than a decade after statehood.

The state capital was not Springfield in the heart of the state. Before statehood, Illinois was governed from Kaskaskia, at the far southern tip of the state. French Jesuits had lived in this Native American village where the Illini Tribe lived, joined by French colonists and European traders, since 1703. It was conveniently located on a waterway, the primary means for transportation to and from the area. Even those who traveled westward often traveled by water until they reached St. Louis, around the bend, on the Mississippi. They bought their wagons and supplies in St. Louis before traveling west, prior to the arrival of the railroads.

When Illinois became a state in 1818, the capital was moved up the Kaskaskia River to what became the city of Vandalia. The new capital building opened in 1820 but burned. It was rebuilt in 1824, but the capital remained in Vandalia.

The earlier Illinois settlers voted to move the capital closer to the geographical center of the state. For the next century, the population center moved progressively north until Chicago became the largest city in the state.

In 1839, Springfield, farther inland near the Sangamon River, a tributary of the Illinois River, became the state capital.[39] It brought the state legislature and the state courts closer to all Illinois residents.

Transportation was an issue as more immigrants arrived in Illinois. Among other things, they needed mail delivery. Months before the State of Illinois addressed railroads, the legislature was still building roads, partly to deliver mail.

During the Dec. 3, 1832, legislative session, the Springfield & Alton Turnpike Road Company was incorporated. It was created with the intention of connecting Springfield to Bloomington, Ill., initially and later to "a point on the Mississippi River in St. Clair County, opposite St. Louis."[40] Upon discussion, the corporation was given the option of building a single or double railroad and they were given a decade to make it happen. Waterways and railroads were treated as a package.

The Springfield & Alton Railroad held out much promise and was granted the use of "so much of the railroad iron now owned by the State, as will be sufficient to lay down a single or double railroad track, from the diverging point of the State works on the Alton & Shelbyville Railroad, to the point of intersection with the Northern Cross railroad."[41] The result would connect Shelbyville, on the Kaskaskia River, with Alton, on the Mississippi, on one end of the rail route with Terre Haute, Indiana, on the other. But, it never amounted to much. In 1867, the state

[39] "Past Illinois Capitols." http://www.ilstatehouse.com/past_capitols.htm, 9 May 2016.

[40] Ackerman, William K. *Early Illinois Railroads: A Paper Read Before the Chicago Historical Society, Tuesday Evening, February 20, 1883*. Chicago: Fergus Print. Co, 1884. Print.

[41] Illinois., Walters, W., & Illinois. (1840). *Laws of the state of Illinois, passed by the eleventh General Assembly, at their special session, began and held at Springfield, on the ninth of December, one thousand eight hundred and thirty-nine: Published in pursuance of law*. Springfield [Ill.: William Walters, public printer.

legislature voted to incorporate the Alton & Upper Alton Horse Railway and Carrying Company, due to lack of rail lines some 30 years later. In fact, in spite of the growing web of interconnected railroads, there were 20 cities in Illinois that incorporated horse railways within their city limits in 1867. They were called railways, but were clearly horse-drawn, such as the Urbana & Champaign Horse Railway Company.[42] At the same time, dummy railroads emerged. According to some sources, these were steam-engine powered locomotives that were made to resemble a passenger coach. Others claim that the railcars were made to resemble horse carts so that they would not frighten horses.[43] In some cases, steam locomotives were referred to as a dummy line.[44]

By 1875, the dummy issue reached the Illinois Supreme Court as Paragraph 90 of the Horse & Dummy Act.[45] The Chicago & Western Indiana Railroad was affected, along with the Chicago Dock Co., the East St. Louis Union Railway (an Illinois line) and others. Primarily at issue, was whether or not railroads had the right to build their roads in the middle of city streets, primarily in Chicago. Paragraph 90 was sometimes considered an act, in itself. It specified that the "city council shall have no power to grant the use of the streets except upon the petition of those owning more than one-half of the frontage of the streets to be used." It is clear, from the law, that the dummy was a steam engine, in contrast to a horse-drawn rail line. This legal issue is just one example of the need for lawyers to be involved in railroading. It seemed everyone wanted railroads—just not in the street in front of their house.

The Galena & Chicago Union Railroad was the next railroad effort undertaken in Illinois, and was incorporated on Jan. 16, 1836. Galena was an especially lightly populated area. When the railroad was built, there were only about 6,000 residents in Galena and only about 18,600 in the entire county of Jo Daviess.

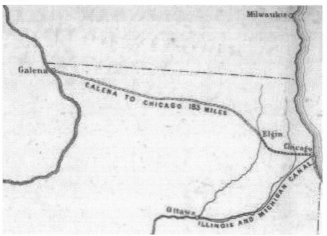

[42] Ackerman, William K. *Early Illinois Railroads: A Paper Read Before the Chicago Historical Society, Tuesday Evening, February 20, 1883*. Chicago: Fergus Print. Co, 1884. Print.

[43] Perna, Michael P. *Remembering Lake Quinsigamond: From Steamboats to White City*. Worcester, MA: Chandler House Press, 1998. Print.

[44] Foreman, Milton J, W A. Evans, Paul P. Bird, Gilbert E. Ryder, and Herbert H. Evans. *The Electrification of Railway Terminals As a Cure for the Locomotive Smoke Evil in Chicago: With Special Consideration of the Illinois Central Railroad*. Chicago: R.R. Donnelley & Sons Co, 1908. Print.

[45] *Reports of Cases at Law and in Chancery Argued and Determined in the Supreme Court of Illinois*. Bloomington, Ill: Supreme Court, State of Illinois distributed by Legal Division, Pantagraph Printing, 1888. Print.

The Original Chicago to Galena Plan, by the Galena & Chicago Union Railroad

The Galena railroad branch was essential for transporting large quantities of mined lead from the area. It wasn't about transporting people.

Lawsuits were not as much of an issue in Galena as open hostilities. Once a railway bridge was built across the Mississippi River, one settler allegedly planted himself on the Illinois side and promised to shoot the first engineer who dared to cross it. It never happened and the threat might only be a folk tale.

But, it does reflect the opposition by Galena residents who feared they would lose trade to Dubuque, Iowa. There was probably good reason for such fear. In 1851, Galena exported 33 million tons of lead.

But, the year before, 1850, is considered the beginning of railroad history in Chicago. It started with a land grant to the Galena & Chicago Union Railroad for property near Elgin, Ill. It took three years for the Galena & Chicago to reach Freeport.[46]

After no small effort, it gradually laid rails six or twelve miles at a stretch, from Chicago inland to Freeport, where it intersected with the Central Railroad. By September 1851, only 42 miles of the line was in operation. The first to go into operation were from the Chicago suburb of Elgin, west 12 miles. Another 12 miles opened and then a second dozen until the railroad reached Belvidere by December. It took until March for the last six miles to reach Cherry Valley. It was reported that the "unfavorable winter and spring" delayed the grading necessary for the line to reach Rockford.[47]

The annual reports from the Galena & Chicago Union Railroad Company reflect the growing business of building railroads.[48] Train depots needed to be built. The earliest expenses were for land—and fences. Since early railroad transportation was focused on transporting goods, weight scales were also at the top of the list.

Keeping those trains operational required more than a little maintenance. Machine shops with tools and paint shops and blacksmith shops were built. Freight warehouses were built of stone and brick. Railroad building was complicated. The railroad crews had to build railroad bridges and, when the G&CU reached the Chicago area, they had to build a drawbridge and a stone sewer.

Already, there were already nine locomotives traveling the juvenile rails. There were seven passenger cars. But, since the transportation of goods were primary, there were 81 covered freight cars, 33 platform cars, eight cars specifically for transporting gravel, 27 small freight cars and eleven hand cars. There were more than 9,000 passengers during 1851 and half of 1852.

Freight, at that time, consisted of flour, wheat, corn, oats, barley, potatoes, butter, pork, hides, "mill stuff," barrels of whisky, paper, and wool, among other general provisions. Animal

---

[46] Andreas, A. T. (1884). *History of Chicago: From the earliest period to the present time*. Chicago: A.T. Andreas.

[47] Galena and Chicago Union Railroad Company. (1858). *Report of the directors of the Galena & Chicago Union Railroad Co. to the stockholders: Read at the annual meeting of the company, June 2, 1858*. Chicago: Culver, Page & Hoyne, 128 and 130 Lake Street.

[48] *Annual Report of the Directors of the Galena and Chicago Union Rail Road Co. to the Stockholders for the Fiscal Year Ending December 31*. Chicago: Dunlop, Sewell & Spalding, 1800. Internet resource.

transport did not begin on the G&CU until January 1852 and during the first four months, only 66 carloads of animals were shipped by rail. But, railroading was just getting started.

The Galena & Chicago Union is just one example of how numerous smaller rail lines created a web of travel and transportation across the state, interconnecting with other states. Sometimes rail lines merged, other times they created contractual agreements. On Dec. 13, 1851, the G&CU contracted with the Chicago & Aurora railroads to carry on joint business.

On June 28, 1856, the G&CU entered into another contract, this one with the Chicago, Burlington & Quincy Railroad. They also formed a contract with the Mineral Point Railroad, connecting Illinois rail lines with Wisconsin. That Wisconsin line was built by the Beloit & Madison Railroad. Another contract between the Fox River Valley Railroad Company, in Illinois, and the Galena & Chicago Union was a cooperative effort with the Fox River providing the equipment necessary for Galena & Chicago Union to carry out construction of the joint project. It was an ambitious project, in effect for 80 years. The area was somewhat late to be populated by Europeans until 1833, when the Winnebago nation ceded their lands to the United States and thereby made the land along Lake Michigan available for other purposes, including the construction of railroads. There was a simple reason to build the Fox River Valley Railroad: "If we don't build one, Milwaukee will."[49]

The Galena & Chicago Union Railroad Lines in 1862

Another small line, the Dixon Air Line, was built as a branch of the Galena & Chicago Union in 1854. An air line was a new term for a direct route, or at least one more direct than a competitor's rail line. Sometimes an air line was created by building rail bridges or cutting a pass through the land.

It was a unique success. Railmen across the country had tried to achieve this kind of success, only to be "driven to the verge of ruin."[50] The Galena & Chicago Union was the only such

---

[49] Andreas, A. T. (1884). *History of Chicago: From the earliest period to the present time*. Chicago: A.T. Andreas.

railroad enterprise that was successful from the beginning.

The Galena & Chicago Union was purchased by the Chicago & North Western. As a result, Chicago, St. Charles & Mississippi Air Line Railroad came into being in 1854. The only work completed over that first decade was grading the road. It was not only a long and unfruitful project, but also some years well over $1 million were spent on the project.[51] In 1864, the Chicago & North-Western was sold to the Galena & Chicago Union after it failed to be profitable.

As a result, the newly-minted Chicago, St. Charles & Mississippi Air Line Railroad came into being in 1854. The only work completed over that first decade was grading the road. It was not only a long and unfruitful project, some years well over $1 million were spent on the project.[52] It was used to connect Freeport to Chicago until 1872 when the Chicago & Iowa Railroad built tracks from Aurora to Forreston, discontinuing the Freeport branch. The result was that this section was part of 400 miles of track that became the Chicago, Burlington & Quincy Railroad Co.

There was a constant trading of railroads. No doubt, investors hoped to replicate the success of the Galena & Chicago Union. Many backers lost money on the railroad while this growing mode of travel brought new prosperity to many escaping famine or regime change in other parts of the world.

The route of the Chicago, Burlington & Quincy Railroad became known as a "Granger Road." As farmers and ranchers moved into the areas along the rail route, Burlington Railroad representatives advised prospective settlers as early as 1854 as to what crops would grow best in Missouri.

Nebraska is known for its vast fields of alfalfa. It was the Burlington Railroad that introduced alfalfa as a commercial crop in Nebraska.[53] The Burlington advanced agriscience by holding seed and soil exhibits, and having special poultry and livestock trains. The Burlington hired farmers in its shops in winter until they were able to develop their farms into full-time operations.

But, it was no afterthought. Congress granted tracts of land in Missouri, Iowa and Nebraska to promote western expansion and settlement. The Burlington hired as many as 250 agents in the eastern U.S., and in England, Scotland, Sweden and Germany. The Burlington sold more than 2 million acres of land to some 20,000 immigrants. Connecting the Burlington to all lines east made it easier for immigrants to travel west and to ship their alfalfa and other farm products to points east. Since the railroad was advertising the land, potential immigrants were likely to travel there by train rather than by Conestoga wagon.

Railroads were on everyone's mind by 1833. Another act, on March 2, 1833, incorporated the Rushville & Beardstown Turnpike-Road Company. The idea was to create a turnpike from

---

[50] *Ibid.*

[51] *Ibid.*

[52] *Ibid.*

[53] BNSF Railway. (1999). *The history of BNSF: A legacy for the 21st century*. Fort Worth, Tex: Burlington Northern Santa Fe Corporation.

Beardstown, through Rushville and Carthage, before passing through Warsaw all the way to Mississippi River.

In 1834, the Chicago & Vincennes Railroad Company came into being legally. But it was years before any action was taken.

Railroads were seen as expensive and impractical. Initially, Illinois' Gov. Duncan told the Illinois House of Representatives in 1834 that canals would be more usual than railroads and generally cheaper to build and to maintain. But, he recanted. The railroad would become king.

Some consider the first functioning railroad in Illinois to be the Coal-Mine Bluff Railroad in 1838. It was a practical enterprise, six miles long, created to haul coal from a bluff near modern-day East St. Louis and the Mississippi River. The Coal-Mine Bluff Railroad was created by Gov. John Reynolds of Illinois, who paid out of his own pocket to build the wooden-railroad and to power it literally by horse-power. The cars were moved by horses. There were no steam locomotives involved.

Reynolds already owned the land and hired an engineer to build it as a private enterprise. Unfortunately, being a new invention, the engineer miscalculated nearly everything.

The railroad needed to span more than 2,000 feet of lake, making this not just a railroad but a railroad with a bridge. Even the governor pondered "strange how it was possible we could construct this road under the circumstances." But, they did—and then he offered to sell it to Congress.[54]

From that humble origin, we see the rise of railroads in Illinois. That little six-mile railroad was extended to 15 miles of rail with three miles of branch rails. It became the Chicago, Peoria & St. Louis Railroad until it was sold at foreclosure in the 1920s.

But, the St. Louis Railroad was a bit behind the times. A charter was granted to the inland Jacksonville & Meredosia Railroad Co. on Feb. 5, 1835. It became the first railway in Illinois to operate a steam engine. Within a decade, the Jacksonville & Meredosia was sold and became part of the Wabash Railroad, which had been incorporated as the Wabash & Mississippi Turnpike Company on Jan. 13, 1836. The Wabash was incorporated on March 4, 1937, in order to create a railroad connecting Upper Alton, in Madison County, with Charleston, in Coles County. [55] But, by 1895, the Jacksonville, St. Louis, and Peoria routes became the St. Louis, Peoria & Northern Railway. But, that was well into the future. In the meantime, railroads literally inched across the state and even across state lines for decades.

The Illinois country was so new that in 1833, the state was still creating roads and bridges and ferry lines. Toll roads, in the form of turnpikes, and railroads were addressed by the state legislature. At that time, the state was voting on creating a toll road connecting Shawneetown with Equality, Illinois. Instead of ordering steel for the railroads, the legislators were devoting time to determining toll rates for ox teams, pleasure carriages and such things to pay for the creation of a road between Shawneetown on the Ohio River and Equality on the Saline River

[54] Ackerman, W. K. (1884). *Early Illinois railroads: A paper read before the Chicago Historical Society, Tuesday evening, February 20, 1883.* Chicago: Fergus Print. Co.

[55] Illinois., Illinois Territory., & Illinois. (1837). *The laws of Illinois: Passed at ... General Assembly.* Vandalia, Ill: Robert Blackwell, Public Printer.

cutting the travel distance to roughly half.

The charter of the Illinois & St. Louis Railroad & Coal Company was approved by the Illinois legislature when the St. Clair Railroad Company was sold. At some point, the name was changed to Pittsburg Railroad and Coal Company.[56]

Obviously, the Illinois railroad history is coal-related, not passenger-related. Prior to the Civil War, a dyke was built on the Mississippi River and the railroad owned a ferry. Between the two, coal was delivered directly into the holds of river barges or steamboats. The inclusion of the word coal in the railroad name was not an afterthought. It was what made Illinois railroads prosperous. The railroad became part of a delivery system by reducing the cost of supplying cheap fuel to river traffic.

Eventually, the I & St. L. began offloading at the Union Depot, competing with other lines. Anyone seeking a wise investment would do well to buy stock in the I & St. L. By 1878, the gross annual earnings were $174, 964.47. Accounting for inflation, that was an estimated $4 million. By then, passengers were a part of the rail transportation system but they only represented about $150,000 out of that $4 million.

Railroads created a boom in real estate sales since speculators began to buy up land where they anticipated a railroad might be laid out and the railroad company might opt to buy the land rather than exercising eminent domain. Entire towns grew up based on the anticipation of a railroad and all the promise it brought for transportation of goods and passengers.

By 1859, the Illinois Central Railroad published a guide to railroad lands for sale.[57] It encompassed 1,400,000 acres of prairie and woods.

From the beginning of the railroad craze, there were lawsuits. There were conflicts of interest including the sale of land where railroads might be built. But, the elevation and other unforeseen factors sometimes altered those plans. In other instances, landowners moved the railroad when it was convenient for them to bring business to their town, or to block business from another town. Unfortunately, moving a railroad had dire consequences. Eventually, the little railroads, being built three, ten or fifteen miles at a stretch, needed to all connect. They simply could not be randomly realigned at the whim of businessmen or the Commissioner of the Board of Public Works.[58]

After an eventual investigation of the Union Pacific Railroad by the Interstate Commerce Commission concluded: "No student of the railroad problem can doubt that a most prolific source of financial disaster and complication to railroads in the past has been the desire and

---

[56] Reavis, L. U. (1879). *The railway and river systems of the city of St. Louis: With a brief statement of facts designed to demonstrate that St. Louis is rapidly becoming the food distributing center of the North American Continent : also a presentation of the great commercial and manufacturing establishments of St. Louis.* St. Louis, Mo: Printed by Woodward, Tiernan & Hale.

[57] Illinois Central Railroad Company. (1859). *A guide to the Illinois Central Railroad lands: The Illinois Central Railroad Company, offer for sale over 1,400,00 acres of selected prairie and wood lands, in tracts of forty acres and upwards, suitable for farms, on long credits and low prices, situated on each side of their railroad, extending through the state of Illinois.* Chicago: Illinois Central Railroad Office.

[58] Illinois., Walters, W., & Illinois. (1840). *Laws of the state of Illinois, passed by the eleventh General Assembly, at their special session, began and held at Springfield, on the ninth of December, one thousand eight hundred and thirty-nine: Published in pursuance of law.* Springfield [Ill.: William Walters, public printer.

ability of railroad managers to engage in enterprises outside the legitimate operation of their railroads, especially by the acquisition of other railroads and their securities. The evil which results, first, to the investing public, and finally to the general public, cannot be corrected after the transaction has taken place; it can be easily and effectively prohibited."[59]

Also by 1838, other railroads were under consideration. Peoria & Warsaw Railroad was to form a west line from Peoria County to Warsaw. The first party was organized in June 1837 and spent the next three and a half months surveying twelve miles. Eventually, the crew surveyed a route from Canton to Farmington. By 1841, the Illinois General Assembly declared that May 1, 1843, was the target date for completing the connecting rail between the Peoria & Warsaw Railroad with the Des Moines Rapids Railroad, of Iowa.[60] But, the Warsaw branch was never built.

On Dec. 1, 1837, work crews began submitting payments due the Northern Cross Railroad (between Illinois and Mississippi Rivers) to the state legislature. From these vouchers, we know that the right of way of the eastern division was surveyed between Quincy and Columbus between February and April of 1838. This was the section between the Illinois & Sangamon Rivers, about 63 miles of track. Soon, it was extended, along with the Central Branch Railroad to connect the Wabash River with the Erie Canal.

The Pekin & Bloomington Branch Railroad was a branch of the Central Railroad which connected Tremont to the Illinois River. The Peoria & Mackinaw Branch Railroad of the Central Railroad was another piece. Other branches were coming aboard. Another ten miles added Carthage to the route.

The Southern Cross Railroad connected Belleville with Lebanon, crossing the Kaskaskia River and including the Great Western Mail Route.

In February of 1841, the legislature legally incorporated the Illinois & Rock River Railroad Company. Their task was to build and maintain a railroad between LaSalle and Dixon, Illinois. It was an impressive undertaking with the goal of "terminating at such points on [the] Rock River, the Illinois, or on the Illinois & Michigan Canal."[61]

The Mount Carmel & Alton Road Company was also incorporated. The goal was to connect with the Southern Cross Railroad. Eventually, it was expected to form a 115-mile connection with the New Albany Railroad Company in Indiana.

The North Cross Railroad was given charge to connect to Jacksonville, Illinois by rail, and with that, it was all starting to come together. The St. Clair Railroad Company was granted permission to extend their line until it extended as far as the Great Western Mail Route. In fact,

---

[59] Brandeis, L. D., & Harry Houdini Collection (Library of Congress). (1914). *Other people's money: And how the bankers use it.* New York: Frederick A. Stokes Co.

[60] Illinois., Walters, W., & Illinois. (1840). *Laws of the state of Illinois, passed by the eleventh General Assembly, at their special session, began and held at Springfield, on the ninth of December, one thousand eight hundred and thirty-nine: Published in pursuance of law.* Springfield [Ill.: William Walters, public printer.

[61] Illinois., Walters, W., & Illinois. (1840). *Laws of the state of Illinois, passed by the eleventh General Assembly, at their special session, began and held at Springfield, on the ninth of December, one thousand eight hundred and thirty-nine: Published in pursuance of law.* Springfield [Ill.: William Walters, public printer.

the railroad was directed to essentially replace the mail route with rail lines. Eventually, the Great Western climbed up the Mississippi Bluffs on the Mississippi River, past Illinoistown with the goal of reaching the Big Wabash River, opposite Vincennes, Ind. But, water always played a role in the location of Illinois railroads.

By 1843, the Illinois state legislature put an end to railroad building at taxpayer expense. Known as the Holbrook Charter, the state abandoned the Great Western Railway Company. The Great Western went from being a direct financial and other concern to the state to one which the state divested itself of all government involvement. In the process, the Cairo project became the Cairo City & Canal Company. The Great Western Railway Company was dissolved on March 3, 1845. Four years later, there was a reversal. The Cairo City & Canal Company and the Great Western Railway Company were joined under the railway's name and tasked with creating a line connecting Cairo to Chicago. By 1850, grand plans were underway as the State of Illinois granted land to construction of a railroad that would connect Chicago with Mobile, Ala.

But, it would take time. Along the way, the state of Illinois donated more than 2.5 million acres of land to the Illinois Central Railroad Company, where they would build 700 consecutive miles of railroad. The Illinois Central Railroad was nicknamed the "Main Line of Mid-America." It was unique in that it was one of only a few railroads running north-south, while the majority of railroads operated east-west. The Illinois Central continues to exist, but it is now owned by Canadian National and transports all the way from Canada to New Orleans.[62]

While land speculators had high hopes, only a little over 100,000 acres were purchased by private parties. As Hon. Lawrence Heyworth, a Liverpool resident and member of the English parliament said after traveling aboard the Illinois Central Railroad, "This is not a railway company; it is a land company."

He became a most extreme speculator, buying every available piece of land for sale by the Illinois Central Railroad. Like most speculators, he never saw a profit. Growth was too slow along the railroad lines and towns. While the railroad succeeded, the public saw no desperate need to live next to a railroad.

But, the Illinois Central Railroad was the first line to reach Chicago. On June 14, 1852, the Illinois Central was granted permission from the City of Chicago to "lay down, construct and maintain within the limits of the city, and along the margin of the lake within and adjacent to the same, a railroad with one or more tracks."[63] Nearly a year later, land on Randolph Street was set aside for a depot. Originally, the land set aside passed through a portion of Fort Dearborn, owned by the United States government. That being the case, an act of congress was required in order for the Illinois Central to build their rail line. Initially, the Illinois Central was given a ten year lease on the land. But, they eventually bought the property for $45,000, an exorbitant price at the time.

---

[62] "The Illinois Central Railroad, *Main Line of Mid-America.*" American-Rails.com.

[63] Railroad Historical Company. (1900). *History of the Illinois Central Railroad Company and representative employes: A history of the growth and development of one of the leading arteries of transportation in the United States, from inception to its present mammoth proportions, together with the biographies of many of the men who have been and are identified with the varied interests of the Illinois Central Railroad.* Chicago.

Illinois Central Railway Ad

Yet another lawsuit was filed. The Illinois Central Railroad sued the U.S. government, demanding a refund of their money since not all of the land was initially required for military purposes. It was already being used as general public lands and therefore should have brought a lower price. But, the court declined to support the railroad's case.

Perhaps the biggest challenge in building a railroad in that early pre-Civil War decade was there were very few people living along the 130-mile stretch directly south of Chicago. Building the railroad instantly created jobs.

There were no hotels, no restaurants, and no stores of any kind. Only half a dozen settlements existed according to the maps.

Railroad laborers had to be enticed from elsewhere or along the railroad route and the company was responsible for their room and board. But, much of the time, the railroad accommodations were rudimentary. The railroad provided camp poles, tents, camp furniture and general camp supplies.[64]

The first railroad engineers were not the people who ran the trains. They were the civil engineers who determined where the railroad should be. They relied on surveyors who mapped out the land.

But there was plenty of room for manual labor such as doing work as an axeman or the all-

---

[64] Illinois. (1837). *Laws of the state of Illinois: Passed by the ... General Assembly at their ... session.* Vandalia, Ill: State Printers.

important role of "compass man" and "leveler." Sometimes there were expenses for such things as "repairing compass case." There were unique jobs like someone to paint rods and targets to mark the surveying.

There was temporary income along the routes for such things as boarding workhands and horses. The cost probably included food and water for the horses. In 1837, one railroad spent what would be the equivalent of about $1,200 on bridles and saddles.

The railroad crews had to haul their own flour, bacon, coffee, sugar, tea, eggs, butter, cheese and a cook or two to prepare the food. The railroad purchased soap, candles, and anything else they needed. In 1837, that included buffalo robes for workmen.

Attracting workers to build the first ever railroad with no other humans in sight was actually the easier task. Nearly 80,000 tons of iron for building those rails were imported from England and began arriving in 1852. They were delivered to the general land office in Washington, D.C. Delivering them to Illinois was more of a challenge. The rails arrived while the final location of the rail line was being surveyed and legally approved. Just getting the iron halfway across the country to Illinois was a task.

Difficulties continued. By 1853, the 61-mile portion of railroad between LaSalle and Bloomington started running trains as the Illinois River Railroad. But, the bridge across the Illinois River was only temporary. According to historic accounts, "[rail] cars were hauled to the top of the bluff with ropes and chains by means of a stationary engine."[65] Unfortunately, the Illinois River Railroad never went beyond Pekin before going bankrupt.

Trains also brought funding for education. By July 1854, trains were traveling 128 miles of rail from Chicago to Urbana. Soon after, the Illinois Central Railroad donated $50,000 toward construction of the "industrial college," Illinois University. This was, of course, the University of Illinois at Champaign-Urbana.

By November 1854, passengers could travel by rail from Chicago all the way to Cairo. That is, railroads finally existed from Chicago to St. Louis. Other railroads helped connect the lines. From St. Louis the Ohio & Mississippi Railroad traveled down to Sandoval on the Illinois Central Railroad and on south to Cairo. The interconnected web of rails now connected Chicago on Lake Michigan to St. Louis on the Mississippi River, and then to Cairo between the Mississippi and Ohio rivers.

The Mobile & Ohio Railroad was not fully completed as far as Cairo until 1874. The Baltimore & Ohio Railroad joined up with the Illinois Central tracks on Nov. 17, 1874.

The Illinois Central Railroad Company connected Jackson, Tennessee to Fillmore, near Cairo. The Cairo line became a means north for escaped slaves. They would cross the Ohio River at Bird's Point, Missouri. (At one point, that portion of land belonged to Kentucky.) Slaves would hide in freight cars or beneath passenger cars. According to the Fugitive Slave Law in effect at the time, they could be returned to their masters. The law was not repealed until June 13, 1864.

---

[65] Railroad Historical Company. (1900). *History of the Illinois Central Railroad Company and representative employes: A history of the growth and development of one of the leading arteries of transportation in the United States, from inception to its present mammoth proportions, together with the biographies of many of the men who have been and are identified with the varied interests of the Illinois Central Railroad.* Chicago.

Escaping via the Illinois Central was risky business.

The Illinois Central Railroad No. 790

It was monumental. For the first time, rail transportation existed from the Great Lakes all the way to Mexico. It had taken some 40 years, but it was a reality.

By 1850, the Great Western Mail Route became the Great Western Railway Company. On Jan. 5, 1851, Sen. Stephen Douglas had a greater vision of the future of railroads. Judge Douglas signed the first charter for a "central road," which did not necessarily mean a railroad at the time. But, he saw that it was essential to connecting the Great lakes with the Mississippi, and the St. Lawrence River with the Gulf of Mexico, as well Chicago with the east. Douglas believed that more roads would benefit the whole country.

The Illinois Central Railroad was ceded a federal land grant in 1853. In 1855, the legislature declared that the "road penetrates the best of Illinois and will cause rapid settlement on its line."[66] Within three years, prairie cities appeared along the railroads.

In 1857, the Peoria & Oquawka Railroad connected Gilman on the Chicago Branch to El Paso on its main line. It took more than a decade but the result was a line forming the Gilman, Clinton & Springfield Railroad.

On June 12, 1861, a federal embargo on the Mississippi River banned river travel between Paducah and Smithland, Kentucky. Illinois Central could transport goods and passengers to the river, but no farther. The rail company lost a great deal of money over this Mississippi River Blockade.[67]

---

[66] Hasse, A. R., & Carnegie Institution of Washington. (1907). *Index of economic material in documents of the states of the United States: New York, 1789-1904*. Washington: Carnegie institution of Washington.

[67] Snodgrass, M. E. (2015). *The Civil War era and Reconstruction: An encyclopedia of social, political, cultural,*

The Civil War impacted the juvenile railway system in other ways. By May 29, 1864, rail travel between Chicago and Cairo was restricted to government employees only. But, make no mistake, the railways profited financially from the war between the North and the South. They were paid to move troops and war supplies. It was war time. The Illinois Central Railroad was placed at the service of the U.S. Government. Most troops from Illinois, Minnesota and Wisconsin joined the Union forces at Cairo, Illinois. Between 1861 and 1865, the transportation of troops and soldiers left the railroads in a poor and unsafe condition.

Perhaps a lesser known fact is that many of the Union officers and privates were previously employees of the Illinois Central Railroad Company. Maj. Gen. George B. McClellan was engineer-in-chief for one year before serving as vice president from 1857-1859. His background was with rivers, not railroads. He was the former Chicago Harbor Master and had superintended the removal of the sandbar across the Chicago River.

A director of the Illinois Central from 1865 to 1868, Maj. Gen. Ambrose Everett Burnside was called to Rhode Island to command the state troops there. Eventually, he was in charge of the Army of the Potomac.

By the end of the war, the Illinois Central Railroad Company had 900,000 acres of land to sell. They wanted to see the population grow, both for increased rider fees and the need for more transportation. They Illinois Central began to promote the "Illinois fruit region" in the Egyptian basin, a common term for the very southern tip of the state.

The little St. Clair Railroad would become the connector between Michigan and Indiana, spanning Illinois.[68]

Cairo was literally put on the map by the railroad. The Cairo City & Canal Company, formed March 4, 1837, was granted real estate in Alexander County. Nestled in the arms of the Ohio River on one side and the Mississippi River on the other, Cairo rail lands were laid off into town lots to form the city. The plan was to create dykes, levees and embankments for security. The Civil War never reached Illinois, but Cairo became a thriving supply base for the Union Army. A canal was built to bring water from the third body of water, the Cache River, through the city. Eventually, it became a central road for the rail lines.

Post-civil war, the Illinois Central Railroad thrived, connecting with the Dubuque & Sioux City Railroad Company. Others followed: connections with the Cedar Falls & Minnesota Railroad Company. Railroad construction was well underway across the country. Illinois was literally right in the heart of it.

The Belleville & Illinois Railroad Company was incorporated in 1852[69] and serves as an example of how diverse the needs of a railroad company are. "Belleville and Illinoistown Railroad Company with perpetual succession, and by that name and style shall be capable in law

---

and economic history.

[68] Hasse, A. R., & Carnegie Institution of Washington. (1907). *Index of economic material in documents of the states of the United States: New York, 1789-1904*. Washington: Carnegie institution of Washington.
[69] Illinois. (1853). *Laws of the state of Illinois: Passed by the ... General Assembly at their ... session*. Vandalia, Ill: State Printers.

of taking, holding, purchasing, leasing, selling and conveying estate and property, real, personal and mixed, so far as the same may be necessary for the purposes hereinafter mentioned, and no further; and in their corporate name may sue and be sued, to have a common seal, which they may alter or renew at pleasure, and may have and exercise all powers, rights, privileges, and immunities which are or may be necessary to carry into effect the purposes or objects of this act, as the same are herein set forth."

Transportation of fuel was at the heart of railroads. At inception, the Belleville & Illinois Railroad Company was permitted to receive, take or hold "any amount of lands, not to exceed twelve hundred acres at any one time, and to mine and work the coal beds therein, and to transport the coal mined therefrom." The legal charter granted the railroad the right to lease or purchase from St. Clair County, Ill. all the ferry rights across the Mississippi River to St. Louis.[70]

So the earliest railroad companies were really in the mining business. The railroads were simply a method of transporting fuel.

While rail lines were interconnecting across the country, making a connection in Cairo remained archaic until Oct. 29, 1889. In order to make a connection between the New Orleans line and the Illinois Central, passengers and freight alike were passed by steamboat between the section that remained unfinished. Finally, in 1889, the railroad bridge at Cairo was opened for traffic. For the first time, a passenger could travel the 938 miles from Chicago to New Orleans by rail.

Years later, Steve Goodman wrote a folk-song about the Illinois Central Railroad route called the "City of New Orleans" when he heard that the route was to close due to lack of riders. In 1972, he played the song for Arlo Guthrie who first made the well-known song popular.

---

[70] *Ibid.*

The Modern Illinois Central Railway Still Connects Chicago & New Orleans

Illinois Central did not close down the City of New Orleans route. It exists today and continues to connect to waterways. The route runs from Chicago's Union Station, across the Chicago River, the Calumet River, along the Kankakee River, across the prairie through Rantoul, Champaign-Urbana, Mattoon, Effingham, Centralia and Carbondale. It arrives at Cairo, the City of New Orleans, crossing to Fulton, Kentucky, and on to Memphis. At the Tennessee and Mississippi state lines, the rail line progresses south through the Lower Mississippi Delta Region. By the time it reaches Greenwood, Mississippi, the Yazoo River is in sight. The Jackson Station, on the Pearl River, was a historic trading settlement and played a role in the Civil War when Gen. Sherman burned it to the ground three times. Further south, the line passes through Brookhaven on the Bogue Chitto River and on to Magnolia on the Tangipahoa River. Before arriving in New Orleans, the route crosses the Louisiana Bayou and then Lake Pontchartrain and the ancient city of New Orleans, on the Mississippi River.[71]

Post-Civil War, railroad repairs were necessary. The rails had been worn thin by military

---

[71] *City of New Orleans Route Guide.* National Railroad Passenger Corporation. 2010.

transportation needs. But, the truly significant improvement, from the passenger's point of view, was the introduction of the Pullman Palace Car Company. These elegant sleeping cars were manufactured in Chicago, and rented to the Illinois Central Railroad. Prior to that, passengers of the Illinois Central had used much more pedestrian sleeper cars. Initially, the Illinois Central was barely even considered a passenger line. But, once the route to New Orleans was completed, passengers were eager to visit the south and to pay for first-class accommodations.[72]

By 1880, the Pullman Palace Car Company had opened ground on land adjacent to the Illinois Central tracks. The same year, they opened the Kankakee & Southwestern Road running from Ottawa to Minonk. Instead of creating sparse rails that needed to be intersected, rail lines were now branching off away from the main line.

Railway labor was again in high demand. The Illinois Central replaced the rails in its entire system with brand new steel rails. Chicago increased its lines from a single line, in and out of the city, to two tracks for freight trains and another pair for passenger trains.

By 1883, when the South Chicago Railroad was completed, it brought a change to way Chicagoans lived. The five-mile long double track made it easier to live in the suburbs and commute into the city.

But, there were ups and downs along the way. In 1876, both the New Orleans and Cairo lines defaulted, resulting in foreclosure. The two were combined and became the Chicago, St. Louis & New Orleans Railroad Company.

Bu the mid-1870s Illinois realized it needed to further regulate railroads. It became law to require railroads to construct fences, within six months of opening a rail line, to prevent livestock from wandering onto the rails. Maintenance responsibility increased with the legal requirement for railroad lines to keep their right-of-way clear of dead grass and weeds, or anything else that might catch fire. And, Illinois required crossing bars on "each public road or street." The signs had to read either "Railroad Crossing" or "Look out for the cars," and the print had to be nine inches tall. Locomotives were required to have a bell and a steam whistle that either an engineer or railroad fireman had to sound within eighty rods of any public highway crossing.[73]

In spite of the law and safety measures, one of the worst train disasters in history happened near Chatsworth, Ill. on August 10, 1887. Because of the widely connected train lines, an excursion to visit Niagara Falls was well advertised. Arriving from west or north, the train stopped in Peoria with 20 passenger cars. A second locomotive was added. There were six Pullman sleeping cars. Prairie fires had been common and railmen were working to prevent fires along the railroads from risk of catching fire as trains passed, sending sparks onto the shoulder.

No one, to this day, can agree on all of the details but the route crossed a railroad bridge near Chatsworth. When the train arrived, the wooden rail bridge was on fire. The train, that day, was a

---

[72] Railroad Historical Company. (1900). *History of the Illinois Central Railroad Company and representative employees: A history of the growth and development of one of the leading arteries of transportation in the United States, from inception to its present mammoth proportions, together with the biographies of many of the men who have been and are identified with the varied interests of the Illinois Central Railroad.* Chicago.

[73] *Laws of Illinois Relating to Railroads and Warehouses with Appendix.* Springfield, Ill: D.W. Lusk, State printer and binder, 1877. Print.

heavy load for even the sturdiest bridges of the day. But, the bridge was wood and it was already on fire when the train approached. The engineer saw the fire too late to respond. [74] There were more than 800 passengers aboard and most of them never reached Niagara. They died a fiery death in what has come to be known as "The Chatsworth Disaster."[75]

Among other things, the Illinois Central Railroad created jobs. Beyond the railroad boards, next came the law departments. There were an array of legal issues pertaining to adhering to the new laws governing the creation and connection of railroad lines. A great deal of the history of railroads involved setting aside land for railroads and much of that was funded by tax dollars. There were auditors and traveling auditors assigned to track all those dollars.

Numerous workers were assigned to manage passengers and shipping. Railway agents became a new way of life, stationed in major cities. Because of the interconnected lines, the Illinois Central Railroad, early on, had passenger agents in Chicago in addition to far flung locations like Louisville, Kentucky; Memphis, Tenn.; Omaha, Neb.; and New Orleans. There was an agent in charge of foreign freight as well as a European agent in Liverpool, Eng. To manage all this, there were superintendents scattered through Illinois and in Cherokee, Dubuque and Council Bluffs, Iowa; Jackson, Tenn.; Durant, Miss; and, again, New Orleans.

But, on the ground and across the Illinois prairie, there were 1.4 million acres "in tracts of forty acres and upwards, suitable for Farms on long credits and low prices, situated on each side of their railroad, extending through the State of Illinois."[76] The railroad guide claimed that the seat of every county in the state of Illinois was within 15 miles of a railroad thoroughfare, with but a few exceptions. "The Chicago branch, 250 miles in length, runs through the Grand Prairie, which, with the exception of occasional groves, presents an almost interminable plain, of which the natural product is prairie-grass."

The first-line railroad builders were the first to turn the soil and dig it deep enough to build bridges and flatten rises to create level surfaces. In the process, it was the railroad crews who discovered that these Illinois properties were covered with vegetable mold between 18 inches and two feet thick "constituting an almost inexhaustible supply of nutriment for crops, for all time."

A mystery still persists that early settlers cut down vast forests in Illinois. But, the early railroad land guide explained that, "It is a popular but mistaken belief that this region was once densely covered with trees, and that their disappearance is to be ascribed to the annual fires that swept over it, long before it became known to the whites, consuming every form of vegetation, except where it was protected by the streams and ravines. There is no evidence that, in the previous physical history of this region, the arborescent vegetation was more extended than it is

---

[74] Burford, Cary C. *The Chatsworth Wreck: A Saga of Excursion Train Travel in the American Midwest in the 1880's*. Fairbury, Ill: Blade Pub. Co, 1949. Print.

[75] Moreno, Richard. *It Happened in Illinois: Remarkable Events That Shaped History*. Guilford, Conn: Globe Pequot Press, 2011. Print.

[76] Illinois Central Railroad Company. (1859). *A guide to the Illinois Central Railroad lands: The Illinois Central Railroad Company, offer for sale over 1,400,00 acres of selected prairie and wood lands, in tracts of forty acres and upwards, suitable for farms, on long credits and low prices, situated on each side of their railroad, extending through the state of Illinois*. Chicago: Illinois Central Railroad Office.

now."[77]

Because of their study of the soil, it was the Illinois Central Railroad that first recommended crops for planting. The deep black soil in the northern part of the state was best for spring wheat, barley, oats, potatoes and domestic grasses for grazing. The grey prairie sod in the more central part of the state was best for winter wheat and fruit. The wooded areas were better for winter wheat, as the forests were felled to build homes and barns.

After listing the current price for wheat, the guide went on to claim that, "It was not until the opening of the Illinois Central Railroad that wheat was cultivated to any considerable extent; it now forms the great staple of the region, and has been the means of conferring upon the farmer, uncounted wealth." Farther south, near the original southern-most section of Illinois, "It has all of the fertility of the Nile, and is well adapted to the growth of Indian corn, broom corn, sorghum, tobacco, hemp…."

They drove home their point by saying, "Migration usually follows lines of latitude. Illinois will, therefore, continue to receive the tide of population from the overcrowded districts of the Old and New World, until her immense capacity for occupation and expansion is fully tested." It was time to move west, because of the railroad and by way of the Illinois Central. Hotels existed along the way. Farmers could stay abreast of farm prices by telegraph on a daily basis.

Lost over the ages is the first precursor to GPS locators and, before that, concrete pins to mark property lines. "In a timber-region, the section corners were blazed onto the trees. On the prairie, sections corners were indicated by mounds containing charcoal, into which a stake was driven."

Imagine arriving by train to the heart of Illinois where there were no homes yet, no farms, and very few little clusters passing as villages. To select a property, one had to search for the emblazoned tree or the stake in a pile of charcoal in order to identify the northeast corner of a forty-acre lot. From that northeast corner, the new immigrant would walk south to the next tree or charcoal pile to find the southeast corner. Then he would turn right, until he reached the next. Then turn right again, and repeat. He would arrive back at the first northeast corner of his forty acres. He was home, thanks to the railroad.

To sweeten the deal, the Illinois Board of Agriculture offered a premium of $6,000 to anyone who could invent a steam-powered farm plow. The Illinois Central Railroad added another $1,500 to the premium.

The railroad was committed to farming and the new lifestyle of Midwestern agriculture. As they mentioned, reaping machines had replaced back-breaking labor. They explained, "The contractor furnishes a driver, raker and horses; the farmer finds binders and shockers." Usually the contractor provided four horses and three threshing operators. The farmer provided four more horses and five farmhands. Jobs were broken down: one driver, one feeder, one measurer, one farmhand to pitch sheaves, one to cut bands and three more to take away the straw left over.

Like a farm director, the Illinois Central Railroad explained that sod "is turned over" in May and June, by farmers who had beat the rush and were already farming the new railroad lands. They continued with a description of the process of when to harrow, when to sow, and when to

---

[77] *Ibid.*

switch from wheat to oats.

Historically, immigrants suffered from the ague, more commonly known as malaria. The Illinois Central Railroad even had a solution to that. The advice was surprisingly sound. Avoid the bottomlands and dense groves near streams. While they perhaps did not fully understand the science behind that advice, they were essentially advising immigrants to stay away from environments that bred mosquitoes that carried malaria. But, ultimately, the responsibility for good health lay with the farmer, not the Illinois Central Railroad and they minced no words about making that point.

"It must be borne in mind too, that, in subduing a farm, the settler deprives himself of comforts, and undergoes exposures at variance with his previous life; and if he finds himself in bad health, he is fain to attribute to the climate what in reality is the result of his own recklessness and folly."[78]

A subtle criticism of the emigrant who arrived in a covered wagon was ticked carefully into the conversation. "He camped in the groves, and beside the sluggish streams, that he might readily obtain wood and water, where miasmatic vapors were sure to be generated." Obviously, the Illinois Central Railroad was the way west, if you wanted to arrive and stay healthy. The Illinois Central went on to explain that the average duration of life is higher in Illinois than in most of the older states, or in most places around the world.

It was the Illinois Central Railroad that advised immigrants about what kind of grasses to plant and the best type of livestock to breed. There were accounts of reportedly true stories. "Jacob Strahn, who came to this country twenty-five years ago, a poor man, when in the full tide of enterprise, has been known to turn off 10,000 head of cattle a year."[79] To punctuate their story, they added, "There are English packers in the State who put up beef for the London market, where it bears a high character." The implication was that beef was being shipped by train to upscale markets in Europe.

Swine came to be associated with Chicago. In 1859, the Illinois Central Railroad, no doubt, helped make that a self-fulfilling prophecy. "Equal facilities exist for fattening hogs, and Chicago will, ere long, press close upon Cincinnati in this respect."

With that, the Illinois Central began selling 40-acre sections in large lots whenever possible. The Illinois Central Railroad started sales of 50,000 acres at a single price of $20 per acre until $1 million of profit had been generated. Prospectors, obviously, would buy the larger acreages and then resell them in smaller portions. Once the Illinois Central had realized their $1 million, they would lower the price to $15 per acre until they earned $5.2 million. At that point, a

---

[78] Illinois Central Railroad Company. (1859). *A guide to the Illinois Central Railroad lands: The Illinois Central Railroad Company, offer for sale over 1,400,00 acres of selected prairie and wood lands, in tracts of forty acres and upwards, suitable for farms, on long credits and low prices, situated on each side of their railroad, extending through the state of Illinois.* Chicago: Illinois Central Railroad Office.

[79] Illinois Central Railroad Company. (1859). *A guide to the Illinois Central Railroad lands: The Illinois Central Railroad Company, offer for sale over 1,400,00 acres of selected prairie and wood lands, in tracts of forty acres and upwards, suitable for farms, on long credits and low prices, situated on each side of their railroad, extending through the state of Illinois.* Chicago: Illinois Central Railroad Office.

staggering 1.3 million acres were available for a mere $8 an acre until $10.4 million of sales were completed. There was money to be made on all those railroad lands and now that the railroad was there to deliver goods to market, it was profitable to move to Illinois. The railroad even published a payment plan, including interest.

Their land sale guide even provided an argument for the man who could not afford to buy land. "If he has no capital, let him not hang about the town, but go to work in the country where there is a demand for his labor, at remunerative prices." The Illinois Central declared that a mere three years of labor in Illinois would be enough for any man to raise enough money to "commence his career as a proprietor of the soil."

The Illinois Central advised migration *en masse*. "The Dane, the Swede, the Norwegian, the Irish, the German, with his liberty-loving principles, in coming here, shall find those to whom he is connected by the ties of country, and with whom he can at once affiliate. To such men, *organized* emigration is preferable."

Ports of entry were identified. The Illinois Central Railroad advised immigrants to arrive in either New York, Boston, Portland or New Orleans. "The map prefixed to this report will show the railway connections between Chicago…and these points of departure."

And if the farm life wasn't for you, the Illinois Central Railroad claimed there were 100 cities and villages with factories, mills, stores, post-offices, schools and churches "affording the comforts of civilized life to the settler, while they open every opportunity and prospect of business to the mechanic and trade."

But the railroads never divested themselves of their connection to coal. The Illinois Central Railroad locomotives burned coal. They reminded readers of their land guide that there was a known seam of coal just 76 miles north of Cairo—on the Illinois Central Railroad. East of Tolono, south of Champaign-Urbana, was another seam, on the Great Western Railroad. There was another on the Main Line at LaSalle.

"The coal is of a fair quality, and besides the local consumption, some of it is sent to Dunleith and Chicago." In other words, there were local customers in addition to the bigger markets where the coal could be shipped by rail.

As mentioned earlier, the Galena lead was of great value. It was the richest lead-bearing region in the United States at the time. The Galena limestone was also of value. It could be used for construction or for burning into quicklime. The Kankakee area quarries were Niagara Limestone. The limestone near LaSalle was good for manufacturing cement. The Chicago limestone was better for construction.

There was iron to be mined just two and a half miles west of the Illinois Central Railroad near Jonesboro. And, the Illinois Central Railroad was ready to haul it to market. Illinois was the place to be.

The Great Fire

A map showing the section of Chicago that burned in the fire, with Mrs. O'Leary's barn marked by a red dot in the southwestern part of the damaged section.

"I was in bed myself and my husband and five children when this fire commenced. I was the owner of them five cows that was burnt, and the horse wagon and harness. I had two tons of coal and two tons of hay. I had everything that I wanted in for the winter. I could not save five cents worth of anything out of the barn. Only that Mr. Sullivan got out a little calf. The calf was worth eleven dollars on Saturday morning. Saturday morning I refused even eleven dollars for the calf, and it was sold afterwards for eight dollars. I didn't save five cents out of the fire. I could not tell anything of the fire only that two men came by the door. I guess it was my husband got outside the door and he ran back to the bedroom and said 'Kate the barn is afire.' I ran out and the whole barn was on fire. Well I went out to the barn and upon my word I could not tell anyone about the fire. I got just the way I could not tell anything about the fire." - Catherine O'Leary

In the wake of the Fort Dearborn massacre and the reoccupation of the site by white settlers, it took only about 40 years for Chicago to grow from a small settlement of about 300 people into a thriving metropolis with a population of 300,000. However, over the course of just two days in 1871, much of that progress was burned to the ground. In arguably the most famous fire in American history, a blaze in the southwestern section of Chicago began to burn out of control on the night of October 8, 1871. Thanks to *The Chicago Tribune*, the fire has been apocryphally credited to a cow kicking over a lantern in Mrs. Catherine O'Leary's barn, and though that was not true, the rumor dogged Mrs. O'Leary to the grave.

Although people who have only passing familiarity with the Great Chicago Fire often know the legend about Mrs. O'Leary's cow, little is actually known for certain about how the fire began. It was pretty clear that the fire began a short while after 9:00 p.m. on Sunday evening, October 8, 1871, but even before the last flame had died down, a colorful legend had grown up around the cause of the fire. While there were many different versions of the original story, the gist of it was that Kate O'Leary went out after dark to care for or check on her cows, and for some reason, she left the kerosene lantern she was carrying with her in the barn. Then, after she went back into the house, one of her cows kicked it over, spilling the oil and igniting the hay.

SUPPOSED CAUSE OF THE CHICAGO FIRE. MRS. O'LEARY AND HER COW.

A *Harper's Magazine* illustration depicting O'Leary and her cow

Although the legend sounds fanciful today, there were several reasons why the story seemed plausible to investigators. First, according to the board who reviewed the evidence, "the fire originated in a two-story barn in the rear of No. 137 DeKoven Street, the premises being owned by Patrick O'Leary. The fire was first discovered by a drayman by the name of Daniel [Dennis] Sullivan, who saw it while sitting on the sidewalk on the south side of DeKoven Street, and nearly opposite O'Leary's premises. He fixes the time at not more than twenty or twenty-five minutes past nine o'clock when he first noticed the flames coming out of the barn. There is no proof that any person had been in the barn after nightfall that evening. Whether it originated from a spark blown from a chimney on that windy night, or was set on fire by human agency, we are unable to determine. Mr. O'Leary and all his family prove to have been in bed and asleep at the time. There was a small party in the front part of O'Leary's house, which was occupied by Mr. McLaughlin and wife. But we fail to find any evidence that anybody from McLaughlin's part of the house went near the barn that night." Furthermore, the O'Leary's did keep cows in that barn, and the cows would have needed care on the farm.

The O'Leary house at No. 137 DeKoven Street

However, except in the case of a cow giving birth, there would be no reason for anyone to have gone to the barn at night. Milking was done in the morning and the evening, but always during daylight hours, meaning there would have been no reason for Mrs. O'Leary to leave a lighted lamp in the barn. Not only would it potentially start a fire, it would also waste oil, which the O'Leary's could not afford to waste.

Of course, the most damning evidence refuting the story came from the man who originally published it. 22 years later, Michael Ahern publically admitted that he had added the story to his original article on the fire to lend some local color to the event.

If indeed the fire was started as a result of someone or something on the O'Leary farm, there were better suspects than Mrs. O'Leary or her cows. According to O'Leary's testimony before the board investigating the fire, there was quite a party going on in another part of the house that night. The family had rented two front rooms to the McLaughlin's, who were the ones throwing the party, and while O'Leary maintained that she was not in attendance, she claimed she could hear what was going on. This led to speculation on some people's parts that there was also gambling going on in the barn, which would at least would present a plausible reason for there being a lit lamp out there. Someone could have knocked it over, especially if there was alcohol involved, and then chose to run rather than try to put it out. In fact, according to an article published decades later, Louis Cohn, then a well-respected world traveler, was honored by Northwestern University's Medill School of Journalism for his large contribution to the college, Cohn maintained for years that he was responsible for the fire: "Mr. Cohn had an interesting connection with the origin of the Great Chicago Fire. He steadfastly maintained that the traditional story of the cause of the fire -- Mrs. O'Leary's cow that kicked over a lantern -- was untrue. He asserted that he and Mrs. O'Leary's son, in the company of several other boys, were shooting dice in the hayloft . . . by the light of a lantern, when one of the boys accidently overturned the lantern, thus setting the barn afire. Mr. Cohn never denied that when the other boys fled, he stopped long enough to scoop up the money."

While O'Leary and Louie Cohn have stories that offer a down-to-earth explanation for the fire, Ignatius Donnelly had a much more heavenly explanation. He speculated that the fire was caused by a meteor shower created when Biela's comet lost its tail. In defending his theory, he pointed accurately to other fires that broke out at that time around the Midwest: "At that hour, half past nine o'clock in the evening, at apparently the same moment, at points hundreds of miles apart, in three different States, Wisconsin, Michigan, and Illinois, fires of the most peculiar and devastating kind broke out, so far as we know, by spontaneous combustion. In Wisconsin, on its eastern borders, in a heavily timbered country, near Lake Michigan, a region embracing four hundred square miles, extending north from Brown County, and containing Peshtigo, Manistee, Holland, and numerous villages on the shores of Green Bay, was swept bare by an absolute whirlwind of flame. There were seven hundred and fifty people killed outright, besides great numbers of the wounded, maimed, and burned, who died afterward. More than three million dollars' worth of property was destroyed." While the meteorite explanation still has a number of defenders, it has never gained wide spread popularity in the scientific community.

Though the fire ultimately spread out of control, the fire department reported that it was able to respond immediately to the reported blaze: "The first information received by the Fire Department came from the alarm struck in the fire-alarm office at 9:30. The alarm sounded Box No. 342, at the corner of Canalport Avenue and Halsted Street, a point in the direction of the fire, but a mile beyond it. There was no signal given by any box to the central office, but the box was given by Mathias Schaffer, from the Court house cupola, he being the night watchman on duty at the time, and having sighted the fire. There was no signal given from anybody until after the Fire Department had arrived and turned in the second and third alarms. If any person set the fire, either by accident or design, he was careful not to give the alarm. The nearest engine-house was six blocks from the fire; the next nearest one was nine blocks away. The nearest hose-house was located eleven blocks from the fire, and, at this hose-house, the watchman had seen the fire before the alarm was given from the Court House, and the company were on their way to the fire before the box was struck."

The Courthouse after the fire

The problem was that Chicago was the scene of a perfect storm of circumstances that conspired together to spread the fire. First, there were the houses themselves; at that time, wood was still the favorite choice of building material in the Midwest, and more than half of all the structures in Chicago were made of wood. Furthermore, even the city's sidewalks were made of wood, providing excellent paths for the fire to travel on from one building to the next. Writing a month after the catastrophe, noted architect Frederick Olmsted blamed the way in which the city constructed its large building for helping spread the fire: "Some ostensibly stone fronts had huge overhanging wooden or sheet-metal cornices fastened directly to their roof timbers, with wooden parapets above them. Flat roofs covered with tarred felt and pebbles were common. In most cases, I am told by observers, the fire entered the great buildings by their roof timbers, even common sheet-metal seeming to offer but slight and very temporary protection to the wood on which it rested. Plain brick walls or walls of brick with solid stone quoins and window-dressings evidently resisted the fire much better than stone-faced walls with a thin backing of brick."

Frederick Olmsted

That said, if the weather and season had been normal, it is unlikely that the fire would have gotten out of hand. Unfortunately, Chicago and much of the Midwest had suffered a severe drought during the summer of 1871, as meteorologists recorded just one inch of rainfall between July 4 and the day of the fire. The effects were still being felt, even in the cities. People had gone from making random comments about the heat to asking each other how long it'd been since it rained. As the drought continued, people started remarking about how important it was to be careful with fire. Public service announcements followed that, with everyone warned to be on the lookout for fire.

Of course, it was impossible during the 19th century to avoid using fire altogether. After all, every morning began with building a fire in the cook stove to make breakfast, and every evening ended around a kerosene lamp or, in wealthier homes, gaslight. In between, fire was used to keep homes warm and even to power steam engines in factories. At the same time, since most people lived with fire all the time, they were more comfortable with it, which could lead to additional care or to carelessness. In October 1871, it may have been the latter.

In addition to the drought, there was also the matter of wind that night. One fireman later wrote, "When they arrived there from three to five buildings were fiercely burning. The fire must have been burning from ten to fifteen minutes; and with the wind then blowing strongly from the southwest, and carrying the fire from building to building in a neighborhood composed wholly of dry wooden buildings, with wood shavings piled in every barn and under every house, the fire had got under too great headway for the engines called out by the first alarm to be able to subdue it…Marshal Williams immediately ordered the second, and, soon afterward, the third, alarm to be turned in, but … before this could be accomplished, the strong wind had scattered the fire into the many buildings, all as dry as tinder, and spread it over so large an area that the whole Department … were unable to cut it off or prevent the wind, which soon became a gale, from carrying burning shingles and brands over their heads, and setting on fire buildings far away from the main fire."

Finally, there was the matter of how close the buildings were to each other. In 1871, Chicago was in the middle of a huge growth spurt as people flocked to the city looking for work. Many were veterans of the Civil War who had growing families and needed places to live. Unable to afford much land, they built rambling houses on small lots, making the best use of the space possible. As a result, many neighboring rooftops nearly touched each other, making it easy for fires to leap from one building to the next.

In the years leading up to the fire, the city had grown to the point of averaging two fires a day somewhere in the area, but this was not overwhelming since the fire department was well-equipped with 17 horse drawn engines and staffed with more than 180 men. However, the frequency with which they were able to put out fires led to a certain complacency on the part of some of the firefighters, including the two Otis brothers. Their sister, Jennie, later recalled, "The room I occupied faced the west, being the back of the house. My two older brothers having the front room on the same floor. I had only been asleep a short while when I was awakened by the fire bells, which we had in those days, and the clanging of engines. My room windows had no shades, but inside blinds. As they were open, I saw the first of this west side fire. The wind was very strong from the south-west, blowing the flames toward the lake and the north side. It grew larger and larger, and after an hour I decided to go and call my brothers. As they had been to the fire the night before and were tired, they did not seem interested, and I returned to my room again, watched the fire leaping and spreading at a terrific rate. In a short while I decided to go again to my brothers' room; this time I was told to go back to bed and forget it."

Tragically, the fire her brothers had fought the night before had also been worked on by many other members of the Chicago Fire Department, leaving them exhausted. This was an important fact to keep in mind when examining any mistakes that may have been made, especially since many members of the department were called upon to give as much as 48 hours of uninterrupted service to very strenuous work, all while being tasked with attempting to use good judgment in making decisions on a scale they had never experienced before.

Though the men were able to put out the initial fire at the O'Leary barn, it had spread to other buildings before they were done. The firemen then changed their tactics and swung their engines around in an effort to stop the fire from the north, but by the time they got to their new location, sometime around 10:30, the fire was already ahead of them and forced them to fall back and move north again. By this time, their efforts were being hampered by the crowds of people flying into the streets and fleeing from the fire with whatever they could carry. Clarence Burley encountered these crowds himself and later recalled, "As I reached Kinzie Street I saw that flames were leaping across Clark Street some blocks South of the river. Many people were coming across the bridge. I thought the tunnel would be a better way to get to the other side. I found the foot passage of the tunnel full of people, with bundles and trunks of belongings, and just as I reached the entrance the gas went out."

Meanwhile, most of the citizens and visitors to Chicago continued to go about their business as if nothing was amiss. The latter group included Alfred Hebard and his family, who were only passing through Chicago and were spending the night at the Palmer Hotel. The building had been open to the public for less than two weeks, and Mrs. Hebard later described the scene: "Returning from an evening [church] service, we were told that another fire had broken out in the western part of the city and was progressing rapidly. We immediately took the elevator to the upper story of the Palmer, saw the fire, but, deciding that it would not cross the river, descended to our rooms in the second story to prepare for sleep. Husband and daughter soon retired; I remained up to prepare for the morrow's journey, and thus gain a little time for shopping before the departure of the train at 11 A.M. Feeling somewhat uneasy, I frequently opened the blinds, and each time found the light in the streets increased until every spire and dome seemed illuminated. I aroused my husband, asking him to go out and investigate once more, which he did, telling me, on his return, not to be alarmed, as there was no danger in our locality."

A picture of the Palmer House before the fire

By around 11:30 PM, the fire had spread well past DeKoven Street and was approaching the Chicago River. At this point, firefighters could only hope that the river itself was wide enough to stop the blaze from spreading any more, and they were encouraged by the fact that the previous night's fire had been in the same area, so much of what might fuel the current fire was already gone. However, their hopes were soon dashed as the bridges themselves caught fire and sent it across the water to the lumber yards and warehouses on the other side. Sparks and the debris from the fire also blew across the river and began landing on other structures, among them the South Side Gas Works. One witness remembered, "The fire on the West Side was fast burning to a point where it must stop--on the grounds burned over the night previous, when all at once the South Side caught, near or at the Gas Works. I would have gone over then--had just seen the C & N Freight houses burn--but wanted the gas works to blow up before I went among the high stone buildings of the South Side. In less than half an hour I went over, after the explosion, and the whole portion of the South Side seemed to be on fire--all west of Dearborn. The burning shingle, pieces of lumber, paper roofing and every conceivable thing came rushing down through the air like snow, all was smoke and sparks and the wind would gather them up again building in huge windows for coals."

The loss of the gas plant only made things even more dangerous for those still trying to survive in the fire's path. In large cities like Chicago at the time, most of the larger houses were lit by gas lighting that was pumped to the houses by the station, so when the station was gone, people were forced to resort other sources of light, even while they continued to try to keep their homes from burning By this time, Alfred Hebard and his family had reached the home of their friends the Hubbard's and joined a large number of people taking refuge there. Mrs. Hebard explained, "The fire, meanwhile, was coming nearer, and just as we began in earnest to pack necessary things for removal, the Gasworks were destroyed and candles had to be resorted to. Everyone thought the house might be saved, standing as it did on a corner and disconnected from every other building, but we worked on through the night, preparing for the worst, and running often to the garret to see if the worst was not over. In the early morning men came, tore up carpets to cover the roof, draining both cisterns to keep the carpets wet, hoping if possible to stop the fire at that corner. Oh, how they worked! The thoughtful family provided refreshments as long as it was possible, and when all supplies were exhausted the men labored on, panting and parched with thirst, drinking the very dregs of the cistern water from tubs in the kitchen as they passed through. All said, 'This house will not burn!' but they might as well have tried to quench Vesuvius. The heat increased. A wooden block nearby flashed into flame, and at 11 A.M. the cornice was blazing, and we were obliged to go out through the alley to escape the heat and cinders; but where to go we could not tell."

Once the fire jumped the river, it was obvious that the fire department would not be able to stop it. Furthermore, the wind itself had become so hot as a result of the flames that it was fanning, and the heat generated by the wind was enough to set fire to buildings before the fire ever reached them. Naturally, more and more people began to panic and evacuate their homes, as Ada Rumsey later recalled: "We hoped the river would prove a barrier to the flames, but this was not to be. Huge burning brands were carried by the wind, starting new fires in places…Christian [a servant to the family] had harnessed our two little black ponies to a phaeton belonging to my older sisters, and into this was put a clothes basket filled with silver and linen with some other things gathered up by Mother and Sister Meme. Also in the carriage were put the portraits of Father, Mother, and Grandfather Turner, and one or two other paintings…By this time houses were burning about us and our own house was on fire. The streets were filled with vehicles loaded with household goods, and with people staggering under big loads. Mother had waited for Father but was feeling that it would not be safe for us to stay much longer, when he appeared begrimed and tired. In his hand he carried a tin box of papers which he gave to Christian, who was just about to drive from the house with his load. Father said he did not know what was in the box, but it represented all the wealth he then possessed. So Christian drove off into the night with all that was left to us."

Sometime between midnight and 2:00 a.m., the mayor of the city, Roswell B. Mason, decided it was time to send to other communities for help, a fact underscored by the fact that the courthouse in which he had been working had been evacuated and caught fire. When the cupola containing the town's great bell collapsed at 2:20, the sound was so loud that it was heard a mile away, but by then, people across the city had to worry about the fact that much of the city was being consumed. William Gallagher noted, "At half-past two I was awakened by a tremendous knocking at my door, and on opening it I found one of my companions of the night before, who told me that Chicago was all on fire, that the Court House was gone, that all the business part of the city was in flames, and that he and his 'chum' were going down town. I dressed hastily, climbed to the roof, and saw a sight such as I never expect to see again, and which few men have had the privilege of witnessing…There was a strip of fire between two and three miles long, and a mile wide, hurried along by a wind that I have never seen excelled except by our September gale, sweeping through the business part of this city. We were situated where we could take in the whole at a sight, and such a view such a magnificent sight!"

Mayor Mason

Part of what drove the fire on through the night was "fire whirl," a meteorological situation that often occurs when large fires sweep across congested areas. As the overheated air rose into the sky, it came in contact with cooler air, which in turn caused it to cool suddenly and fall to earth. This created a sort of burning tornado that not only lit things on fire but also threw burning debris toward other areas, thereby starting new fires. When some of the debris kicked up by the fire whirl landed in a railroad car full of kerosene, it spread the blaze further and helped the fire jump the river again so that it began burning the north side of the city. According to Julia Lemos, "[A]bout five o'clock in the morning was woke up by a rumbling noise, so as I was awake I got up and threw open the shutters, I thought I was dreaming, the whole street was crowded with people, with hats and shawls on, a neighbor who stood in front of our house called to me, and said Mrs. Lemos, are you just getting up? I said yes, what is the matter? The sky was reflecting fire, she said the city has been burning all night, and the fire is coming to the north side, Well, that startled me, and I ran to the back room and called my father and mother up, I said the city is burning…by that time the fire was advancing on us, I wanted to leave the house, but father said, O, the wind will change. People were running in crowds past our house, I stood with my baby in my arms and the other children beside me, when a woman running past with three children, said to me, Madam, ain't you going to save those children, that started me, I went to Father and said I was going to leave at once…"

Although the situation was becoming increasingly hopeless, the firefighters continued to fight in an effort to save what they could. One of their main concerns was trying to keep the city's water supply flowing, not only to fight the fires but to ensure people still had water to drink. Unfortunately, the efforts were futile once a burning piece of wood from one building fell onto the roof of the facility and set it on fire. As the roof burned and fell through, pieces of it fell into the machinery and broke it, bringing the pumps to a halt. For the next few weeks, the citizens of the city were wholly dependent on the few older wells still in use around town for water.

Even worse, there was no more water with which to fight the fires. William Carter was among the first to see the damage: "Between one and two in the morning I went home, took Kate and the children to a place of safety, ordered the bedding and other things to be packed--went for teams--a difficult thing to find at that time of the night and then drove with all speed to the water works. My anxiety for the water works was due not more to save the buildings than to save a supply to the people to drink. It was too late, after going around in order to reach a spot of safety nearly five miles, I had to abandon the attempt and turned back almost in despair. The flames were rushing most frantically, leaping from block to block--whole squares vanishing as though they were gossamer."

Without water, the fire department quickly began trying to think of another way to stop the fire, and they decided to try to create some sort of fire break between where the fire was burning at the time and the rest of the city. In order to do this, they would have to take a very large chance by blowing up several buildings that were still standing. According the official report filed after the fire, "The engines had all been working on the West Side; and they could not reel-up six hundred feet of hose each, and cross the river, and get to work soon enough to prevent it spreading, literally, on the wings of the wind. Blowing up buildings in the face of the wind was tried, but without any benefit. The Court House and the Water Works, though a mile apart, were burning at the same time. Gunpowder was used in blowing up buildings, with good effect, the next day, in cutting off the fire at the extreme south end of it, and preventing it backing any further. After the Water Works burned, the firemen could do little good with their engines, except on the banks of the river."

From that point forward, the fire burned with no resistance, constantly perpetuating itself through the spread of ash and sparks. It spread across the city to areas that had not yet been burned, brought by the winds that continued to blow unabated through the night. Cassius Wicker later remembered, "Tops of all the buildings as well as the street were all a blaze. Chamber of Commerce and cupola of the C & N were a blaze, and flying embers and sheets of flame were born against the Skinner house, and falling would break into a thousand pieces, only to be born again into some basement, or further down the street by the perfect hurricane of a wind."

Though they had no water, the firefighters continued to fight on through the night by taking the hoses and pumps to the river and getting as much water from there as they could in order to keep up their battle against the spreading flames. These efforts were complicated by the fact that they had already lost a bunch of their equipment, and there was only so much they could do under those circumstances: "After the Water Works burned, the firemen could do little good with their engines, except on the banks of the river. They had lost seven thousand five hundred feet of hose and one steam fire engine. Two more engines had been in the repair shops…and, after daybreak, only one-half of our hose remained. This would not [allow] an engine conveying water very far from the river. The firemen and their officers were sober, and did all that men could do. They worked heroically to save the property of others, when their own houses were burning and their families fleeing from the flames. A large part of the Department had worked on Saturday night, and Sunday until 3 p.m.--eighteen hours' steady work,--and they were nearly exhausted when this fire commenced; but they responded to the call with alacrity and worked with all their remaining energy."

People were already terrified before word began to spread that the fire was out of control. However, while there was still water, there was hope that their brave firemen could get the fire under control, and that even if others' houses were burning, their own homes might be spared. Likewise, the Hebard's and the other visitors staying in the Palmer Hotel continued to hope for the best. After all, many had heard that its developer, Potter Palmer, called the hotel "The World's First Fireproof Building," but he was about to being proven terribly wrong. Mrs. Hebard later wrote, "About 11 P.M. I retired, but could not sleep, and it seemed not more than half an hour before there was a rapping at every door, and finally at ours, to which my husband responded very coolly, 'What's wanted?' 'Fire, sir!' was the answer, and the same moment we were on our feet. Our daughter was awakened, toilets soon made, and no time wasted in gathering together bags and shawls ready for departure. By this time my husband, who had stepped out to reconnoiter, returned, saying that everyone was stirring, and that he saw gentlemen dragging their own trunks down the stairs. The clerks at the office assured him there was no immediate danger, but they thought it well enough to be prepared. Then we all went once more to the seventh story, looked in vain for any evidence that the fire was decreasing, returned to our room, picked up our parcels, including the trunk (for no porters were to be found), descended to the office, paid our bill, and sat down to watch and wait. Finally, leaving our daughter in charge of the baggage, I went with my husband into the street, and around to the rear of the building where the fire was distinctly visible and apparently only two blocks from us."

At that point, the family soon reached the decision to join the many others thronging the streets and running away from the fire. While some either owned a carriage or cart, others tried in vain to hire one, but as the flames rose, so did the prices, so many were forced to make their way with their trunks and other belongings on their backs. Cassius Wicker was a bachelor and only responsible for his own safety, so he found his escape to be easier than that of many others: "My trunk was soon filled with the most valuable portion of my clothing, etc. and my hand bag packed for a camping out expedition, but all was done quickly and I assure you that I disposed of many an old garment, book and trinket that under other circumstances should not have [been] deserted in their old age. The bottle of brandy…was found while emptying my trunk of worthless trash and safely placed in the bag and it did good service the balance of that night and forenoon at Dick's, and many a stranger took courage from it. After helping my halls chamber girl down, and many another trunk before I could get my own down, I reached the street and started east as the heaviest portion of the fire was not yet there…everybody knew the town was doomed to destruction.

Not surprisingly, Wicker soon realized that the few worldly goods he was able to save were getting heavier by the minute. He explained, "Down to State Street, hailing every man or team for assistance, but all had…theirs to save. Dragging the trunks a block I would set down on it, only to be run over by others equally as anxious as I to get away from the devouring element. Would have given $10 for a rope five feet long--I never knew the value of such a rope until my back was nearly broken and hands so tired I could no longer stir the trunk." Fortunately, help soon arose from an unexpected corner, as he later related: "At last I came to a light wagon with a horse and obtained the assistance of a one-handed man to put the trunk into it, but the owner, or a man stronger than I claimed it. But my one-handed man would work for money and away we went, quite bravely until I could no longer lift my end. We rested more than we walked. Soon I could not stir my end and had a handkerchief through the handle and around my arm. This worked well until…both gave out entirely. Soon an Englishman, fleeing from the wrath,...in a large U.S. Express wagon, himself as motive power, with a few household goods and a sick wife came slowly along. I saw he was about exhausted and could not hold out much longer, so speedily compromised with him--adding our two loads together as well as our united strength, and the way we did the jackass business…"

Of course, only a small number of any person's belongings could be saved, so people made choices, leaving behind expensive oil paintings in favor of old daguerreotypes of dead relatives and wearing heavy wool coats instead of soft silk shawls. Likewise, beautiful churches were blown up in the hope of saving simple homes and offices. There would never be any way of knowing the full value of all the property lost, but there are a few records of some of the most mourned artwork and architecture. Wicker spoke of the losses, as well as the brave work of some who risked everything to save what they could: "The magnificent painting 16 by 32 feet of the Baron of Gillingsbury just behind the hotel was burned about this time. Hurrying to Dick's after seeing church after church, stone block after block blown up in vain endeavor to save what remained and after seeing the flames come from Dick's store, Pullman Palace Car Co. Building, and the Union Depot, we had just time to kick the fine pictures from their frames, load two wagons and be off up the avenue amid fire engines, everybody's last team and crowds of departing homeless people. Not until the flames came into the dining room and leaped over the roof did we leave the house. Never did I work as hard as for the last team--never did I see the avenue so full, to say nothing of crazy people. Never did I see such a wind carrying flames across the broad avenue."

Of course, even the best efforts of people to protect their valuables often failed. Many larger businesses during that era stored their receipts and record books in safes, many of which were supposed to be fireproof, so rather than carry large sums of money and bonds on them, many of the wealthier citizens of the town chose instead to lock these items, along with fine jewelry and other small but valuable possessions, in these safes and leave them behind. This strategy often proved to be a mistake, as Francis Test later explained: "The iron safes stood the heat well, but many were burned to a white heat; their contents were destroyed. I can safely say over two thirds of them were found to contain nothing but charred masses of what once were thousands in bonds and notes…Large safes may be seen walled in at a height of three and four stories. Some of the walls tell the place where a safe once was. The intense heat had made loose the bricks around them and they fell bursting or jammed in such a way that the fire searched out their contents. Many a man has awaited, buoyant with hope, the cooling and opening of his safe, and very many have been disappointed--thousands and thousands of dollars have been taken out charred and burned. I have seen safes completely melted and by one tap of the hammer would crumble like mortar. This fire has taught many lessons, especially in regard to iron safes and fire proof buildings."

As important as it was that the fire be put out, the city leaders also understood it was imperative for everyone's health and safety that order be restored. To that end, they made the following proclamation on Monday afternoon as the fire finally began to burn itself out:

❖ WHEREAS, In the Providence of God, to whose will we humbly submit, a terrible calamity has befallen our city, which demands of us our best efforts for the preservation of order and relief of suffering, be it known that the faith and credit of the City of Chicago is hereby pledged for the necessary expenses for the relief of the suffering.

❖ Public order will be preserved. The police and special police now being appointed will be responsible for the maintenance of the peace and protection of property.

❖ All officers and men of the Fire Department and Health Department will act as special policemen without further notice.

❖ The Mayor and Comptroller will give vouchers for all supplies furnished by the different relief committees.

❖ The headquarters of the City Government will be at the Congregational Church, corner of West Washington and Ann Streets.

❖ All persons are warned against any act tending to endanger property. Persons caught in any depredation will be immediately arrested.

❖ With the help of God, order and peace and private property will be preserved.

❖ The City Government and the committee of citizens pledge themselves to the community to protect them, and prepare the way for a restoration of public and private welfare.

❖ It is believed the fire has spent its force, and all will soon be well.

Damage on Washington St.

Though the fire finally burned itself out, aided by a light rain on Monday night, the city was still in great danger. The rain was not enough to thoroughly wet the buildings, and there was still no more water to be had. As Francis Test wrote, "We have the fire departments from all the larger cities in the West but the water has not been introduced into the pipes sufficient to put out the smallest fire. Water is being forced into the mains from the river by the fire engines. They have laid four inch mains above ground to a great distance on the South Side and the water is forced into them by the same means."

As a result, harsh laws against kindling any fire were put into effect. Not only were they enforced by the police officers and other government officials, they were also enforced by the citizens themselves, often with tragic results. As Test wrote, "The city is not strictly under martial law but it reminds me of the first days of the rebellion. Soldiers march our streets; the citizens are patrolling the squares; every alley is guarded and woe be to him that lights a match or smokes a cigar on the street after nightfall. Those who have this matter in charge will not permit any such thing. Fires in the house were prohibited for a long time but the rule is not so strictly observed now as it was. There have been a few men killed and I only wonder that the number is not greater, so intensely excited are the people. Some who have been shot deserved their fate, others were not guilty but indiscreet."

Fortunately, rain came again on Wednesday evening, giving people hope and much needed relief. Test continued, "It commenced raining last night and it is a Godsend. We have caught a supply of water, enough to do washing…The people of the West Side get water from Union Park. There is a small ornamental lake there, but this is fed by the water mains and was almost dipped out till the fire engines began forcing the water from the river into it. On the South Side they have the Lake and as I have said they are conveying water by means of a four inch main around the destroyed property and for a distance beyond."

Nonetheless, the water was only a drop in the bucket toward meeting the needs of the citizens, many of whom were in frightful condition and also needed food and shelter. As always during a disaster, there were those who wanted to take advantage of the situation with price gauging, but they were quickly and harshly dealt with. Test recalled, "I saw a farmer's wagon standing near a market store. It was loaded with bagged beans and a calf. He offered the beans at an exorbitant price and the calf he wanted $50.00 for. A crowd gathered around him and drove him from the city. It was with difficulty he got away unharmed."

Another need that had to be met was for care for the sick and injured. O.W. Clapp was charged with trying to organize locations suitable for medical care and later wrote, "It was there, and then I learned the usefulness of church basements for hospital uses, whereupon I ordered signs to be put on all churches south of the burnt district pointing to the next church basement south for food, beds and clothing. Within a few days all church basements on the south side acted as hospitals, as well as the hospitals and many schoolhouses and private homes." Fortunately, there were many others who just wanted to help, and Test praised these generous souls when he wrote, "Our sister cities are sending us food and everything we want. If it were not for this aid God knows what we should do. Provisions are plentiful and they are being properly disbursed."

In fact, a committee was soon organized to manage the donations being received. A poster informed the public, "J.W. Preston, Esq., President of the Board of Trade, is hereby authorized to receive on account of this Committee, all supplies for the relief of the destitute, and distribute the same to depots of supplies established in the city, under the control and upon the order of this Committee. He is also authorized to hire or press into service, if necessary, a sufficient number of teams to handle such supplies."

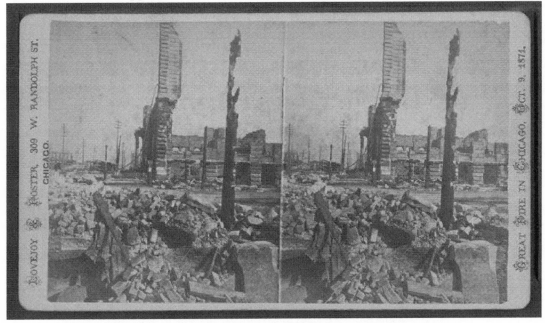

The remains of Chicago's Chamber of Commerce

Damage on Michigan Ave. in the northwestern section

With food and water in place, the third concern for the surviving refugees was shelter, which was a dire situation since cities could not simply provide people places to live as they did with food. Furthermore, it was October, so the days and nights in Chicago were quite cold. Wicker described the first terrible night after the fire: "It's fearful. All down through Lake Park people were strung out on their few things saved, many of them fast asleep with the sand blowing over them…All day long, part of the night before and in many cases, Monday night, hundreds and thousands of people lay out on the sand in the wind strong enough to blow a chair left alone clear across the park. The air was so full of dust and sand that it was impossible to see the fire, and there, utterly exhausted, lay the lowly and the proud."

Unfortunately, at least one businessman thought he could make a profit off of people's misfortune, but according to Test, he quickly learned otherwise: "General Sheridan has control here now and this has done much to stay the confidence of the people. He is a little God here. Hotel and boarding housekeepers were trying to make money out of the misfortunes of the people. Sheridan went to one of our hotels, asked the proprietor what he asked for room and board per day. 'I am charging $10.00, sir. Will you register your name?' 'No sir, but I will inform you that if you cannot give room and board at $3.00 per day I can find someone that can. I suppose you understand that.'"

Fortunately, by Tuesday morning, help had been put in place for those left destitute by the fire. A public notice informed them, "The headquarters of the General Relief Committee are at the Congregational Church, corner of Washington and Ann streets. All of the public school buildings, as well as churches, are open for the shelter of persons who do not find other accommodations. When food is not found at such buildings, it will be provided by the committee on application headquarters." Moreover, the city did not have to provide shelter for everyone because some were able to find housing elsewhere in the area. Julia Lemos explained, "[F]ather told me that the government was giving free passes on the railroads, so people could go to their friends and that he could take us to New York to my aunt there. As all the firms I worked for were burned I knew it would be very long before I would have work to support the family, but might get work in New York, so I told father to get the pass and we would go. The next morning he went after the pass…Well how were we to get to the train for New York? There was no way--so the janitor of the church had a wagon and horse, and offered, if father would let him have the dog … he would take us to the train, in his wagon, so father arranged it, and he put our two trunks in the wagon then we got in…"

The railroads did indeed offer free passes to people, but they soon had to limit the policy to only women and children since the men were needed to help with repairing the city. The fire had destroyed more than 120 miles of sidewalk and 70 miles of road, and 2,000 lampposts were gone, leaving the city in eerie darkness each evening. A third of the city's buildings were gone, and more than 100,000 people left homeless.

Considering all the damage, the estimated death toll of close to 300 was surprisingly low, and Frederick Olmsted found the number so low that he mentioned it in his writings: "That the number should be small can only be accounted for by the fact that there was an active volunteer rear-guard of cool-headed Christians, who often entered and searched houses to which they were strangers, dragging out their inmates sometimes by main force, and often when some, caught unawares, were bewildered, fainting, or suffocating." He continued praising those left in Chicago, writing, "For a time men were unreasonably cheerful and hopeful; now, this stage appears to have passed. In its place there is sternness; but so narrow is the division between this and another mood, that in the midst of a sentence a change of quality in the voice occurs, and you see that eyes have moistened. I had partly expected to find a feverish, reckless spirit, and among the less disciplined classes an unusual current setting towards turbulence, lawlessness, and artificial jollity, such as held in San Francisco for a long time after the great fire there--such as often seizes seamen after a wreck. On the contrary, Chicago is the soberest and the most clear headed city I ever saw. I have observed but two men the worse for liquor; I have not once been asked for an alms, nor have I heard a hand-organ. The clearing of the wreck goes ahead in a driving but steady, well-ordered way. I have seen two hundred brick walls rising, ten thousand temporary houses of boards, and fifty thousand piles of materials lifting from the ruins…"

There was a good reason why Olmsted observed so little drunkenness; during the days following the fire, the city's first order was "that no liquor be sold in any Saloon," and the city later decreed, "All saloons are ordered to be closed at 9 P.M. every day for one week, under a penalty of forfeiture of license."

Determined to protect the citizens in his community, Mayor Mason issued a notice as the fire was dying down that the city would be divided into districts and that each district would recruit 500 citizens to act as Special Policemen. Furthermore, he announced, "The Military are invested with full Police power, and will be respected and obeyed in their efforts to preserve order." In effect, he declared martial law and put General Philip Sheridan, a Union hero during the Civil War, in charge of keeping order in the city. Charles Holden later wrote, "For two weeks Sheridan oversaw a de facto martial law of dubious legitimacy implemented by a mix of regular troops, militia units, police, and a specially organized 'First Regiment of Chicago Volunteers.'

They patrolled the streets, guarded the relief warehouses, and enforced curfews and other regulations. John DeKoven, cashier of the Merchants' National Bank of Chicago, wrote to his wife of his experience as a sentry, 'I have not had my clothes off for a week, the city is patrolled every night, you should have seen me last night patrolling our alley with a loaded revolver in my hand looking for incendiaries for there are many about.' Illinois Governor Richard Oglesby, among others, strongly questioned whether such measures were justified and legal, but the calming effect of Mason's actions in the days right after the fire was evident, especially among the well-to-do. Former Lieutenant-Governor William Bross, part owner of the Tribune, later recollected his response to the arrival of Sheridan's soldiers: 'Never did deeper emotions of joy overcome me. Thank God, those most dear to me and the city as well are safe.'"

Illustration depicting the ruins of the National Bank of Chicago

Sheridan

Unfortunately, the citizen police officers were not thoroughly trained in handling difficult situations like the police often encountered. In fact, they were not really trained at all. Many were former Union soldiers who had fought in the Civil War and as such had developed a certain willingness to shoot at a fellow American that many past and future generations would find hard to understand. Others had fought in the Indian Wars and had not fired a gun in decades. Still others had never been in any kind of organized conflict and had no clue how to give and take orders. The only thing that the mayor could hope for was that most were armed with some sort of common sense.

O.W. Clapp was one of those deputized, and he made the following observation about his service, which centered primarily on the first wave of food distribution: "Mayor Mason then clothed me with a lead pencil order on the back of an old envelope and a Policeman's star and a verbal order to act on my own responsibility and not bother him. I proceeded to ask the views of those I thought my peers in this emergency and visited certain sections of the south side driving through parts of the burnt district…Next morning … I went to the Plymouth Congregational Church, corner Wabash Ave. and Eldridge Court and found Rev. Wm. Alvin Bartlett at breakfast and applied to him for men in the basement of his church to go with me to the Warehouse and help unload cars and load wagons… The Doctor at once went to the basement of his church, mounting a chair called for recruits to aid the distribution. About 20 men volunteered… Coming out we saw one of Farwells, and one of Fields big truck wagons. I ordered the driver to take these men on their trucks to the 18th St. warehouse, near the river. They rebelled, but soon repented being persuaded by the minister and men and my showing of a police star."

As the weeks wore on, there was more and more to protect and distribute. Towns from around the state and cities from around the country began to send donations to Chicagoans. New York City send food, clothing and $450,000 in cash, while Milwaukee, St. Louis, Cleveland, Buffalo and Cincinnati provided hundreds of thousands of dollars worth of money and goods. Even London, on the other side of the world, sent more than £7,000 to Chicago. To his credit, Mason was sensitive to the need to manage these donations well and formed yet another committee. As Holden pointed out, "The Relief and Aid Society's fire activities were considerably more long-lived, extending into 1874. Dividing the city into districts, the Society opened offices and supply depots connected by telegraph. It separated its work into different areas--contributions, shelter, employment, transportation, distribution, and health--each overseen by a designated committee. The Society not only distributed food and clothing, but also made available the materials for several thousand simple 'shelter houses,' erected four barracks in different places throughout the city for the homeless poor, helped secure necessary tools and appliances to skilled workers, and vaccinated tens of thousands of Chicagoans against smallpox. Its work was a model of a new kind of 'scientific' charity, conducted by paid professionals carrying out the policies of an executive board."

CHEER UP.

In the midst of a calamity without parallel in the world's history, looking upon the ashes of thirty years' accumulations, the people of this once beautiful city have resolved that CHICAGO SHALL RISE AGAIN

Part of an article in *The Chicago Tribune* after the fire

Fanny Boggs Lester was 11 when Chicago burned, and she recorded her memories in a letter written about 75 years later: "Opposite us on the S.E. corner of Michigan Ave. and Twenty-third was a vacant lot. When we looked out in the morning it was filled with refugees from the hotels with their belongings in bags, sheets and pillow cases. In front of our house was a hearse filled with baggage and on the driver's seat a man with his marble mantle clock. I remember my mother saying, 'I certainly would not have chosen that heavy thing to carry,' so as one of the letters said 'there were amusing things too.' I remember my mother with others feeding these sufferers, in the Michigan Ave. Baptist Church which was two doors from us, and for many following weeks, because a distributing center to give out clothing and food that came so generously from many places. The danger from incendiary fires made my father and the other residents of our blocks watch night after night. One was discovered near us. I to help, got my new shoes and put all the silver and napkins in these and was ready to go. For weeks we had to use candles which mother put in bottles with water in them and card-board to catch the wax. When my father let me ride down with him to see the wreck the cedar blocks of the pavement were still smoking in many places which our horse did not like..."

As is always the case with a tragedy, the story is not complete until someone has been blamed. While this seems cruel and mean-spirited, there is also a practical reason for establishing blame, because if people can determine what went wrong in the situation, there is hope that corrections can be made in the future and that such a hardship will not have to be experienced again. One of the first reports issued about what could have prevented the fire, or at least minimized its damage, came from those at the forefront of fighting it. The official report of the board of the Chicago Fire Department observed, "We believe that had the buildings on the West Side, where the fire commenced, been built of brick or stone, with safe roofings (the buildings need not have been fire-proof) the fire could have been stopped without great danger, and certainly would not have crossed the river. After it did cross, the wooden cornices, wooden signs of large size, the cupolas, and the tar and felt roofs, which were on most of the best buildings, caused their speedy destruction, and aided greatly in spreading the conflagration." The board then went on to add, "The single set of pumping works, upon which the salvation of the city depended, were roofed with wood, had no appliance by which water could be raised to the roof in case of fire, and was one of the earliest buildings to burn in the North Division."

In order to bolster its case, the board went on to point out, "The Board of Police have, year by year, in annual reports to the Mayor and Common Council, endeavored to point out the great defects of the manner in which our city was being built up. We advised and entreated before such an immense amount of combustibles was piled around the heart of the city. We reported mansard and tar roofs to be unsafe; that the water supply was insufficient; that our fire hydrants were twice too far apart; that we ought to have Fire Department cisterns at the intersections of the streets, so that we should always have water at fires; that we ought to have floating fire engines, with powerful pumps, in the river, to enable the firemen to wet down fifteen hundred feet on either side of the river or its branches; that wooden cornices were an abomination; that the Holly system of pumping the water and sending it through the pipes, with a pressure of forty pounds on ordinary occasions, with power to increase it to one hundred pounds in case of fire, would give us four sets of pumping works in different parts of the city, and not leave us to the mercy of chance, or, accident, with a single set."

Of course, the changes suggested in the report would have been expensive, and then as now, small local governments were reluctant to spend the money to make the upgrades. Also, the Civil War had ended a mere six years earlier, and the entire country was in the midst of a post-war economic crisis that even affected growing cities like Chicago. That said, the report was quick to point out the flaw in the "costs too much" excuse: "We showed that the four sets of Holly works could be built for less than one year's interest on the cost of the present Water Works, and, when built, would admit of the dispensing with every engine in the Fire Department where the water was in the street, allowing us to get rid of most of the horses and all the engines of the Department, and to reduce the number of men one-half--saving two-thirds of the expense of the Fire Department, and making it as efficient as it would be with one hundred steam fire engines."

Having gotten the readers' attention, the authors of the report then went in for the kill, writing: "None of these things was noticed by the mayor, the Common Council, or the newspapers. No heed being paid to our suggestions, so far as any improvement of our plan of extinguishing fires was concerned, the only thing we could do was to ask for an increase of the engine companies, in order that we might be prepared as well as possible to contend with the great fires to which we were and are still liable." They closed with a summary of their concerns: "Our engines have always been too few in number and too far apart. The Fire Department should be very much enlarged, or the system of putting out fires by steam engines be abandoned. If the citizens do not believe this now, they will after the next great fire sweeps out of existence the greater portion of the wooden city which now remains."

This time, the city leaders listened. Within weeks of the fire, committees began to draft new laws concerning where and how new buildings could be built. They also consulted fire prevention expert Arthur C. Ducat and others on how to reform the fire department. Before long, the Chicago Fire Department earned a reputation for being one of the best fire departments in the United States.

Meanwhile, Gordon Hubbard, who had sheltered the Hebard's and many others until his own home burned, threw his money and efforts into rebuilding the city. In fact, he ordered lumber delivered to town before the last fire had even gone out. Francis Test also tried to assure those he was writing to: "The heart of our city is gone, but our business men are not discouraged. Soon we will begin again. Even now over the smoldering ruins they are placing new buildings. Our houses may be burned but our energies are just the same, they cannot be destroyed. It looks like rain tonight. The clouds are very dark and on these the light from the burning coal heaps reflect a living red that is surely visible for miles. We have the fire departments from all the larger cities in the West but the water has not been introduced into the pipes sufficient to put out the smallest fire. Water is being forced into the mains from the river by the fire engines. They have laid four inch mains above ground to a great distance on the South Side and the water is forced into them by the same means."

Mayor Mason, who saw the city through its darkest days, stayed on to help with the rebuilding, but not as mayor. He was soon replaced in office by his successor, Joseph Medill, and less than two weeks after the fire, he issued his last order related to the incident: "In view of the recent appalling public calamity, the undersigned, Mayor of Chicago, hereby earnestly recommends that all the inhabitants of this city do observe Sunday, October 29, as a special day of humiliation and prayer; of humiliation for those past offenses against Almighty God, to which these severe afflictions were doubtless intended to lead our minds; of prayer for the relief and comfort of the suffering thousands in our midst; for the restoration of our material prosperity, especially for our lasting improvements as a people in reverence and obedience to God. Nor should we even, amidst our losses and sorrows, forget to render thanks to Him for the arrest of the devouring fires in time to save so many homes, and for the unexampled sympathy and aid which has flowed in upon us from every quarter of our land, and even from beyond the seas."

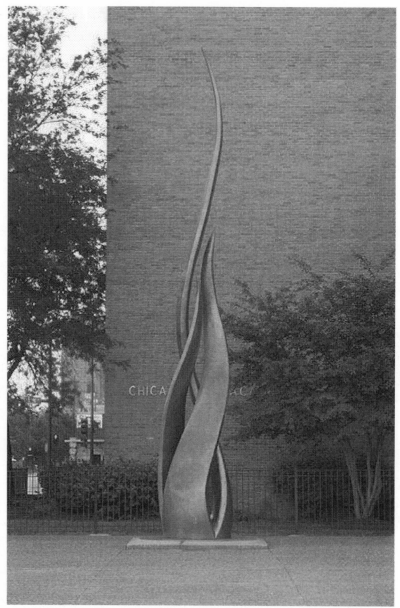

Picture of a sculpture commemorating the site where the fire started

The Chicago World's Fair

Chicago proved resilient enough after the Great Fire that within 20 years, it was being considered for the world's fair, a popular celebration of global culture. The first world's fair was held in London in 1851. The primary goal was to entertain, but world's fairs also served to enlighten and inspire.[80] World's fairs are one of the three largest international events, the other two being the Olympics and the World Cup. Such colossal affairs take a tremendous amount of work to organize.

It was not until 1928 that the Bureau International des Expositions was established. The bureau manages international expositions on behalf of more than 100 member nations. Since its

---

[80] World's Fair Historical Society. Web. 22 April, 2016.

inception, world's fairs have been held only in years ending in "0" and "5." Other international expositions, occurring in all other years, are now referred to as smaller expositions.[81] Thus, when Chicago hosted the 1933-34 Century of Progress Exposition, it was not a world's fair, but in 1893, the exposition in Chicago had the title of "world's fair" despite of not occurring in the correct year, as it predated the nomenclature for designating world's fairs versus international expositions.

The designation of the "World's Columbian Exposition" came about as the result of an act of Congress. "The holding of an International Exposition or World's Fair in the city of Chicago, in the state of Illinois, to commemorate on its four hundredth anniversary the discovery of America."[82] Politically, the 1893 world's fair met a number of obstacles. Pres. McKinley had previously signed a tariff bill, discouraging European countries from sending exhibits as it was just too costly and some countries were unsure if they would be allowed to ship the exhibit items they wanted to include in their exhibit.

Fortunately, Europe wanted to penetrate American markets, and being seen at the world's fair, on American soil, guaranteed immediate exposure to thousands of people. Countries quickly decided to participate after all. There were other congressional issues, but in the end, the fair was approved and funded, and shipments to the fair were exempted. The final issue was not resolved until shortly before the fair opened, resulting in many exhibits arriving shortly before the fair's opening day. But shipping was the least of the worries the fair administrators had to deal with.

The Illinois state legislature voted to create the "World's Columbian Exposition" as a legal entity on April 25, 1890, with a board of 45 members. They elected the Hon. Lyman J. Gage to serve as president, with the Hon. Thomas P. Bryan serving as vice-president, and the Hon. Benjamin Butterworth as secretary.

Though it might seem like a really large board, there were also two commissioners and two alternates from each of the 44 states, plus U.S. territories, plus two from the District of Columbia, and eight commissioners-at-large, with their alternates. The 45-member board was just the beginning of a staff of the hundreds required to create and manage such a huge undertaking. There was also separate board of Lady Managers or Lady Commissioners, led by Mrs. Potter Palmer, who, despite her seemingly lofty position, was little more than a socialite. After completing finishing school at a convent, her greatest claim to fame was that she married well. Many of the art exhibits at the world's fair were items on loan from the private art collection that she and her husband owned, but primarily, the Lady Managers were responsible for the Woman's Building, and the events and exhibits located in that one building.

---

[81] "Bureau International des Expositions." Web. Expomuseum. 22 April 2016.

[82] Handy, Moses P. *The Official Directory of the World's Columbian Exposition, May 1st to October 30th, 1893: A Reference Book of Exhibitors and Exhibits; of the Officers and Members of the World's Columbian Commission, the World's Columbian Exposition and the Board of Lady Managers; a Complete History of the Exposition. Together with Accurate Descriptions of All State, Territorial, Foreign, Departmental and Other Buildings and Exhibits, and General Information Concerning the Fair.* Chicago: W.B. Conkey Company, 1893. Print.

Mrs. Palmer

The Woman's Building

That said, more accomplished women did play a significant role in the Chicago World's Fair, and though women technically had their own exhibition hall, women's inventions and other contributions to society were on exhibit throughout the fair. Women stepped up from the beginning, and not just the socialites. Miss Phoebe Couzins was secretary of the Board of Lady Managers. She graduated in 1871 from the Washington University School of Law, in St. Louis. She practiced law for a time before she opted to devote her time to lecturing in support of women's rights.[83]

Couzins

Rather than simply materialize, the Board of Lady Managers was created by an act of Congress, to whom they reported. When Mrs. Palmer presented the Board of Lady Managers' report to the U.S. Congress on March 30, 1892, she pointed out something that had perhaps been lost, or at least overlooked, and that was that the Lady Managers were paid employees of the World's Columbian Exposition - these were not voluntary positions. Mrs. Palmer made specific mention in her report of their "salaries or compensation, the dates of their employment, the nature of their duties, and the States or Territories from which they were severally appointed." Between Nov. 19, 1890, and March 15, 1892, the Lady Managers were paid a total of $47,811.89, which, accounting for inflation, would be about $1.2 million dollars by today's standards.

The World's Columbian Exposition is remembered as much for the role these women played

---

[83] Campbell, James B. *World's Columbian Exposition Illustrated: Devoted to the Interests of the Columbian Exposition, Art and Literature.* Chicago: J.B. Campbell, 1891. Print.

as perhaps anything else. The Woman's Building exhibition hall was designed by Miss Sophie Hayden of Cambridge, Massachusetts, who was presented a $1,000 award for her work, in addition to her salary.

Mrs. Palmer also noted that it was the intention of the Lady Manager to show "that the women among all primitive peoples were the originators of most of the industrial arts and that it was not until these became lucrative that they were appropriated by men and women pushed aside."[84] But even Mrs. Palmer, in all her liberal views, did not respect the contributions of black women. She had grown up in Kentucky, after all.

By contrast, after having survived slavery, black women inherited a different experience than did the white women, and they did not hesitate to point this out to Mrs. Palmer, with respect to the World's Columbian Exposition. Women from two different African American women's groups made a concerted effort for the Lady Managers to grant African American women the right to display their successes. They specifically requested to be included alongside the Lady Managers selected by each state. As an alternative, they would have been willing to participate as separately and uniquely as any other cultural or ethnic group.

Mrs. Palmer was in a quandary over how to placate the women, but she clearly had no intention of advocating on behalf of African Americans. To assuage her conscience, Mrs. Palmer explained that the Board of Lady Managers lacked the authority to include women of color when two groups representing them presented requests. Mrs. Palmer pleaded that a decision for one over the other would simply be unfair. Her perception of what was the right thing to do clearly differed from the women appealing to her good sense. She opted not to honor the request of either group, rather than honoring both.

Eventually, the Lady Managers passed the question of whether to include African American women on to the state boards, who'd selected all managers of exposition. The states would ultimately have to select them anyway, just as they had selected the white men and white women.

At no point did it seem to occur to Mrs. Palmer that by not allowing African American women to participate, she was also preventing them from earning the pay that the white Lady Managers were receiving. It was probably not her intention to reserve the payroll for whites, any more than the president was actively preventing black men from being selected, and therefore, compensated. But it was clear that Mrs. Palmer had no intention of advocating for minorities, regardless of who they were, or what their contributions to society might have been. It was the beginnings of the recognition of an issue between the perception of African Americans by and of themselves, when compared to non-African Americans. Though most people, all the way up to the president of the United States, paid lip service to freedmen and equality when it came to governing and compensating elected positions, when a leader was needed and government funds were set aside to pay them for services rendered, only white men and women were considered.

In the end, New York was the only state that appointed a black woman to serve on the Board of Lady managers. Her name was Miss Imogene Howard. Miss Howard graduated from the Girls'

---

[84] *United States Congressional Serial Set*. Washington: U.S. G.P.O, 1892. Print.

High Normal School in Boston. She was the first African American to do so.[85] Armed with a degree, Miss Howard moved to New York City, where she was hired as a teacher at Colored Grammar School No. 4. Howard continued her own education, earning her master's degree from the College of the City of New York in 1879, while she continued to teach, full-time. She later earned a second master's degree in Pedagogy, from the University of the City of New York.

As a result of her professional experience, she was appointed to the Board of Lady Managers' Committee on Education at the World's Columbian Exposition, but she was not singled out for being a successful black woman. By some accounts, Miss Howard was marginalized by the other Lady Managers, as if her career had not been considered the equivalent to that of a white woman with the same education and experience. Few people are even aware of Imogene Howard. Yet she was there, alongside Mrs. Palmer and all the women who refused to include women of color in the World's Columbian Exposition of 1893. And the U.S. government paid Imogene Howard for her services to the World's Fair.

Howard's experience was emblematic of many minorities' experiences during the coming world's fair. By 1893, there were two African Americans serving in the House of Representatives, and blacks were more fully integrating into American society, but it certainly didn't seem that way at the World's Columbian Exposition, nor did it go unnoticed. 30 organizations lobbied for all appropriations to be withheld unless "ample" provisions be made for the "representation of the colored people's interest at said Exposition." The demand wasn't even for equal provisions. African Americans protested until the Exposition's authorities consented to include one solitary black man on the board, a school principal from St. Louis named Hale G. Parker, as an alternate national commissioner.

No doubt, African Americans were surprised when they were not treated equitably for their advancement over more than a quarter of a century following emancipation, whether anyone else was or not. Reportedly, blacks in Georgia had organized and incorporated a Colored World's Fair Association by 1890. Three years before the World's Columbian Exposition, Georgian blacks had assumed they would be equally represented, and began to actively organize exhibits.[86]

One African American who is often overlooked in the record books is Dr. Daniel Hale Williams, a black physician who founded Chicago's Provident Hospital, at the intersection of Dearborn and 29th Streets in Chicago. During the very time when blacks were being omitted from the World's Columbian Exposition, half a dozen black nurses graduated from Provident Hospital, just blocks from the fairgrounds. Dr. Williams served on the Sanitary Board of the World's Columbian Exposition for a time. He stood as a prime example of black equality the 1890s. Though Williams only served on the board during 1892 (the year prior to the World's Columbian Exposition), his name appears as one of the seven members of that World's Fair Sanitary Board who presented a report on zymotic diseases in Chicago, published in 1893.[87]

---

[85] Majors, Monroe A. *Noted Negro Women: Their Triumphs and Activities*. Freeport, N.Y: Books for Libraries Press, 1971. Print.

[86] Reed, Christopher R. *All the World Is Here!: The Black Presence at White City*. Bloomington: Indiana University Press, 2000. Print.

[87] *Zymotic Diseases in Chicago: Sanitary Exhibit of the Illinois State Board of Health*. Springfield, IL, 1893. Print.

Dr. Williams

The makeup of the exposition board did not reflect the attitude of Chicagoans toward minorities, which in 1893 meant primarily freed slaves who had migrated to the north in search of jobs, far from the plantations. The down payment for Dr. Williams' Provident Hospital came from Philip Armour, owner of the meatpacking enterprise, who recognized that Dr. Williams was as respectable and capable as any physician. Armour hired many of those new arrivals to the city to work at his meatpacking plant.

Though the World's Columbian Exposition may not have welcomed blacks with open arms, there were those who did. The Provident Hospital board members included Florence Pullman, daughter of the inventor of the Pullman Rail Car; Marshall Field, founder of the iconic department store; the aforementioned meat packer, Philip Armour; and Henry Herman Kohlsaat, co-owner of the *Inter-Ocean* newspaper. They served alongside Ferdinand Barnett, husband of Ida B. Wells Barnett; African American dentist, Dr. Charles Bentley; and black Unitarian Fannie Barrier Williams, and her husband.[88]

The *Chicago Tribune* took notice when Dr. Williams opened the doors of Provident Hospital, with its 12 beds. It was the first African American-owned hospital in Chicago, and it exercised desegregation. Patients of any race were admitted, inspiring the *Tribune* to call Provident Hospital an "opening attack on race discrimination." By the time the World's Columbian Exposition fairgrounds opened, Provident Hospital had treated some 200 patients.[89] But its contributions went unsung by the world's fair.

The main part of the fair, especially the section devoted to culture and education, consisted of buildings covered with brilliantly shining coats of Plaster of Paris, a quick-setting plaster coating

---

[88] Giddings, Paula. *Ida: A Sword Among Lions : Ida B. Wells and the Campaign against Lynching*. New York, N.Y: Amistad, 2008. Print.

[89] Gustaitis, Joseph A. *Chicago's Greatest Year, 1893: The White City and the Birth of a Modern Metropolis*. Carbondale: Southern Illinois University Press, 2013. Internet resource.

often used to make casts for sculptures.[90] The central section became known as the White City, which continues to serve as the one of the best known nicknames for the World's Fair of 1893. The buildings of the White City were never intended to survive for more than 10 or 15 years, and it was clear they were not intended to reflect any color whatsoever.[91] The sole exception to this was the Golden Doorway, designed by the creators of all those gleaming white buildings.

The Golden Doorway

Somewhat ironically, given that it had nothing to do with the color of the buildings and continues to be a colloquial name for the entire event, the White City came to represent more than was perhaps intended. Even at the time, it was seen as being in contrast to African Americans and to women, and the committee selections did little to assuage that perception - African Americans submitted proposals for exhibits, but the all-white committees rejected them with little respect.

Moreover, planning such an event as an international fair with participants from every country imaginable was no small venture, even a century ago. The first session of the World's Columbian Exposition Commission was held June 26, 1890, nearly three years before the gates would open.[92] There was much to do, and a country doesn't just decide to hold one; a decision is

[90] *Encyclopaedia Britannica: Ultimate Reference Suite*. London: Encyclopaedia Britannica, 2003. Print.
[91] Shaw, Albert. *Review of Reviews*. New York: Review of Reviews, 1894. Print.
[92] Moses, John, and Paul Selby. *The White City: The Historical, Biographical and Philanthropical Record of Illinois*. Chicago: Chicago World Book Co, 1893. Print.

made at the international level, and then at the national level. In the United States, Congress selected a state to host.

In 1890, a Board of Reference and Control, composed of the National World's Columbian Commission and the World's Columbian Exposition, formed committees and boards, and broke down the tasks necessary to coordinate the six-month long fair so that everything went as smoothly as possible.

People and talents from around the world and across the country joined forces. The work was divided into 16 different departments:

- Agriculture
- Electricity, Electrical and Pneumatical Appliances
- Fine Arts
- Finance
- Foreign Exhibits
- Grounds and Buildings
- Liberal Arts
- Legislation
- Mines, Mining and Fish
- Manufactures and Machinery
- Press and Printing
- Transportation
- Ways and Means

Among other things, the World's Columbian Exposition brought jobs to the city. The fair itself started out with a $15 million budget from Congress, and the board and committee members were paid staff members. The security staff, maintenance crews, and ticket-takers were paid out of tax dollars, which were paid back by the expo's profits. The World's Columbian Exposition Corporation, and its many stockholders, received the remaining profit dollars.

Private businesses profited as well. Chicago hotels and restaurants benefited from the increased tourism. As a result, waiters, concierges, bellboys, maids, and every type of service industry that could possibly connect itself to the fair, saw an uptick in income. In the same vein, the fair had its own publicity department that published, among other things, the aptly named Official Directory to the Fair, complete with advertisements.[93] Major Moses P. Handy was editor of the directory, published by W. B. Conkey. In addition to the massive directory of the fair proper, Handy published smaller catalogues for individual departments. The publishing was done for the fair and by the fair.

Moses Purnell Handy grew up in Virginia. He was young enough that he had fought during

---

[93] Handy, Moses P. *The Official Directory of the World's Columbian Exposition, May 1st to October 30th, 1893: A Reference Book of Exhibitors and Exhibits; of the Officers and Members of the World's Columbian Commission, the World's Columbian Exposition and the Board of Lady Managers; a Complete History of the Exposition. Together with Accurate Descriptions of All State, Territorial, Foreign, Departmental and Other Buildings and Exhibits, and General Information Concerning the Fair.* Chicago: W.B. Conkey Company, 1893. Print.

the Civil War, and for the Confederacy at that. Perhaps his political leanings helped to influence his rare coverage of the black perspective of the World's Columbian Exposition, but regardless, the fair organizers were happy with Handy, and he successfully established a reputation for himself in spite of the fact that he had no formal training for the position. As a young man, he had determined to become a reporter and he took advantage of every opportunity to insinuate himself into journalistic affairs until he became a paid reporter. After the 1893 fair, he was tapped to serve in the same capacity for the Paris Exposition of 1900, and went to Paris to make early preparations. Unfortunately, he passed away on Jan. 8, 1898 and thus never saw the 1900 fair.[94]

Handy

In 1892 and 1893, Handy did, however, create a huge directory for the White City, consisting of 1,254 pages. The directory was quite well-organized, including every single entry, in every single exhibit, in every single building. The entries were interspersed with paid advertisements, and Handy listed the more than two dozen dates set aside for "state, foreign and other celebrations." They consisted of days honoring the various states, some countries, and a handful of organizations, like a general "College fraternities" day. On August 25, it was announced that "Colored people" were to have a celebration day, and Handy did point out that what would be referred to today as historically black colleges and universities would be included in the Liberal

---

[94] *Year-book*. Paris, 1879. Print.

Arts Exhibits in the Main Building. "Distinct exhibits are presented by thirty States and Territories; about forty colleges and universities, including six for women, and seven distinctively for the colored race, more than thirty normal schools; a series of manual training and trade schools; sixteen art schools; collective exhibits from thirty business colleges; fifty schools for the deaf; schools for the blind; schools for those of feeble mind, etc."

The interesting aspect of this group is that there were more colleges and universities for blacks than there were women, yet it was women who were granted their own building. Also, Liberia was given its own ceremonial day, but it was granted an "unclassified collective exhibit," in the Agricultural Building. Handy explained, "Liberia is the only civilized Christian negro state in Africa, and is exerting a wide influence in the enlightenment of those parts of the continent with which it comes in contact." No such respect or admiration was granted to African Americans. That unclassified Liberian "African" exhibit was Group 176, consisting of three exhibits. One consisted of Eastern European costumes "donated by the women of Bohemia to the permanent memorial building at Chicago," and exhibited by the Lady Managers of the World's Columbian Commission. Another was a vaguely described "collection of ancient articles," from Mrs. L. P. Hunt of St. Paul.

Illustration of the Agricultural Building

The African Exhibit, with no additional detail mentioned in the directory, was under the direction of M. French Sheldon of Boston.[95] Mrs. Mary French Sheldon was not an African. Her claim to fame was that she was the second white woman to explore Africa without a chaperone, following Alexine Tinne.[96] Moreover, Sheldon was not an anthropologist by training. She was

---

[95] Handy, Moses P. *The Official Directory of the World's Columbian Exposition, May 1st to October 30th, 1893: A Reference Book of Exhibitors and Exhibits; of the Officers and Members of the World's Columbian Commission, the World's Columbian Exposition and the Board of Lady Managers; a Complete History of the Exposition. Together with Accurate Descriptions of All State, Territorial, Foreign, Departmental and Other Buildings and Exhibits, and General Information Concerning the Fair.* Chicago: W.B. Conkey Company, 1893. Print.

[96] Sheldon, Mary F. *Sultan to Sultan: Adventures Among the Masai and Other Tribes of East Africa.* Boston, Mass:

not much more than a tourist, backed by her wealthy husband's finances. She was, in many ways, an antagonist of Africa, if not African Americans. French's primary interest in Africa was the exploitation of resources. Though she did brave East Africa on foot, rather than by train like some early women explorers, Sheldon has been described as "the only professed feminist among the women travelers in Africa [who] clearly travelled to Africa in order to find a stage adequate to the drama of her feminist heroism."

Sheldon

Six months before the World's Columbian Exposition, the *New York Times* took Sheldon to task, asking "who but an American woman would have conceived the idea of making a Worth

Arena Pub. Co, 1892. Internet resource.

gown help her win her way into the interior of Africa? But that gown was a part of a well-devised plan, based upon the penchant of savage and semi-barbarous persons for finery in dress and ornaments."[97] It was not a compliment, but nevertheless, she was ultimately honored with three awards. One was for the litter she traveled in, physically carried aloft by African natives. A second was for a book, *Sultan to Sultan: Adventures Among the Masai and Other Tribes of East Africa*. The third award was for her collection of artifacts on exhibit, the African Exhibit in her name, in the Agricultural Building. Clearly, this was no African American exhibit.

After she spoke at the World's Columbian Exposition, the elaborate gown and some of her equipment were put on display but not in the African Exhibit tucked away in Agriculture. It went on permanent display in the Woman's Building instead. This was no khaki outfit with pith helmet; she dressed ridiculously inappropriately for the jungle and demanded to be treated like a white queen.

On top of all that, she was a double-agent in the Congo, performing the bidding of Belgium in obtaining lands for them, and in reward, garnering her the equivalent of a knighthood. She further profited from developing 1,200 square miles of Liberia into her own rubber business. After the World's Fair, French incorporated the Americo-Liberian Industrial Company, under Oklahoma state law. Her intention was to create a sort of reverse slave trade, transporting freed American blacks to Africa, where they would become slaves, once again, only this time on her Liberian plantation, harvesting timber and agricultural products. Needless to say, this had nothing to do with the Agricultural Building in 1893.

Any hint that Sheldon's African Exhibit was in any way flattering to African Americans would be insultingly offensive, but like other whites and other white women, she was a paid presenter at the fair while African Americans were not. For the most part, African Americans were subjects at the World's Columbian Exposition. The Fine Arts Department exhibited a watercolor by Clara Weaver Parrish, entitled "A Study of a Southern Negro." Parrish was a white woman from Alabama who'd donated large sums of money to the poor in Selma and elsewhere, but her painting represented a distant and mild curiosity about blacks, rather than an opportunity for blacks to speak for themselves.[98] Similarly, the illustrator Arthur Burdett Frost[99] exhibited his ink drawing, "The Negro Leaned, Exhausted Against the Wall." Frost is best known for illustrating Uncle Remus' *Brer Rabbit*.

Perhaps nowhere were they missing quite as blatantly as in the Woman's Building, which housed "a well-filled library of printed works and original manuscripts in many languages, by women writers." Individual states sent books by authors hailing from their state. While the above-mentioned African American women were invited to speak and paid to do so, their writings were apparently not included in the library, nor in the Department of Liberal Arts. As historian Christopher Robert Reed laments, "Colored American Day brought no redemption to

---

[97] *New York Times*. Dec. 11, 1892.

[98] *World's Columbian Exposition, 1893: Official Catalogue. Part X. Department K. Fine Arts*. Chicago: W.B. Conkey, 1893. Print.

[99] *A. B. Frost*. Morristown, NJ: Morristown & Morris Township Public Library, The North Jersey History & Genealogy Center, n.d.. Internet resource.

African Americans for past sufferings, it established no new dialogues with whites in the present, and it resulted in no ameliorative framework for the future."[100] African Americans were subjects and topics for paintings, books, and illustrations, but real African Americans were missing throughout the World's Columbian Exposition.

Even though there were black newspapers in print in Chicago at the time, none dwelled on the World's Columbian Exposition, though there were two factions emerging. One school of thought advocated participating in every aspect of the fair, to whatever extent they might be permitted, as a means of protest. The other school of thought vehemently urged African Americans to boycott the fair. The issue became such a large one, that it was unavoidable for anyone to omit the situation from their publications. The black perspective of the World's Columbian Exposition was clearly different from the festive celebration of human successes, inventions, and accomplishments as viewed by anyone else in the world.

That is not to say that the fair was not spectacular, because it was, but it revealed the discrepancy between world viewpoints in a way that white Americans and many African Americans didn't want to admit. It was the ongoing news coverage that laid open the facts which have become fodder for much research. Numerous books have also been written about the subject of the black perspective of the White City.

---

[100] Reed, Christopher R. *All the World Is Here!: The Black Presence at White City*. Bloomington: Indiana University Press, 2000. Print.

A picture of the White City

Entrepreneurs saw dollar signs with the coming of the World's Fair. There was to be an official directory printed in English, French, German and Spanish. The fair promised six months' worth of content, and more drawings and photographs than any editor could have dreamed prior to the World's Fair. Without this and other publications serving as firsthand documentation, there would not have been such a clear perspective of the World's Columbian Exposition.

James B. Campbell, who began publishing a periodical in February of 1891, long before the World's Fair gates opened, was among the first to see the opportunities ahead and to diligently promote the international event. He was a visionary who realized there were going to be so many things for fairgoers to see that they would need a guide, but first they needed the *World's Columbian Exposition Illustrated*[101] to pique their interest and allay their fears of venturing to the big city.

Campbell made no bones about how great he thought his new home, Chicago, was. "With her expansive thoroughfares, her majestic buildings, her public and private institutions, outdone by none, she stands without a peer."[102] Campbell was not averse to acknowledging, in print, the

---

[101] Campbell, James B. *World's Columbian Exposition Illustrated: Devoted to the Interests of the Columbian Exposition, Art and Literature.* Chicago: J.B. Campbell [etc., 1891. Print.

struggle for the selection of Chicago as a World's Fair destination. He covered the disagreements over plans and site locations, with every corner of the city vying to be selected. After the Lake Front and Jackson Park were selected, the fair board wanted the Illinois Central Railroad Company to remove its railroad tracks, among other things, in the area. Eventually a decision was made among the states, and a location was decided on. The international administration eventually agreed—the 1893 World's Fair was to be held in Chicago. And no one covered the event quite as well as Campbell did.

During this time, Campbell ran a photograph of the Hon. Thomas Witherell Palmer, president of the World's Columbian Exposition, on the cover. Fittingly, Palmer was an attention-grabber; He was a former senator from Michigan who'd chaired the Committee on Fisheries during the Forty-ninth Congress, and was on the Committee on Agriculture and Forestry during the Fiftieth Congress. President Benjamin Harris had appointed Palmer as the United States' Minister to Spain in 1889. Palmer returned stateside in time to relocate to Illinois and become president of the National Commission of the World's Columbian Exposition at Chicago.[103]

Palmer

In Chicago, excitement was high, and Campbell was at the forefront, but he certainly was not alone. A number of men had hopes of getting rich off the coming attraction. After all, Chicago

---

[102] Campbell, James B. *World's Columbian Exposition Illustrated: Devoted to the Interests of the Columbian Exposition, Art and Literature*. Chicago: J.B. Campbell, 1891. Print.

[103] *Biographical Directory of the United States Congress, 1774-Present*. Washington, D.C: The Congress, 1998. Internet resource.

was considered "a crude western metropolis,"[104] by some. The World's Fair just might be the chance for the City by the Lake to overcome her sooty history as a meatpacking and manufacturing town. As if by some mythical consensus, none of the 70 periodicals that cropped up during that time "of aesthetic character" dared use the word "western" in its title.[105] It was an opportunity for the Windy City to create the illusion of being as cosmopolitan as its European counterparts.

In a pre-fair edition covering March 1892 to March 1893, Campbell mentions an African American woman who might design a box for jewels, but that, apparently, never happened. He also listed a number of topics the Columbia Catholics' Congress were considering. Among them was an address on "The Condition and Future of the Negro in the United States," which failed to make the cut, but thanks to Campbell's publication, a record exists proving that there was, indeed, an effort to include African Americans. It also served to acknowledge the race issue.

Campbell was just one of the three primary periodical publishers. The first publication was *Halligan's Illustrated World's Fair*, a promotional effort, published in 1890 by Mr. Jewell Halligan, who hailed from Denver. Halligan jumped the gun in assuming, and copyrighting, the name of his publication. It was already in print bearing the wrong name when Congress opted to call the event the World's Columbian Exposition, rather than the World's Fair. Before Halligan's second edition appeared in August 1891, Campbell was publishing his weekly as the *World's Columbian Exposition Illustrated*.

Regardless of the name on the masthead, *Halligan's* was unique among the publications at the time in that it implemented a new process, one of many of the innovations of the age, called half-tone illustrations. Enamored with the technique and eager to set his publication apart, *Halligan's* was published exclusively with half-tone photographs, published on extra-large paper.[106] It was assumed that *Halligan's* would continue as a magazine after the fair. Unfortunately, Halligan lost some $30,000 in the *Illustrated World's Fair*'s excessive cost for all those extra-large, half-tone photographs which, a century later, would be the equivalent of about half a million dollars.

---

[104] Fleming, Herbert E. *Magazines of a Market-Metropolis: Being a History of the Literary Periodicals and Literary Interests of Chicago*. Chicago: University of Chicago Press, 1906. Print.
[105] *Ibid.*
[106] Fleming, Herbert E. *Magazines of a Market-Metropolis: Being a History of the Literary Periodicals and Literary Interests of Chicago*. Chicago: University of Chicago Press, 1906. Print.

A *Halligan's* half-tone picture of the Ohio State Building at the fair

A *Halligan's* half-tone picture of the German Castle at the fair

By contrast, the World's Fair was profitable for Campbell, in spite of the weekly format that ran from February 1891 through February 1894.[107] Also unlike Halligan, Campbell did continue publishing after the fair, changing the name to *Campbell's Illustrated Journal*. He capitalized on his experience with a successful World's Fair publication by continuing to cover other fairs, and he later received a gold medal at the Paris Exposition at the turn of the century.[108]

The third competitor was G. P. Engelhard. His effort, the *Graphic*, was considered to be a more artistic publication. Engelhard stepped into the publishing business with a local newspaper in the Chicago suburb of Hyde Park. Shortly prior to the 1893 World's Fair, Chicago annexed Hyde Park, and it became the fairgrounds. The *Graphic* later absorbed other publications, but circulation dropped to half in 1893, and it also failed to survive after the gates closed in October.

There were several smaller publications that enjoyed various successes. One that came out of the World's Fair was the chap-book, small booklets issued intermittently and sold by chapmen, or peddlers. The Chicago *Chap-Book* was the brainchild of Herbert S. Stone and H. I. Kimball. Stone was the son of Melville E. Stone, who helped establish the *Associated Press*. The younger Stone, however, saw only a short-lived success with *Chap-Book* that barely survived the life of the fair, even though the concept remains today.

---

[107] *Ibid.*
[108] *Ibid.*

The three days from October 21-23, 1892 were set aside for the dedication of the various White City exposition buildings. On the third day, 300,000 people arrived by train, and with that, more than a quarter of a million visitors were in the city of Chicago. Many of them attended the Grand Inaugural Ball, held in the Manufactures Building.

A lithograph depicting the Manufactures Building

The interior of the Manufactures Building

Thursday morning, the crowds spilled into the streets when a parade was held on the streets of Chicago for the general public, clogging the city streets for three hours. Friday, more celebrations took place, and this time, there were military maneuvers on display. Afterward, a crowd of 100,000 took their seats for the opening addresses, poems, songs and music. At the conclusion, the World's Columbian Exposition transferred the buildings to the United States government for the duration of the fair. That evening, Friday night, there were three fireworks displays. Three bombs simultaneously lit up the air above Washington, Lincoln, and Garfield parks, followed by the release of 100 balloons.

After the dedication, there was much yet to do in order to complete the rest of the White City by May 1. Exhibits began arriving to fill the newly-completed buildings. Staff members were needed to direct exhibit items to the correct buildings, unpack the boxes, and help organizers set up their displays. An estimated 10,000 workers set to work with that deadline in mind. Before the fair even opened, $2.2 million was spent on non-construction items, including salaries. Janitors alone earned $34,690 before the gates even opened.

There was a lot of work to do, but plenty of people eager to do it. The population of Chicago had swollen by the tens of thousands since the Civil War, and the country was on the verge of financial failure. Finding workers to fill all of those positions was perhaps the simplest task for which the fair organizers were responsible.

Among the many accounts given of the event was that of Hezekiah Butterworth, author of several series of books. He devoted the 16th volume of his ZigZag series to *Zigzag Journeys in the White City*.[109] Being a member of the Folk Lore Society, Butterworth could not resist waxing eloquent about the scene before him: "When the President arrived shortly before eleven o'clock, the sun, for the first time in several days, broke through the dark, low-lying clouds; but trailing fogs still half veiled the domes, towers, and finials of the gigantic buildings. Never, as it seemed to those who have marked their progress toward completion, had these huge structures looked so enormous, as now that their foundations were encompassed and blackened by the innumerable multitudes, while their domes and roofs were looming, half concealed, in the mist-clouds."

Poetic or not, the essence was nevertheless accurate. The weather cooperated and the public thronged through the gates and into the White City. Once it started, investors in the World's Columbian Exposition felt a sense of relief. In April 1893, the U.S. Treasury gold reserves fell drastically, generating a financial panic among investors, and while the World's Fair was essentially a government effort, it was held in place by stocks, making it an investment company. Thus, in the weeks before the doors opened, the investors in the 1893 World's Columbian Exposition Company were faced with the very real possibility that they might not ever see a profit. In fact, they could very well lose the money they had invested in the fair. The government had to be paid, and any profit—or loss—beyond that would come out of their pockets.

The World's Columbian Exposition investors were largely wealthy American men who held

---

[109] Butterworth, Hezekiah. *Zigzag Journeys in the White City: With Visits to the Neighboring Metropolis*. Boston: Estes and Lauriat, 1894. Print.

their breath as some 50 U.S. railroads failed, 30 North American steel companies collapsed, and 4,000 American banks failed. The fair simply had to be a success for those investors, as they stood to lose everything. Bringing the issue closer to home, the financial failures affected the bank branch in the Administration Building on the fairgrounds. Foreign visitors had deposited money in the bank, and the World's Columbian Exposition officials had to return the money from their own pockets.

Perhaps fortunately for them, the eventual impact resulted in working class layoffs and wage reductions. Employment by the end of the fair had reached 20 percent, and an estimated 2.5 million men migrated to urban areas in search of jobs. In Chicago, there were local strikes, including confrontations between workers and the Pullman Railcar Company. Altogether, the country saw 1,300 strikes, involving 750,000 workers. [110]

For the fair, that meant they could hire cheaper labor, and on top of that, African Americans - in particular those arriving from the South where wages were traditionally lower - were migrating north in search of work. Even if it was temporary work, the World's Fair meant jobs, and the employment situation guaranteed the availability of workers desperate for a paycheck, no matter how small.

The World's Columbian Exposition organizers anticipated, and saw, large crowds. The fairgrounds were designed with 326 turnstiles, in and out of the grounds, with 97 ticket booths and 182 ticket windows throughout. Their anticipation was that 2,000 visitors per hour would be able to enter the grounds, and they needed the money this would provide. Given the economic environment, the fair was no longer the guaranteed profit-maker its investors had anticipated four years earlier when the plans were still in their infancy.

Innovations to save money, time, and labor were in high demand, and not just for exhibits. They were needed in order to save money and bring in more dollars. No one could be turned away from visiting. Indeed, the ticket gates used in at the World's Columbian Exposition were a brand new invention. They consisted of automatic turnstiles operated by tickets, which cut the tickets in such a way that they could not be reused.

Those tickets represented quite an investment on their own. Five million advance order tickets were lithographed to prevent forgery. The remaining 35 million tickets were printed much like railroad tickets of the time, except that each was printed for a given day and were good only on the day they were sold.

---

[110] "Panic of 1893." American Eras. 1997. *Encyclopedia.com.* 26 Apr. 2016<http://www.encyclopedia.com>.

A ticket to the fair

The turnstiles, of course, saved money by replacing workers. Every one of those turnstiles took the place of two or more employees each day. Nevertheless, the Department of Admissions alone required 400 men, and they literally meant "men" rather than "workers," because ticket-taking at the time was not considered respectable work for women. A woman in that position would have to have a mind capable of handling money, and the tenacity to deal with the public, besides.

As the summer approached, even more work was created that required human labor. There were walkways to sweep, and general maintenance tasks to perform. Large numbers of workers had to clean a new innovation known as the Comfort Station, and there were bigger crowds in summer. Though summer was a more traditional time of year for vacations in general, it was also true that farmers waited until their crops were harvested and sold before determining if they had enough money to attend the fair.

The fairgrounds were divided into sections. There were three entrances at the North End, six at the South End, and five at the Midway Plaisance. There were transportation-based entrances at terminal stations, elevated railroad stations, commuter train stations, the casino pier, and the naval pier. To further facilitate the process of getting all of the fairgoers through the door, tickets were also on sale at the more upscale hotels and retail stores, from passenger trains into the city, and boat lines.

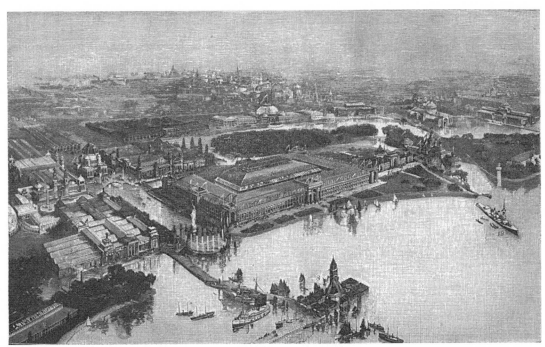

An aerial view of the fair from Jackson Park

The Great Wharf at the fair

One single company was awarded the concessions for selling food and drink throughout the fairgrounds. There were restaurants on the fairgrounds that were not owned by the Wellington Catering Company, but they were required to buy their provisions from Wellington. A staff of

2,000 waiters, cooks, and dishwashers were required by the concessions center, and someone was needed to hawk popcorn, crackerjacks, peanuts, ice cream, and water. Trainloads of perishable food arrived daily, just to keep the agricultural displays fresh, and there were 50 cattle slaughtered every morning for the six-month duration of the fair, in order to feed the hordes. There was plenty of need for manual labor.

It has been said that the modern day use of the word "midway" for a carnival originated with the Midway Plaisance of the World's Columbian Exposition. The French term was a holdover from a previous world's fair held in Paris, but Americans shortened the term to "midway." The White City, with all its museum-quality exhibits, was built at a right angle to the Midway Plaisance, which was fashioned after the 1889 Paris Universal Exposition midway.

In Chicago, the Midway was populated with native villages created by Harvard University professor Frederic Ward Putnam. His vision was quite different from that of showman Sol Bloom, with whom he was partnered in managing the Midway.[111] Putnam was a serious anthropologist, while Bloom was more of a carnival promoter.

A modern picture of the Midway Plaisance with University of Chicago buildings in the background

[111] Giddings, Paula. *Ida: A Sword Among Lions : Ida B. Wells and the Campaign against Lynching*. New York, N.Y: Amistad, 2008. Print.

The Midway Plaisance during the fair

The Chicago Midway Plaisance became home to ethnological villages representing Europeans, Africans and Asians. There was a German Village, an Irish Village, a Ferris wheel, gondolas on the lagoons and the lake, wheelchairs for those who were tired of walking and had the funds to pay someone to wheel them around the fairgrounds, and souvenir shops.

The original Ferris wheel at the fair

The Midway placed the European villages at the "top" of the racial order. It was followed by Chinese, Turkish, Arabic, Persian, Algerian and Egyptian villages. By opening day, entrepreneurs had turned all these villages into concessions, though Putnam had intended for them to be outdoor museums. To make matters worse, the Midway soon became the amusement center, much as we know it today. The "primitive" villages were placed near the Ferris wheel, belly dancers, and ethnic cuisine.

Unlike the White City events, there were additional charges for most experiences on the Midway, which became home to the first ever sideshows featured at a world's fair event. As is the case with most midways, there was a Ferris wheel, a ride that generated a huge profit even amidst the financial collapse happening all across the United States. When the accounts were settled, the fair had made a profit of $300,000 off of the Ferris wheel alone.

But there was also a more exciting ride. Every 30 minutes, fairgoers could splurge on the most expensive attraction at the entire fair, which allowed them to float 1,500 feet into the air in a hot-air balloon tethered to the Midway. For a mere quarter, the more timid could step up and simply look at the craft, but the brave and adventurous put their money down and rode the daredevil ride, high above the Midway and the White City, and even had their pictures taken.

When a windstorm flattened the balloon, the attraction was replaced with a trapeze act. The new entertainment was free, but still offered the thrill of impending risk.

The Midway was also the place for fairgoers to have their photos taken, proving they had been to the World's Fair. Natives from 40 different countries, decked out in their country's attire, would pose with fairgoers for a quarter apiece.

Entertainment was everywhere along the Midway, whether it was drummers from an African village, or a female animal trainer putting her bear, lions, tigers and dwarf elephant through their paces. Gypsy bands from Hungary also performed. If that didn't increase the adrenalin enough, there was also a replica of a spewing, Hawaiian volcano.

The Midway was also home to the earliest chamber of horrors, featuring the re-enactment of the execution of Marie Antoinette. Fortune tellers were at the ready.

As this all suggests, the Midway became a source of entertainment that was thinly disguised as anthropology or international experiences, while remaining clearly targeted toward the less-educated. The villages located there were cheapened by the food, trinkets, and performances offered there, and it became fair game in the press to speak disparagingly of the natives, just as it had become commonplace for the village occupants to mock their own traditions of sword-fighting or ritual.

At the Midway, the exhibits were easy to comprehend, unlike the paintings, sculptures and mechanical inventions housed in the White City, which defied the imagination.

The White City was perceived and experienced differently by African American leaders of the day, who were enraged about being excluded. They personally blamed President Harrison for appointing 208 national commissioners and their alternatives, while he "refused to appoint a single representative of seven and one half millions of colored people."[112] While he had a reputation for being fair to minorities as a practice, when it came to the World's Fair he inexplicably chose only white Americans for every single position charged with presenting American culture to the world. He did not seem to do it intentionally, which was even more disturbing. It appeared that it simply never occurred to him to include African Americans, because he did not see them as professionals.

Various groups of people were honored with their own, special day. In perhaps an effort toward inclusionism, the managers designated August 25, 1893 as "Colored People's Day."Although there were other ethnically-related days. it appears lost to many, even today, that August 25 was significant. It was a Jubilee Day, a day for prayer, speeches, and song. To the African Americans, Emancipation was known as the Year of Jubilee.

But the date was given a collection of names, no one seeming to know quite what to call it. The Chicago *Herald* called August 25 "Colored Folks' Day,"[113] but the fact that no one was even sure what term to use should have made the administration realize that there was a race issue at hand, and it was not being resolved. Even the Chicago *Herald* took notice, albeit two days after the fact, saying, "That a colored man, Douglass, Langston or Bruce, should have been named a National Commissioner, will be admitted by fair-minded Americans of all political parties. That President Harrison should have omitted to name one of them is apparently inexplicable. That the race has made extraordinary progress will also be conceded."[114]

---

[112] "The Reason Why the Colored American Is Not in the World's Columbian Exposition: the Afro-American's Contribution to Columbian Literature." *Lse Selected Pamphlets*. (1893). Print.

[113] Abbott, Lynn, and Doug Seroff. *Out of Sight: The Rise of African American Popular Music, 1889-1895*. Jackson: University Press of Mississippi, 2002. Internet resource.

Regardless of the name, some 2,500 people attended the Colored Folks' Day program in Choral Hall, intended to show respect toward black Americans, but only about 2/3 of those who attended the entertainment program were African American.[115] Blacks were not honored as Americans on Colored Folks' Day, or at any point during the fair. They were still perceived as "others" by the World's Columbian Exposition.

On Colored Folks' Day, Frederick Douglass spoke from the podium as a guest speaker in the Choral Building on "The Race Problem in America." Frederick Douglass took the opportunity to demand that the country adhere to the Constitution, and carry through on their promise of social justice for former slaves. Douglass was granted a position of honor at the fair, having been selected by the Republic of Haiti to serve as its representative. That decision resulted in being a "courtesy the Colored American received from a foreign power the place denied to him at home."[116] Douglass had also been present on Opening Day, but he was not given an opportunity to speak. In fact, he and Buffalo Bill Cody were paraded, together, as caricatures. Besides Douglass, Paul Laurence Dunbar read a poem he had written for the event. The composer Will Marion Cook presented portions of his opera, *Uncle Tom's Cabin*.

---

[114] Editorial. Chicago *Herald*. August 27, 1893.
[115] *Ibid*.
[116] "The Reason Why the Colored American Is Not in the World's Columbian Exposition: the Afro-American's Contribution to Columbian Literature." *Lse Selected Pamphlets*. (1893). Print.

Douglass

The Jubilee Singers took time from the Chautauqua circuit to entertain the crowd with spirituals.[117] Just a few years after the Civil War, they had introduced slave songs to the world. The original Jubilee Singers were all former slaves. On Colored Folks' Day, the singers were invited to revive songs from the most shameful period of American history. While some have pointed out that it is important to remember the slave songs helped African Americans survive the heartbreak of being a slave, those songs would not have existed had slavery not also existed.

It has also been said that the White City led to the separate-but-equal laws that soon followed the World's Columbian Exposition, in 1896. Those laws came into being even though Ida B. Wells was so incensed by the treatment of blacks in White City that she organized black leaders, and left her home in Memphis, specifically to object to the treatment of African Americans at the World's Fair. She thought she had fought and won a legal battle guaranteeing equality, but that battle would rage on long after the White City had closed its doors.

Black businesspeople advocated that, since blacks were not being included alongside whites,

---

[117] Appelbaum, Stanley. *The Chicago World's Fair of 1893: A Photographic Record, Photos from the Collections of the Avery Library of Columbia University and the Chicago Historical Society*. New York: Dover Publications, 1980. Print.

perhaps the exposition board should establish a Department of Colored Exhibits. They proposed exhibiting the progress of blacks, only since emancipation, but that suggestion was also dismissed. The message was clear: modern, free blacks were not to be visible in the White City.

As a result, for Ida B. Wells and many others, the White City as a whole was an affront. The famous civil rights crusader noted, "Our failure to be represented is not of our own working and we can only hope that the spirit of freedom and fair play of which some Americans so loudly boast, will so inspire the Nation that in another great National endeavor the Colored American shall not plead for a place in vain."[118] She went on to note, "The exhibit of the progress made by a race in 25 years of freedom as against 250 years of slavery, would have been the greatest tribute to the greatness and progressiveness of American institutions which could have been shown the world. " She also pointed out that the New World had established international trade credit based on labor production provided by slaves. She wanted visitors to understand that the wealth of white Americans and their progress in art, education, industry, invention, and science were all achieved with the help of the hard labor of black slaves.

---

[118] "The Reason Why the Colored American Is Not in the World's Columbian Exposition: the Afro-American's Contribution to Columbian Literature." *Lse Selected Pamphlets*. (1893). Print.

Wells

To bring home the point, she published her explanation in English, French, and German, for the benefit of foreigners attending the World's Columbian Exposition. Other voices joined her, penning entire chapters of *The Reason Why the Colored American Is Not in the World's Columbian Exposition.* One chapter was written by attorney F. L. Barnett, who Ida B. Wells married two years after the World's Fair.

Other leaders of the day, in addition to Ida B. Wells, urged African Americans to boycott the fair. Not only were they not being represented alongside white Americans, they were not even offered employment in clerical positions where they would interact with the public. Only three people, one man and two women, were hired for clerical jobs.

The administration of the World's Columbian Exposition did pass a resolution, "Resolved: That the Director General be requested to lay before the Local Directory the expediency of having the department of Publicity and Promotion employ a colored man and a colored woman to promote the interests of the World's Columbian Exposition throughout the United States."[119] In retrospect, this might have only served to make the situation worse, as it only advocated that a single man and a single woman be employed. But as it turned out, even this resolution was not honored. The board reasoned that there simply were no available funds, in spite of having spent $90,000 building floats for opening day, which were used for no more than a few hours during the ceremony.

During the fair, the Columbian Guards (World's Fair security) rejected black applicants. An appeal was ignored, creating the perception that, though it was "[t]heoretically open to all Americans, the Exposition practically is, literally and figuratively, a 'White City,' in the building of which the Colored American was allowed no helping hand, and in its glorious success he has no share."[120] Blacks were only hired as janitors, laborers, porters and chair men, rolling visitors around the acres of fairgrounds.[121]

The one little-known exception was George Washington Carver. Possibly not realizing who he was, the fair exhibited one of his paintings in the Art Palace. His work, "Yucca and Glorioso," earned an honorable mention.[122] Edmonia Lewis, who holds the honor of being the first professional African-American sculptor—not just the first female African-American sculptor—exhibited her sculpture, "Hiawatha," in the Women's Building.[123]

---

[119] "The Reason Why the Colored American Is Not in the World's Columbian Exposition: the Afro-American's Contribution to Columbian Literature." *Lse Selected Pamphlets*. (1893). Print.

[120] *Ibid*

[121] Reed, Christopher R. *All the World Is Here!: The Black Presence at White City*. Bloomington: Indiana University Press, 2000. Print.

[122] Wells-Barnett, Ida B, and Robert W. Rydell. *The Reason Why the Colored American Is Not in the World's Columbian Exposition: The Afro-American's Contribution to Columbian Literature*. Urbana: University of Illinois Press, 1999. Print.

[123] Wells-Barnett, Ida B, and Robert W. Rydell. *The Reason Why the Colored American Is Not in the World's Columbian Exposition: The Afro-American's Contribution to Columbian Literature*. Urbana: University of Illinois Press, 1999. Print.

Carver

Perhaps African Americans had hoped that the meeting of the Parliament of the World Religion during the World's Columbian Exposition would garner some respect. But Bishop Benjamin William Arnette, with the African Methodist Episcopal Church, delivered the invocation and benediction. He also gave two speeches: "Africa and the Descendants of Africa: A Response in Behalf of Africa," and "Christianity and the Negro."[124] He was the only African American man to speak.

Race was one of many topics of the World's Congress of Representative Women. Fannie Barrier Williams was just getting started when she spoke at the World's Columbian Exposition. She participated in the World's Congress of Representative Women at the fair, giving the address, "The Intellectual Progress of the Colored Women of the United States Since the

[124] Evans, Curtis J. *The Burden of Black Religion*. Oxford: Oxford University Press, 2008. Internet resource.

Emancipation Proclamation."[125] Speaking about women of color, she said, "Less is known of our women than of any other class of Americans."

She went on to explain, "No organization of far-reaching influence for their special advancement, no conventions of women to take note of their progress, and no special literature reciting the incidents, the events, and all things interesting and instructive concerning them are to be found among the agencies directing their career. There has been no special interest in their peculiar condition as native-born American women. Their power to affect the social life of America, either for good or for ill, has excited not even a speculative interest."

Williams brought unique experiences with her to Colored Day. A New York native, she did not grow up with racism. She was only 15 years old when she graduated from the Brockport State Normal School (now SUNY Brockport) in 1870. In the early post-Civil War era, she moved to Washington D.C., with the goal of teaching recently freed blacks arriving there from the South. Instead, she found it impossible to adjust to the racism aimed at her in the nation's capital. She enrolled in Boston's New England Conservatory of Music where she began studying piano. She did not graduate, because the administration asked her to leave when her white schoolmates threatened to leave if she stayed. She eventually returned to her teaching mission in Washington, D.C., where she married Samuel Laing Williams, a law student. When they moved to Chicago, Samuel opened a law practice, and they joined the All Souls' Unitarian Church. Fannie Barrier Williams became the first African American, and the first woman, to serve on the Board of the Chicago Public Library.[126]

[125] Eagle, Mary K. O. *The Congress of Women: Held in the Woman's Building, World's Columbian Exposition, Chicago, U.s.a., 1893 : with Portraits, Biographies and Addresses*. Chicago, Ill: International Pub. Co, 1895. Internet resource.

[126] Hendricks, Wanda A. *Fannie Barrier Williams: Crossing the Borders of Region and Race*. , 2014. Internet resource.

Williams

The congress did give her special notice. They named her Honorary American President of the World's Congress of Representative Women. If anyone took the Lady Managers and the attendees of that congress to task, it was Fannie Barrier Williams, pointing out that there were documentable facts and figures about African American women. "Among the white women of the country, independence, progressive intelligence, and definite interests have done so much that nearly every fact and item illustrative of their progress and status is classified and easily accessible. Our [black] women, on the contrary, have had no advantage of interests peculiar and distinct and separable from those of men that have yet excited public attention and kindly recognition."

It was Williams who most fittingly explained the white perception of the White City, and of America: "The most important thing to be noted is the fact that the colored people of America have reached a distinctly new era in their career so quickly that the American mind has scarcely had time to recognize the fact, and adjust itself to the new requirements of the people in all things that pertain to citizenship."

Had the Lady Managers, and the administration in general, taken that to heart in creating the World's Columbian Exposition, the black perspective and the black participation in the World's Fair could have been so different. But it was too late; the fair was already underway, the administration was already in place, the committees had largely finished their work, the buildings had been built, and the exhibits were in place.

Another African American woman, Mrs. Anna Julia Cooper, continued the discussion with her own address to the women's congress. Like Williams, Cooper's story varied from the narrative of most black women, even though she had been born a slave in 1858 in North Carolina. She was still a child when the Civil War ended, and she went on to earn a B.A. and an M.A. at Oberlin College. Eventually, she earned a Ph.D. at the Sorbonne.[127]

Cooper

Cooper took the opportunity to inventory what the World's Columbian Exposition had overlooked. She listed schools established by and for colored people, noting that these African American schools were co-educational from the beginning, partially because of their commitment to equality, but also for a very practical reason: "[f]unds were too limited to be divided on sex lines."[128]

---

[127] "Anna Julia Cooper." *Black Past: Remembered and Reclaimed.* , n.d.. Internet resource.

[128] Eagle, Mary K. O. *The Congress of Women: Held in the Woman's Building, World's Columbian Exposition, Chicago, U.s.a., 1893 : with Portraits, Biographies and Addresses.* Chicago, Ill: International Pub. Co, 1895.

Without diluting Fannie Barrier Williams' message, Cooper did have figures and statistics at the ready, pointing out what the Lady Managers had overlooked. By 1893, six African American women had earned college degrees from Oberlin, and three African American women had graduated from the University of Michigan at Ann Arbor and Wellesley. After Vassar had refused admission to one of Cooper's own Washington High School students from Washington, D.C., that young African American woman went on to graduate with honors from Chicago University.

Cooper continued listing, by name, one African American female after another who was an actively participating and productive member of American society—and whose absence was shameful. Her speech was followed by another in the same vein by Fannie Jackson Coppin.

Coppin was born into slavery in Washington, D.C. in 1837.[129] She was freed when her aunt bought her when she was only 12 years old, though she continued to work as a servant, albeit a paid one, for author George Henry Calvert. In 1860, prior to the Civil War, she enrolled at Oberlin College, the first college to accept black and female students. She married Rev. Levi Jenkins Coppin in 1881.

Coppin devoted her life to education, and in 1869, became principal of the Institute for Colored Youth, an all black high school in Philadelphia. She was the first African American school principal, yet she was not considered appropriate for the Lady Manager's position at the World's Columbian Exposition a quarter of a century later.

Following her address, Frederick Douglass, the only man who'd spoken during the congress, was asked to speak. He said, "I have heard tonight what I hardly expected ever to live to hear. I have heard refined, educated colored ladies addressing—and addressing successfully—one of the most intelligent white audiences that I ever looked upon."

The evening was not over. Two more African American women were on the agenda. Following Douglass, Sarah J. Early took the podium. Sarah was born in 1825 near Chillicothe, Ohio. Some historians speculate that she was the child of a controversial relationship between Sally Hemmings and Thomas Jefferson. When Thomas Woodson was a young man, he bought his family's freedom while they were in Virginia. Soon thereafter, the Woodsons moved to Ohio.

Sarah grew up as a free and educated woman. She'd begun teaching by 1859. She joined the faculty of Wilberforce University. She served as a school principal, hired for the position after her predecessor, a white woman, reportedly had a nervous breakdown after school buildings were torched by someone who'd objected to the education of African Americans.[130]

A few years after the Civil War, Early moved to North Carolina to teach at an all-black girls' school, supported by the Freedman's Bureau. She also married Jordan Winston Early, a widowed AME minister. By the end of her life, Sarah had taught an estimated 6,000 children, and served as principal for several black schools in four different cities, as she followed her husband's ministry.

Internet resource.

[129] "Fannie Jackson Coppin." *Black Past: Remembered and Reclaimed.* , n.d.. Internet resource.

[130] Smith, Jessie C. *Notable Black American Women: Book Ii*. Detroit: Gale Research, 1996. Print.

Sarah was also active in the Women's Christian Temperance Union, and urged black women to participate. She was also tapped to speak at the women's congress, being invited to speak, but not to participate as a Lady Manager.

The next and last speaker was Hallie Quinn Brown of Alabama. Hallie was born in Pittsburgh in 1850, to former slaves who'd migrated to Ontario, Canada, when Hallie was a teenager. The Browns returned to the U.S., settling in Ohio.

During the Civil War, Hallie enrolled in the Chautauqua Lecture School, graduating in 1866. She went on the lecture circuit, speaking on behalf of temperance, women's suffrage, and civil rights. Hallie enrolled in Wilberforce College, earned a degree in 1873, and became an educator. She taught in the K-12 system before becoming a faculty member at Allen University, where she taught for ten years before being promoted as Dean of the University. During 1892-1893, she was Dean of Women at Tuskegee Institute.

She published four books in her lifetime. In 1884, roughly a decade before the World's Columbian Exposition, she published *Bits and Odds: A Choice Selection of Recitations,*[131] but that was not what had brought her to the world's fair--she was there to speak on behalf of women of color.

In her address, Hallie recited the words of Frances Harper:

> "Yes, Ethiopia shall stretch
> Her bleeding hands abroad;
> Her cry of agony shall reach
> The burning throne of God.
> Redeemed from dust and free from chains
> Her sons shall lift their eyes,
> From cloud-capped hills and verdant plains
> Shall shouts of triumph rise."

The lines were from the poem "Ethiopia," written in 1850 by Harper. More than a decade before the Civil War, Harper was known for turning scripture into poetry in protest against slavery.

Hallie ticked off name after name of African American women leaders to the largely Caucasian women's congress, including Sojourner Truth, poet Phyllis Wheatley, and singer Amanda Smith. She left the audience with a friendly warning: "Talk not of the negro woman's incapacity, of her inferiority, until the centuries of her hideous servitude have been succeeded by centuries of education, culture, and refinement, by which she may rise to the fullness of the stature of her highest ideal."

And that was the conclusion of the speeches categorized as "Chapter XI. The Solidarity of Human Interests." Perhaps it was a reflection of the times that poet Katherine Lee Bates reportedly was so inspired by the World's Columbian Exposition that she wrote *America the Beautiful,*[132] but the White City was not quite as beautiful for those who were black.

---

[131] Brown, Hallie Q, and Faustin S. Delany. *Bits and Odds: A Choice of Selection of Recitations for School, Lyceum and Parlor Entertainments*. Xenia, Ohio: Chew Printers, 1884. Print.

The original plans for the closing day of the World's Columbian Exposition were to be elaborate, but unfortunately, the festivities were marred by the assassination of Mayor Carter H. Harrison by Patrick Eugene Prendergast just two days before the scheduled date. "Everything partook of the solemnity of death"[133] as a result.

Harrison

The Ferris wheel was a lonely site, remaining in place until the end of April 1894, some six months after the World's Columbian Exposition closed, when the decision was made to move it to Lincoln Park. It took 86 days to dismantle at a cost of $14,833. Finally, in July, 1895, the process of rebuilding it began. It was not back in service until October, nearly 2 years after its last ride was offered at the fair.

Though the Ferris wheel had been an exciting addition to the World's Fair, it had lost its appeal to Chicagoans. Fewer and fewer people bought tickets and the Ferris Wheel Company was rapidly losing money. The inventor, George Washington Gale Ferris, died of tuberculosis just

[132] Bolotin, Norm, and Christine Laing. *The World's Columbian Exposition: The Chicago World's Fair of 1893*. Urbana: University of Illinois Press, 2002. Print.

[133] Campbell, James B. *Campbell's Illustrated History of the World's Columbian Exposition*. Chicago, Ill: The author, 1894. Internet resource.

before Thanksgiving 1896, at the age of only 37, and in 1903, a decade after all those eager fairgoers saw amazing views of the city at the World's Fair, the remaining metal was sold at auction to the highest bidder for a mere $1,800. The engine, the boilers and the 2 tons of steel frame and cars were reduced to scrap. Ferris left a debt of $400,000 after the sale of his world famous Ferris wheel.[134]

Ferris

Of the hundreds of buildings erected in the White City, only two survive in their original location. The former Palace of Fine Arts survives as Chicago's Museum of Science and Industry. The World's Congress Auxiliary Building was constructed with the intention of becoming the Art Institute of Chicago, and continues to house the museum and art school. The remainder of the White City, and the Midway, are long gone.

---

[134] Meehan, Patrick. "Ferris Wheel in the 1893 Chicago World's Fair." Hyde Park Historical Society. http://www.hydeparkhistory.org. 26 April 2016.

Palace of Fine Arts

Much of the White City would burn down over the years, and the Cold Storage Building was one of the first structures in the White City to catch fire. It burned during the summer fair season, on July 10, 1893. The fire at the Cold Storage Building resulted in the loss of 17 lives, and thousands watched the five-story building burn. The construction of the building's boiler flue had already been cited as cause for concern, and after smaller incinerations occurred, most of the insurance policies were cancelled just weeks before the building's major fire. A number of firemen died when they were left with no alternative but to jump from the gallery above the ice skating rink to the ground below. The 60 foot drop killed or seriously injured every single man who had to make the jump.[135]

[135] "Remembering 12 Chicago Firefighters: The White City Fire of 1893." Honoring Heroes: The American First Responder Institute of Heraldry. Web. http://www.honoringheroes.com. 26 April 2016.

The Cold Storage Building

Crews began intentionally dismantling the fair immediately after the exhibits closed and the Midway went dark. Within two weeks, exhibits were gone from some buildings and many of the villages and concessions in the Midway Plaisance had already been razed. The Chicago Wrecking and Salvage Company bought most of the White City for $100,000, a high sum back then, with the intention of scavenging the wreckage.[136]

Unfortunately, shortly after the end of the fair's run, the grounds continued to burn. A fire broke out in the Casino at the southeast corner of the Court of Honor on January 8, 1894. The fire spread until it eventually destroyed the Music Hall. The flames then leaped over to the Manufactures Building. By January, 1894, French exhibitors estimated they had lost $80,000 worth of exhibits, including some irreplaceable, rare art.[137]

---

[136] Appelbaum, Stanley. *The Chicago World's Fair of 1893: A Photographic Record, Photos from the Collections of the Avery Library of Columbia University and the Chicago Historical Society.* New York: Dover Publications, 1980. Print.

[137] *The Insurance Times.* Calcutta: Insurance Times, 1894. Print.

The Court of Honor

Music Hall

On February 9, 1894, the White City burned four times in one night, including the Colonnade between the Agriculture and Machinery sections. It was alleged that the fires were intentionally set.[138]

The Court of Honor buildings were completely incinerated on July 5, 1894. The fire spread until it burned the Terminal Station, Machinery, Administration, Electricity, Mining and what was left of the Manufactures buildings. Bits and pieces of whatever buildings were left were gradually destroyed, also by fire, perhaps the last of them being the Japanese Hooden Palace Exhibit, now the Osaka Garden or "Garden of the Phoenix."[139]

The White City remained until the end of September 1896, except for the Golden Doorway of the Transportation Building in Jackson Park. The Golden Doorway was an arch decorated in an array of red, orange, and yellow tones. Ribbons on either side of the arch bore quotations by Bacon and Macauley. The heart of the arch was decorated with angels. Built by Louis Sullivan, inventor of the skyscraper and former employer of Frank Lloyd Wright, it was located on the side of the Transportation Building, facing the Lagoon designed by Frederick Olmstead (who famously designed New York City's Central Park). It was subsequently purchased by an art dealer, who in turn offered it to the city of Cleveland.

Of the buildings that do remain are those like Chicago's Field Museum. Initially, when it opened in 1894, it was housed in the World's Columbian Expositions Palace of Fine Arts. Later, the building was altered to become the Museum of Science and Industry. The Art Institute of Chicago was established in a building that was the living quarters for delegates to world's congresses.[140]

Only three works of art remain in the Midway Plaisance. The statue of Czech President Masaryk stands near Jackson Park, and a bit farther down, there is the statue of Linne, the Swedish naturalist. At the far end, just inside Washington Park, is a work by Lorado Taft, the only remaining bit from the Horticultural Building, called *The Fountain of Time*.[141]

The Creation of the Chicago Canal and Reversing the Chicago River

Along with providing safe drinking water, the river had always been a means of transportation between the Great Lakes and the rest of the United States. The Chicago River connects the Illinois River with Lake Michigan, and all the Great Lakes via the Illinois & Michigan Canal.

In 1822, which was very early in Illinois history, the legislature authorized construction of the Illinois and Michigan Canal. The state was only four years old.

There were no railroads in Illinois at that time and there was no easy way to connect the Great Lakes to the Mississippi River. Pioneers took a southern route, even to Chicago, via the Ohio River.

[138] *Ibid.*

[139] "Relic of 1893 World's Columbian Exposition found by Chicago Park District." Chicago Now. Web. http://wwwchicagonow.com. 23 April 2016.

[140] Grossman, James R, Ann D. Keating, and Janice L. Reiff. *Electronic Encyclopedia of Chicago*. Chicago: Chicago Historical Society, Newberry Library, 2005. Internet resource.

[141] Appelbaum, Stanley. *The Chicago World's Fair of 1893: A Photographic Record, Photos from the Collections of the Avery Library of Columbia University and the Chicago Historical Society*. New York: Dover Publications, 1980. Print.

There is a lot of land in between the lakes and the Mississippi, plus there was the entire Illinois River that flows across the entire state. But there were lots of little riverways and some damming that would need to be done.

Prior to 1852, the depth of the Illinois River reached as little as one and a half feet between La Salle, IL and the Mississippi River. Today, silt builds up so easily in the Illinois River that it needs to be frequently dredged in order for river traffic to navigate in spite of the promise that the I&M Canal would solve that problem.

The solution proposed was the Illinois and Michigan Canal. The purpose of that canal was to make possible commercial transportation on the Illinois River. But, the Chicago River still stood in the way of progress. The only way to travel from the Illinois River to the Great Lakes by boat was by portage where travelers had to get out and carry their boats across the Chicago Divide. Obviously, this restricted travel to canoes and very small boats meaning it could not be used as a shipping route.

It took 26 years and $7 million to build the I&M canal and, during that time, the population of Chicago grew significantly. All the sewage from Chicago residents was being naturally flushed down the Chicago River and into Lake Michigan. It turns out that was actually by intent.

The Illinois and Michigan canal

Lake Michigan was also Chicago's water supply source. Clean water became a huge issue.[142] Typhoid and cholera were common due to the lack of proper sewage disposal. Water used to wash patients' clothes or bedding eventually reached Lake Michigan and was pumped back in as fresh drinking water. The city was infecting itself.

The size of the population was a large contributor, but so was industrial waste. In 1848, the first stockyard opened in Chicago. Sewage from livestock pens and meat butchering was not

---

[142] Chicago and Alton Railroad Company. (1895). *A guide to the Chicago Drainage Canal with geological and historical notes to accompany the tourist via the Chicago & Alton Railroad.* Chicago: Chicago and Alton Railroad Co.

regulated and regularly polluted the water. As Chicago became the Hog Capital of the World, blood and discarded animal parts ended up in the Chicago River, and eventually Lake Michigan.

In 1858, Ellis Chesbrough constructed the nation's first comprehensive sewer system to deliver water to residents and to dispose of it. He had already designed a water distribution system for the city of Boston. But this was a little different. Chicago also needed a better way to remove wastewater and sewage, not just pipe water to the city.

Ellis Chesbrough

Chesbrough's plan turned out to be a disaster. He devised a system for collecting the sewage from Chicago and discharging it into Lake Michigan.[143] Chesbrough's plan was a simple solution that relied on gravity. Unfortunately, the city streets were too low for water to flow downward to the lake. The solution was that, during the 1850s and 1860s, the city raised the streets.

Nevertheless, Chesbrough's plan is considered the beginning of the field of sanitary engineering. That facet of engineering is said to have begun in Chicago. Prior to the Chicago Canal project an engineer was simply an engineer, and often uneducated.

Eventually the concept of sanitary engineering, or civil engineering, spread to cities throughout the country.[144] As it did, more trained civil engineers were needed. When the Boston Society of Engineers formed in 1848, only three members had college educations and only one had a civil engineering degree. Even Chesbrough was self-taught.

But his work in Chicago inspired students to work toward engineering degrees. And, it opened doors for new jobs in the field as municipalities recognized the need for more specialized engineers to build and maintain what was becoming increasingly more complicated infrastructure.

---

[143] Russell, J. S., & American Society of Civil Engineers. (2003). *Perspectives in civil engineering: Commemorating the 150th anniversary of the American Society of Civil Engineers*. Reston, Va: American Society of Civil Engineers.

[144] Russell, J. S., & American Society of Civil Engineers. (2003). *Perspectives in civil engineering: Commemorating the 150th anniversary of the American Society of Civil Engineers*. Reston, Va: American Society of Civil Engineers.

Chesbrough's first solution sufficed for a couple of decades. But, it did mean that sewage was flowing into Lake Michigan. Since the City of Chicago continued to use the lake for its water source, it was polluting the city's drinking water, as it removed sewage.

Chesbrough's next solution was to dig a two-mile long, 60-foot wide tunnel beneath Lake Michigan. Sewage would leave the city underwater and be dispersed into the mighty Lake Michigan, diluting it until it was no longer a safety issue. By simply pumping sewage two miles away from the shore, the water drawn from Lake Michigan for use by city residents and businesses was clean. But it did not help much in times of extreme flooding. Chesbrough also miscalculated that a two-mile tunnel would be long enough. Plus, there was still the issue of flooding.

In the meantime, in1871, the Illinois state legislature opted to deepen the I&M Canal by eight feet. It cost tax payers another $3.5 million. But, it was also not enough to address severe flooding in Chicago. Because of the natural elevation, Chicago's excess water flowed down to Lake Michigan, with or without assistance. It just didn't always flow quickly enough to avoid flooding.

In August 1885, a six-and-a-half inch rainfall flooded both the Des Plaines and Chicago rivers. Flooding had been occurring from time to time, but this event was different. As floodwaters rushed downhill to the lake, this flood washed debris out into Lake Michigan beyond the two-mile radius, where the Chicago water supply tunnel commences. Chicago was again dumping sewage into its own drinking water and there was no quick solution.

Two years later, Dr. John H. Rauch, Secretary of the Board of Health, conducted a plumbing inspection. In 1887, he found that 85% of the 31, 171 occupied dwellings surveyed in Chicago had defective plumbing.[145] The situation was becoming dire. Without good plumbing between the homes, businesses and the city's sewage system, wastewater drained downhill as best it could. But, with the city's growth there were now buildings and roads in the way. The sewage and other wastewater pooled rather than draining away. The city was becoming a cesspool.

---

[145] Chicago Medical Society & Stanton A. Friedberg, M.D. Rare Book Collection of Rush University Medical Center at the University of Chicago. (1922). *History of medicine and surgery, and physicians and surgeons of Chicago*. Chicago: Biographical Pub. Corp.

Workers in the Union Stock Yards

Mortality rates skyrocketed when a severe outbreak of influenza struck the city in 1891. The following year, Chicago experienced the highest typhoid fever rate in history, at that time, with a death of 173.8 people out of every 100,000. Then smallpox took 1,000 children. City residents were infecting themselves through no fault of their own. There was no other option, at that time. There was no vaccine. And many of the illnesses of the time had no cure, in addition to disease spreading quickly through lack of sanitation.

The Citizens' Association of Chicago,[146] an umbrella association had been formed back in 1874, after the second great Chicago fire. It was initially created to ensure honest and cost-effective governance of Chicago. But, its first task had been to secure the city against another fire. The city had already experienced two major fires and numerous smaller ones.

In the mid-1880s, the CAC took time away from the fire issue and, instead, focused on the task of studying the water issue and finding a solution to supplying clean water to Chicago residents. Chicago was making history and causing the creation of laws still in effect governing sanitation, thanks to the hard work of residents serving on the CAC.

A more immediate need was solving the sanitation issue. There was yet another cholera scare reported by the Chicago Department of Health. They had asked the city for $100,000 to attempt to clean the city.[147] But, the health problem was so much worse than residents realized. There wasn't even clean water to clean with.

Soon the Citizens' Association of Chicago's Committee on Drainage and Water Supply reported the work on the Chicago River to the health department. The CAC stressed that it was

---

[146] *Ibid.*

[147] Chicago (Ill.). (1885). *Report of the Department of Health of the City of Chicago*. Chicago, Ill: Dept. of Health of the City of Chicago.

important that the "first attention called to flies as carriers as disease (was) by Dr. F. W. Reilly."[148] For that, Reilly became known as the original "Swat the fly" advocate of Chicago.[149] But, swatting flies was not enough.

One reason people were flocking to Chicago was that jobs were available in factories, working on roads and building homes and skyscrapers. Hundreds of workers arrived to fill positions in the meat-packing district. They added to the residential waste at home, and the industrial waste at work. The lower the unemployment rate, the higher the rate of pollution.

It seemed no solution could keep up with the increasing amounts of sewage generated by the Union Stock Yards, and other industrial culprits. Industrial pollution created what is still known as Bubbly Creek, a tributary of the Chicago River that literally bubbles. It was this pollution from the stock yards that Upton Sinclair referred to in his novel, *The Jungle*, in 1906. He published this work half a dozen years after the Chicago Canal opened with its promise of clean water.

In spite of efforts to solve the pollution problem, in spite of the canal, "grease and chemicals that are poured into it undergo all sorts of strange transformations, which are the cause of its name; it is constantly in motion, as if huge fish were feeding in it, or great leviathans disporting themselves in its depths. Bubbles of carbonic acid gas will rise to the surface and burst, and make rings two or three feet wide. Here and there the grease and filth have caked solid, and the creek looks like a bed of lava; chickens walk about on it, feeding, and many times an unwary stranger has started to stroll across, and vanished temporarily." In spite of more than a century of effort, Bubbly Creek still bubbles.[150] It was Bubbly Creek.

Chicago was not the only city facing pollution issues and related health safety, but it was the first U.S. city to address the issue for such a large metropolitan area. Seven years after the Chicago Canal project started, St. Louis was still in the midst of resolving the issue. Their mayor said, "By general law of the United States all cities must, sooner or later, be prevented from polluting the natural watercourses of the country with sewage."[151] When it comes to waterways, cities, states and countries are connected by the all-important flow of water and what is deposited in it. It was a different view of the world that did not end two-miles away.

The impact of pollution was becoming clear. An undertaking like the Chicago Drainage Canal brought to light ongoing issues like whether a sanitary district should be paid for by state funds or the local community—or even more than one state where a waterway divides two or more states. The city of Chicago shared Lake Michigan with Indiana, Wisconsin and Michigan and, via the inter-connected Great Lakes, the argument could be made that Chicago indirectly shared responsibility for the water with Canada. As Lyman Cooley, one of the engineers on the Chicago Canal project, said, "A full understanding of the waterway possibilities and of the interests

---

[148] *Ibid.*

[149] *Ibid.*

[150] Chicago (Ill.). (1999). *Chicago River Corridor design guidelines and standards*. Chicago: Dept. of Planning and Development.

[151] American Society of Civil Engineers, American Society of Civil Engineers, International Engineering Congress, & International Engineering Congress. (1867). *Transactions of the American Society of Civil Engineers*. New York: American Society of Civil Engineers.

therein of the State and the Nation, as well as of the Sanitary District, has been deemed an essential preliminary in defining the policy of the District."[152]

The Chicago Drainage Canal began with experts who best understood the geological and sanitation issues at hand. They were joined by committee members who possessed additional expertise as well as a vested interest. They owned businesses in Chicago. They lived in Chicago. They, too, were impacted by the canal. In the end, they literally turned the Chicago River around.

At the time of its construction, the Chicago Canal was truly a marvel. Other significant canals had been built all around the world, like the Suez Canal. But the Suez was built from excavated sand. The Chicago Canal needed to be built by excavating sections of solid rock. It would require different equipment, much heavier equipment.

The Chicago Canal is wide. It was built 160 feet wide. The Chicago Canal is twice the width of the 82-foot wide Suez.[153]

Construction of the canal

But the greatest feat of the Chicago Canal was reversing the flow of water. No one had ever attempted that before. The idea was to reverse the flow so that sewage and wastewater would flow down the Illinois River, and away from the city, instead of out into Lake Michigan.

Rivers have a natural direction of flow, based on elevation. Even a school textbook at the time explained, "If the land over which a river flows slopes toward the north, the river must flow north; if toward the south, the river flows south. You may know which way the land slopes by observing the direction of the rivers."[154]

---

[152] Cooley, L. E., & Chicago. Sanitary District. Board of Trustees. (1891). *The lakes and gulf waterway: As related to the Chicago sanitary problem. The general project of a waterway from Lake Michigan to the Gulf of Mexico ... A preliminary report with appendices, maps and profiles.* Chicago: Press of J.W. Weston.

[153] Chicago and Alton Railroad Company. (1895). *A guide to the Chicago Drainage Canal with geological and historical notes to accompany the tourist via the Chicago & Alton Railroad.* Chicago: Chicago and Alton Railroad Co.

All they had to do was change the elevation. That meant changing the elevation of miles of streets and roads, and the Chicago River.

The Chicago River passes through a valley that was formed by glaciers that were probably half a mile to a mile wide before they stopped on the shore of what is now Chicago. As they melted, glacial streams deposited their primordial debris. As the glaciers crept from Lake Superior, far to the north, they deposited stones from Michigan and Canada, ranging from pebble-size to 100-ton boulders. These rocks were composed of sandstone, quartzite and granite, among other hard stone.

The original Chicago valley was limestone. The harder stone debris carved out the land we see today. Because of the rolling nature of the glacier, clay, sand, gravel and boulders from far away were randomly dumped along the Illinois River Valley, as it formed.

This is visible to the geologist's eye. At Lemont, the rock remained on the surface. At Summit, IL, the glacier left a bank of boulder-size gravel some 30 feet deep. In between, a 12-mile long glacial lake formed. In the early days of construction, tours of the geology were organized, the different layers of rock were so interesting and so starkly exposed as the canal went deeper and deeper.

Because of the digging and dynamite-blasting, it was possible to see far more of the effects of the glaciers than early discoverers could ever imagine. Sediment, from erosion and runoff, is an ongoing issue in the Chicago River and the Illinois River and has been for eons. The Des Plaines River, nearby, once emptied into Lake Michigan alongside the Chicago River. But sediment built up, near Kedzie Avenue, blocking the Chicago River with a naturally-occurring dam. A small body of water, known as Mud Lake, received overflow water during flooding and, at those times, it connected with the Chicago River. During drier times of the year Mud Lake was merely a marsh.[155]

The first Frenchmen to travel from the Illinois River to Lake Michigan were Joliet and Marquette back in 1673. But, because of the array of smaller waterways and the damming that was occurring, they had to carry their boats on foot from Summit, IL, to the Chicago River, across the Chicago Divide. So, even though they found a passage, it was not completely a water passage.

On March 30, 1675, when the Chicago area flooded, Marquette and his men set out in canoes to study the various waterways converging at Summit. Today there is a monument at Summit commemorating the history of that spot, built from granite boulders that traveled all the way from Lake Superior aboard a glacier.[156] The monument was built by the Chicago & Alton Railroad Company and can be found directly across from the train depot in Summit, IL.

Three experts served on the aforementioned committee of the Citizens Association of Chicago in order to make the Chicago Canal happen. Each played a very distinct role and brought unique

---

[154] Warren, D. M., & Sumner, A. (1878). *A brief course in geography*. Philadelphia: Cowperthwaite & Co.

[155] Chicago and Alton Railroad Company. (1895). *A guide to the Chicago Drainage Canal with geological and historical notes to accompany the tourist via the Chicago & Alton Railroad*. Chicago: Chicago and Alton Railroad Co.

[156] *Ibid.*

talents to the table.

Ossian Guthrie became known as the "Father of the Drainage Canal."[157] His obituary called him the "Father of Chicago's Drainage System."[158] Guthrie was enamored with the Chicago River.

He was born in New York in 1826. When he arrived in Chicago at the age of 20, he brought with him the model of a steam engine. The model was produced and propelled the first tugboat up the Chicago River. He became the engineer in charge of building, not just the Illinois and Michigan Canal, but the machinery that would be used to build it. [159]

Inventing things was a family tradition. Guthrie's grandfather invented chloroform, arguably before Dumas[160] who is usually given that credit. He also invented percussion priming powder used in cannons in the Civil War.[161] Ossian Guthrie himself patented a device for preserving ice using pooling water.

Guthrie was joined by Lyman Edgar Cooley, one of Chicago's best-known consulting hydraulic engineers and editor of the journal *The American Engineer*. He was a consultant with the Isthmian Canal Commission which oversaw construction of the Panama Canal. He served in a similar capacity on the Rochester Barge Canal and the Erie Canal.[162] Canals were Cooley's life.

After graduating from Rensselaer Polytechnic Institute, he arrived in Chicago, in 1874, to serve as a professor of engineering at Northwestern University. [163] But first, Cooley took some time off to serve as assistant United States Engineer working on Missouri and Mississippi River improvements. Three years after the work on the Chicago Drainage Canal started, in 1895, President Cleveland appointed Cooley as a member of the International Deep Waterways Commission.[164] This meant Cooley was in charge of investigations and surveys for ocean navigation from the Atlantic to Chicago and Duluth via the Great Lakes[165] before the Chicago Canal project was even completed. He had a lot of hats to wear.

The third committee member was Dr. Frank W. Reilly, the same Dr. Reilly who warned people to swat flies. He was assistant health commissioner for the City of Chicago.[166] Reilly had come

---

[157] Citizens' Association of Chicago, Crane, R. T., Singleton, S. M., Municipal Voters' League (Chicago, Ill.), Committee of One Hundred (Chicago, Ill.), & Citizens' Community Conference (Chicago, Ill.). (1874). *Citizens' Association of Chicago records.*

[158] "Death Calls Ossian Guthrie: 'Father of Drainage System' Expires After Long Illness." Obituary. *Chicago Tribune.* 26 Oct. 1908: A4. Print.

[159] *Ibid.*

[160] "The Discoverers of Chloroform." Editorial. *The chemist and druggist.* 6 Jan 1894. London: Publisher of Chemist & Druggist.

[161] Guthrie, O. (1887). *Memoirs of Dr. Samuel Guthrie, and the history of the discovery of chloroform.* Chicago: G.K. Hazlitt.

[162] Hager, W. H. (2016). *Hydraulicians in the USA 1800-2000.* CRC Press.

[163] Waterman, A. N. (1908). *Historical review of Chicago and Cook county and selected biography: A.N. Waterman ... ed. and author of Historical review.* Chicago: Lewis Pub. Co.

[164] *Ibid.*

[165] *Ibid.*

[166] International Waterways Commission (U.S. and Canada), & Chicago Sanitary District. (1924). *Copy of the report of the International Waterways Commission upon the Chicago Drainage Canal: Issued at Toronto, Ontario, on January 4, 1907 ... entitled International Waterways Commission progress report.* Chicago: The Board.

to the United States as an English immigrant. He studied medicine at the College of Charleston Medical School, in South Carolina. Afterward, he attended lectures at Rush Medical College in Chicago and eventually graduated from the Chicago Medical School, at Rosalind Franklin University of Medicine and Science in 1864, just prior to the Civil War. He was hired by his alma mater as Demonstrator of Anatomy.

Since the Civil War had broken out, he entered the United States Army. He was sent immediately to the front, where he was seriously wounded in the Battle of Shiloh. When he recovered from his own wounds, he became an Assistant Surgeon in the military. He worked his way up through the ranks until he was in charge of general and field hospitals.[167] He resigned from the military the very day the Civil War ended and returned to Chicago where he opened a private doctor's office on Archer Avenue, in the Bridgeport area.

The Chicago Canal project was a couple of decades away still, but sanitation was an immense issue. In 1867, Reilly was appointed as a Sanitary Inspector for the City of Chicago. It was a terrible year to live in Chicago.

Asiatic cholera struck. In common cholera, it is estimated that about six to seven percent of patients fail to survive. The loss of life due to Asiatic cholera was ten times that—sixty to seventy percent.[168] By early 1868, just a year later, smallpox broke out.

Overwhelmed, Dr. Reilly resigned. It was his responsibility to enforce sanitary laws. He was said to dislike contention or dealing with departmental finances, to the point that he would disappear while on the job. Reilly was highly regarded as a physician and as an advocate of fly-swatting. But, he was ill fit for the job of Sanitary Inspector.[169]

Reilly gave up medicine, determined to devote his life to sanitation. He left Chicago and attempted to start a monthly magazine in New York City, called *Hygiene* and devoted to public health. His goal was to convince insurance companies that, if policyholders better understood hygiene, they would be at less risk of health problems. But the idea never caught on. Reilly's message had fallen on deaf ears, in spite of the money that good hygiene could save the insurance industry.

Reilly returned to medicine. For the next three years, he served as a surgeon in the Marine Hospital Service. While he was there, the hospital published a book, *The Nomenclature of Diseases*. The book was actually the work of Dr. Reilly.[170]

When he again returned to Chicago, there was no better person to serve on a committee to solve the sanitation issue than Dr. Reilly. It was once said that he was the most useful citizen of Chicago. When he passed away in 1909, the *Bulletin* of the Society of Medical History of Chicago published pages and pages of condolences and detailed accounts of his life.

It was these three brilliant minds, Cooley, Reilly and Guthrie, that ultimately came together to

[167] Society of Medical History of Chicago. (1911). *Bulletin of the Society of Medical History of Chicago*. Chicago: The Society.

[168] *The Medical and surgical reporter*. (1867). Burlington, N.J: S.W. Butler.

[169] Society of Medical History of Chicago. (1911). *Bulletin of the Society of Medical History of Chicago*. Chicago: The Society.

[170] *Ibid.*

solve the sanitation problem that resulted in the Chicago Canal. They were supported by five special representatives.

Water was on the mind of Special Representative Charles A. MacDonald, long before he was tapped to serve on the committee. He was a Scottish immigrant who had arrived in Chicago in 1870. When the canal committee first came together, MacDonald was the owner of Hercules Iron Works, in Aurora, IL. He had already invented a gas pump and a compress cylinder[171] and was focusing on refrigeration machines and the Hercules Ice Machine, garnering $1 million a year. That was a lot of money for the late 1800s.

His efforts on the Citizens' Association Committee barely garnered a mention. He focused his life on a large number of activities. But, water was his bread and butter. He needed pure water for his ice machines.[172] The work of the CAC was important to his company.

Another committee member, David Bradley, was the founder of David Bradley Manufacturing. When the company was later sold and relocated to North Kankakee,[173] the city changed its name to Bradley,[174] in honor of the company. But, that was still far in the future when David Bradley became interested in Chicago city water.

He and his parents moved from Syracuse, NY, to Chicago when he was young. In 1835, Bradley founded the first foundry in the city. Later he was the first person to ship a bar of pig iron into Chicago.[175] Bradley saw the Chicago Canal as an important shipping route for his equipment. Therefore, he had a vested interest in water.

Another committee member, John J. Glessner, is not nearly as well-remembered as his house is. Today, the Glessner family home is a museum, the Glessner House.

He was born in Zanesville, OH, and moved to Chicago as a young man. Glessner became a founding partner of Warder, Bushnell & Glessner, who were successful farm implement manufacturers. Few people remember that name today, but in 1902 they merged to become part of the well-known International Harvester Company and Mr. Glessner remained as vice president.[176] Transportation was an important issue for transporting large equipment. He also served as president of Rush Medical College.

At times, Glessner served on the boards of Chicago Relief and Aid Society, Chicago Orphan Asylum, and the Art Institute of Chicago. He also participated in the Union League, Quadrangle and Chicago Literary Clubs as an active member and as a trustee of the Chicago Orchestra Association. Suffice it to say that Glessner loved Chicago.

Lastly, Edwin Lee Brown rounded out the committee. Brown was more involved with animal

---

[171] *Industrial refrigeration.* (1953). Chicago: Nickerson & Collins Co.

[172] World's Columbian Exposition. (1893). *Columbian Exposition dedication ceremonies memorial: A graphic description of the ceremonies at Chicago, October, 1892, the 400th anniversary of the discovery of America.* Chicago: Metropolitan Art Engraving & Pub. Co.

[173] Farm Implement News Company. (1895). *Farm implement news buyer's guide: A classified directory of manufacturers of farm and garden implements.* Chicago, Ill: Farm implement news company.

[174] *The Iron age.* (1899). New York: David Williams.

[175] *Ibid.*

[176] Bright, Wendy. "The Glessner House: How Forward-Thinking Homeowners Helped a Revolutionary Architect Make His Mark in Chicago." *Chicago Architecture.* Web. 1 Feb 2016.

rights than with water. In 1870, he founded the Illinois Humane Society. A Massachusetts native, he remained an honorary member of the Massachusetts Society for the Prevention of Cruelty to Animals when he relocated to Chicago. When the International Humane Society was formed, he was elected the first president of that organization.[177]

Part of his work was related to the humane shipping of cattle. When Brown spoke before the Illinois Humane Society, he explained "conclusively how closely the health of the community was related to the supply of wholesome meat, and that the crueltees practiced on cattle in transit made them really unfit for human food."[178]

Brown was born in Maine. When he was only 14 years old, he entered Bowdoin College before studying law for a while. He moved to New York City for time where he became a partner with Thaddeus Hyatt, who patented a sidewalk system made of illuminated basement windows, basement extensions, sidewalks and roofs.[179]

Edwin Lee Brown parted ways with Hyatt and set out on his own with his brother, Frank, and formed Brown Brothers Manufacturing Company in 1870. They were in the business of making lights for sidewalks. At the time, it was the largest such company in the world.

He moved to Boston, preferring to study architecture instead. While there, he was instrumental in forming the Boston Art Club. He demonstrated his public spirit.

Edwin Lee Brown also owned the Western Sand Blast Company, manufacturers of ornamental glass. Plus, he owned Ohio Handle Works which made, of course, handles. He owned Western Seed Company and he was president of the Evanston Gas Company.[180]

In his spare time, he was president of the Young Men's Library Association of Chicago for two years prior to the Great Fire. One source declares Brown "as much as any other person, is indebted for its free library system."[181]

Ever busy, Brown became connected with the Interstate Industrial Exposition of Chicago. In 1877, he served as president. The exposition was host to numerous companies needing better transportation methods. That was one of the two-fold purposes of the Chicago Canal, in addition to public safety.

It was this small group of talented and educated men who were tasked with solving a very complicated issue. There was no time to waste. As Chicago continued to grow, as did the need for commercial transportation via inland waterways.

Like most committees, progress was less than smooth. In the end, Lyman Cooley published a book detailing the entire process less than a year after the original report was completed. He explained in the preface that, "This report was practically completed months ago but as the policy herein was not in harmony with that of the Board of Trustees of the Sanitary District, it has not been published."[182] Cooley still did not cope well with confrontation and felt the need to

[177] *Voice of masonry and family magazine.* (1859). Chicago: J.W. Brown.

[178] Starrett, H. E. (1880). *The Western magazine: Vol. 1, no. 2.* Chicago: Western Magazine Co.

[179] American Institute of Architects. (1882). *The California architect and building news.* San Francisco, Calif: San Francisco Architectural Pub. Co.

[180] *Voice of masonry and family magazine.* (1859). Chicago: J.W. Brown.

[181] *Ibid.*

[182] Cooley, L. E., & Chicago. Sanitary District. Board of Trustees. (1891). *The lakes and gulf waterway: As related*

defend the decisions made by the CAC.

To begin with, the committee had not been allocated funds to even collect and organize the data. But, before they could even collect information, Brigadier-General William L. Marshall, of the U.S. Army Corps of Engineers, "antagonized" the interests of both the Sanitary District and the people of the Des Plaines and Illinois River Valley by questioning the committees' plans.

He charged in an official report that efforts to simply make the Illinois River deeper, from Lake Michigan to the Mississippi River, was "adverse to the interests of the United States." Marshall was a voice to be reckoned with. He invented automatic movable dams, lock gates and valves, like those already being used by the Illinois & Michigan Canal.[183] Perhaps more importantly, Marshall was personally responsible for the Illinois River and the Lake Michigan harbor.

Cooley disrespected Capt. Marshall's viewpoint, saying, "If his views are to govern the policy of the United States, a waterway is hopeless for this generation."[184] It should be remembered that the Chicago Canal project would impact work Capt. Marshall had been conducting on the Illinois River for 20 years.

Cooley charged that the deep-water solution was actually a covert attempt by Chicago to hide the sanitation problem under the guise of a deep waterway.[185] Debates in the legislature devolved into matters of language. Cooley wrote, "It appears that the 'interests of commerce' require the terminus to be at Chicago while the 'interests of navigation' require it to be in the Calumet region."[186] Also, the Calumet Harbor, built in 1870, had served as a refuge for boats needing to escape storms. No sooner had work begun on that project, than those using the refuge harbor claimed it should have been built 12 miles north of the Chicago River.[187] This added just one more detail the committee would need to resolve. The committee determined that the existing refuge harbor should remain in the city, "in other words, such a site is the cheapest, as well as the best."[188]

Cooley, feeling he was being rushed to choose a route without sufficient time to study the facts, resigned his post.[189] He was replaced by William E. Worthen, M. Am. Soc. C. E., who reported two alternative routes to the trustees.[190] The canal trustees chose one of the routes, but then the project languished. Worthen too resigned. Without funding, no route could be

to the Chicago sanitary problem. The general project of a waterway from Lake Michigan to the Gulf of Mexico ... A preliminary report with appendices, maps and profiles. Chicago: Press of J.W. Weston.

[183] *Engineering news*. (1902). New York: McGraw-Hill Pub. Co.

[184] Cooley, L. E., & Chicago. Sanitary District. Board of Trustees. (1891). *The lakes and gulf waterway: As related to the Chicago sanitary problem. The general project of a waterway from Lake Michigan to the Gulf of Mexico ... A preliminary report with appendices, maps and profiles*. Chicago: Press of J.W. Weston.

[185] *Ibid.*

[186] *Ibid.*

[187] *Ibid.*

[188] *Ibid.*

[189] Hill, C. S., & Engineering News Pub. Co. (1896). *The Chicago main drainage channel: A description of the machinery used and methods of work adopted in excavating the 28-mile drainage canal from Chicago to Lockport, Ill*. New York: Engineering News Pub. Co.

[190] Hill, C. S., & Engineering News Pub. Co. (1896). *The Chicago main drainage channel: A description of the machinery used and methods of work adopted in excavating the 28-mile drainage canal from Chicago to Lockport, Ill*. New York: Engineering News Pub. Co.

implemented.[191]

Samuel G. Artingstall, M. Am. Soc. C. E. replaced Worthen. Artingstall submitted four routes. Again the trustees selected one. And, again, they failed to proceed beyond that. So, Artingstall resigned—and so did three members of the board of trustees.

Ossian Guthrie also opposed making the current Chicago Canal deeper. He had carefully studied the area and the impact the movement of the glacial drift had on the land. He was the first engineer to suggest diverting the waters of the Des Plaines River as an alternative, in addition to reversing the direction of the Chicago River.[192]

But, first, governing bodies had to agree on who was in charge. The City of Chicago insisted that work on the Lower Illinois River should not be disturbed, or dams removed, until the city's sanitary project was completed. The state legislature perceived that the project from Lake Michigan to the Mississippi should be considered as a single entity. Bickering continued until finally the work on the Chicago Canal began in earnest.

---

[191] *Ibid.*

[192] Citizens' Association of Chicago, Crane, R. T., Singleton, S. M., Municipal Voters' League (Chicago, Ill.), Committee of One Hundred (Chicago, Ill.), & Citizens' Community Conference (Chicago, Ill.). (1874). *Citizens' Association of Chicago records.*

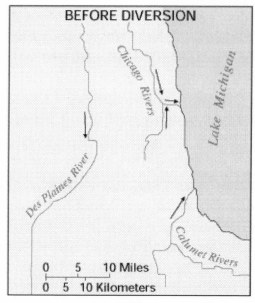

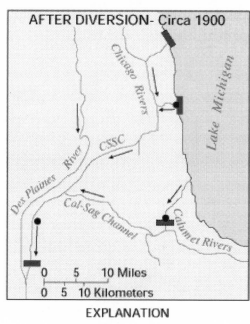

EXPLANATION
← Direction of Flow
▬ Control structure
● Acoustic velocity meter

A map indicating the flow of the river before and after the construction

    On September 14, 1892, seven years and seven days after the plan was devised, the first shovelful of dirt kicked off construction of the Chicago Canal. Known as "Shovel Day," the groundbreaking took place just below the city of Lemont, IL. Lyman Cooley, who served on the original committee, gave an address. "This is the logic of our policy. Today we cut the Chicago Divide for an urgent sanitary need which rouses our city; and in so doing we sever the Gordian knot which has fettered all projects, loosen possibilities of which statesmen have dreamed for a century; and in the manner of our doing, we set the gauge which shall govern the waterway of a continent."[193]

Lyman E. Cooley was back on board. The Board of Trustees of the Chicago Drainage Channel included businessmen, politicians, attorneys and physicians. Frank Wenter, as president, was a German immigrant. He ran for mayor of Chicago, but lost, settling instead for a position with the Civil Service Commission.[194] The Board Clerk was Thomas P. Judge. William H. Russell, a Chicago attorney, served as treasurer. Attorney for the board was George E Dawson. Chief Engineer was Isham Randolph, Thomas T. Johnston was First Assistant Chief Engineer and Uri W. Weston was Superintendent of Construction. Other members were John J. Altpeter, who was another German immigrant. He was a watchmaker and worked in the jewelry business.[195] William Boldenweck, was a German immigrant who worked in the cut-stone and contracting business. A.P. Gilmore was a Chicago physician. Bernard A. Eckhart was a senator and director of the Chicago Board of Trade. Thomas Kelly was owner of Thomas Kelly & Bros., who sold sanitary products. Richard Prendergast was an attorney and last, but certainly not least, Melville E. Stone was one of the owners of the *Chicago Daily News.* [196]

The work was divided into four sections and the contractors who submitted the lowest bid were hired. Division Engineers were hired to supervise for the Summit Division, the Willow Springs Division, the Lemont Division and the Lockport Division.

Cooley had intended for test pits to be dug first, but he was overruled by the original Board of Trustees. "The error of this action of the Trustees had far reaching results, for, owing to a combination of peculiar material and inefficient inspectors to record the borings, an entirely misleading idea was obtained of the hardness of the glacial drift in certain sections. In fact, it is doubtful if, with the most careful attention to conducting and recording the borings, they would have indicated with any truthfulness the exact character of some of this material. From the information obtained from these borings, however, the relative quantities of solid rock and glacial drift to be excavated were calculated and specifications were prepared." Instead, contractors were warned they were taking on all the risk in any variation from what they anticipated finding. When they objected, the phrasing was changed but probably not the risk.

The work itself was precisely laid out, right down to how many cuts with a channeling machine were to be made. The instructions varied according to the type of rock or soil, whether there were trees or structures nearby. As they worked, the excavated debris was built into 19 miles of levee along the canal. Progress was measured every other month.

It was never easy going. There were streets and railways crossings to consider. Trustees failed to take this into account and did not secure the right of way in advance.

The work brought jobs to Chicago and innovation to the waterways. It cannot be stressed enough what an enormous project this was in a fairly early time in the history of construction. In many cases, clay had to be blasted with dynamite before it could be removed by heavy

---

[193] Seeger, E. (1893). *Chicago, the wonder city.* Chicago: G. Gregory Print. Co.

[194] "Frank Wenter, Former Canal President Dies." *Chicago Tribune.* 10 Oct. 1929.

[195] *Chicago and its resources twenty years after, 1871-1891: A commercial history showing the progress and growth of two decades from the Great Fire to the present time.* (1892). Chicago: Chicago Times Co.

[196] Hill, C. S., & Engineering News Pub. Co. (1896). *The Chicago main drainage channel: A description of the machinery used and methods of work adopted in excavating the 28-mile drainage canal from Chicago to Lockport, Ill.* New York: Engineering News Pub. Co.

equipment during long days.[197] There were crane operators, pitmen, trainmen (dirt was hauled out by locomotive), shovel engine operators, firemen, dump men, drillers, blasters, and an array of machinists and blacksmiths to keep the project moving ever forward.

Initially, excavation work was done by scrapers. The Excelsior Iron Works, a Chicago manufacturing firm, built one of the first dredges specifically for the Chicago Canal. One might imagine an entirely metal dredge, but it was actually built of oak timbers braced together inside an iron hull and was steam operated. Excelsior was owned by Scottish immigrant John McArthur who, during the Chicago Fire, had served as Commissioner of Chicago Public Works. Five of the six dipper dredges used were all made by McArthur's Excelsior.

Soon, the Vulcan Iron Works of Chicago built two steam shovels for the project, to be used by contractors Shailer & Schniglau. Together with a novel bridge conveyor, they removed one million cubic yards of glacial drift.[198] Vulcan Foundry survived the Great Fire but eventually the name changed to Vulcan Iron Works. Founded by Henry Warrington, an English immigrant, by the time the Chicago Canal project was under way, Vulcan employed 175 men who turned 1,500 tons of pig iron and 150 tons of other steel and iron, into dredges and other machinery.

No doubt the new canal was a boost to Vulcan. The company exists today and among other things, they still make dredging equipment but they are owned by Bucyrus, who was originally a competitor.

Several types of steam shovels were used. The Bucyrus Special Contractor's, Bucyrus No. 1 Boom was used in conjunction with the Barnhart's AA for some of the most difficult excavation. Together the Barnhart's AA and Bucyrus No. 1 Boom worked 29 ten-hour shifts for two months to excavate solid rock.[199]

The Barnhart's AA type, was built by the Marion Steam Shovel Co. This Ohio-based company also built an excavator for moving dirt. It included a steam shovel built of wood and iron and weighed 250,000 lbs. It was 50 feet long and 23 feet wide.[200]

The Bucyrus was built by the Wisconsin-based company of the same name. Bucyrus originally was located in Ohio, but later moved to Wisconsin. A century later, Bucyrus acquired the Marion Steam Shovel Company, but not before Marion built transporters for the Apollo moon rocket.[201]

The canal was a big project. It required massive-sized equipment to accomplish the tasks set forth.

Grading was performed with equipment manufactured by the Western Wheeled Scraper Company. Originally an Iowan farm implement company, Western Wheeled moved to Aurora, IL. They owned the patent on the wheeled scraper, the original model for all road graders.[202]

---

[197] Gillette, H. P. (1920). *Earthwork and its cost: A handbook of earth excavation.* New York: McGraw-Hill Book Company, Inc.

[198] Hill, C. S., & Engineering News Pub. Co. (1896). *The Chicago main drainage channel: A description of the machinery used and methods of work adopted in excavating the 28-mile drainage canal from Chicago to Lockport, Ill.* New York: Engineering News Pub. Co.

[199] *Engineering news and American railway journal.* (1888). New York: Engineering News Pub. Co.

[200] *Engineering news.* (1902). New York: McGraw-Hill Pub. Co.

[201] Haddock, K. (2005). *Bucyrus: Making the earth move for 125 years.* St. Paul, MN: MBI.

[202] *Railway review.* (1914). Chicago: The Railway Review.

Part of the cost of the canal was reduced thanks to an invention by Eyvind Lee Heidenreich, a Swedish immigrant. The Heidenreich Incline was a complex system of an inclined track for moving dump cars full of dirt. Heidenreich was later hired by the Federal Government to construct the Hennepin Canal.[203] But, he devoted much of his career to the construction of large grain elevators. He was considered a world expert on reinforced concrete and went on to write a book about it.[204]

Construction of the canal

Some of the equipment was so new that it did not yet have a name. The Hoover & Mason Company created what might "be called a double cantilever conveyor for want of a better name."[205] It consisted of a 320-foot long bridge across the channel with a continuous belt of cars that carved away the banks. The contraption was so large that it slipped off its jacks and sunk. It was rebuilt, only to be damaged by a severe gale. It was then rebuilt a third time. The device became the most elaborate and expensive device on the entire river channel.

The builders, Frank K. Hoover and Arthur J. Mason, from Kansas City, MO, were the

[203] *A history of the city of Chicago: Its men and institutions. Biographical sketches of leading citizens.* (1900). Chicago: Inter ocean.

[204] Sundby-Hansen, H. (1921). *Norwegian immigrant contributions to America's making.* New York: The International Press.

[205] Hill, C. S., & Engineering News Pub. Co. (1896). *The Chicago main drainage channel: A description of the machinery used and methods of work adopted in excavating the 28-mile drainage canal from Chicago to Lockport, Ill.* New York: Engineering News Pub. Co.

designers of this patented contraption.[206] Hoover & Mason primarily focused on coal excavation. A waterway proved to be a very different process. The canal was inspiring invention on a scale never seen before.

A rubber conveyor built system was invented by Lindon W. Bates, owner of American Hydraulic Dredging Co.[207] It was only one of half a dozen dredgers he patented. Before the Chicago River project was even completed, Bates presented a paper on hydraulic dredges "and their relation to sea and inland navigation" at the International Congress on Navigation in Brussels, in September 1898.[208]

Bates' father was a shipbuilder in Chicago. After earning a degree from Yale, he spent a year working for the Chicago, Burlington & Quincy Railroad. He then spent the next few years working construction on the Oregon Railway, and other lines, across Oregon, Washington, Montana and California. He learned the dredging business while working on the Kaw River in Kansas City, MO, where he invented the first Bates Dredge that he patented. After his work on the Chicago Canal, he went on to dredging work on the Mississippi River. His travels even took him to Europe where he was hired to dredge rivers and harbors.

Water was a way of life for the Bates family, and it came in the way of death. Their son, Lindon W. Bates, Jr., drowned when the Lusitania sank. His father was chairman of the American Commission for Relief in Belgium, and young Lindon was on his way there to assist.[209]

An existing piece of equipment, the Lidgerwood Cableway, was adapted for use on the canal. It was manufactured by a New York company with more than half a dozen branch offices in the United States and Europe.[210] But the traveling cableway was first employed on the Chicago Drainage Canal.

The development of the first electric telegraph took place in the old Speedwell shops. John H. Lidgerwood inherited Speedwell Works from Judge Steve Vail, his stepfather, a couple of decades prior to the Chicago Canal project. Lidgerwood continued growing and exists today as the Superior-Lidgerwood-Mundy Corporation (SLM Corp.).

Unlike some of the manufacturers involved with the canal construction, Lidgerwood was very familiar with large projects. In 1890, prior to the beginning of the drainage work, Speedwell built a steam ship, the *Savannah*—the first steam ship to cross the Atlantic Ocean.[211] But most of their work focused on hoisting engines, such as those needed for the Chicago Canal.

Even though it was stipulated that contractors were not allowed to subcontract work, they did, nevertheless. Between that, and the coming and going of contractors, a vast number of people were employed in some fashion on the canal project.

---

[206] *Ibid.*

[207] *Engineering news.* (1902). New York: McGraw-Hill Pub. Co.

[208] American Society of Civil Engineers. (1956). *Journal of the Power Division: Proceedings of the American Society of Civil Engineers.* Ann Arbor, Mich.: The Society.

[209] "The Lusitania Resource: history, passenger & crew biographies, and Lusitania facts." Web. rmslusitania.info 2 Feb 2016.

[210] Lidgerwood Manufacturing Company. (1900). *The Lidgerwood cableway.* New York: Sackett & Wilhelms.

[211] United States National Museum, Smithsonian Institution, & Smithsonian Institution. (1884). *Report of the United States National Museum.* Washington: U.S. G.P.O.

Not only did the Chicago Canal project improve the river situation, it brought new business and innovation to the construction industry. Some of those businesses continued providing equipment and expertise long after the project was completed.

After a great deal of trial and error and really hard work, the Chicago Drainage Canal was finally finished. But it was far from complete.

A picture of the finished canal

Since the Chicago River is a tributary of Lake Michigan, one of the Great Lakes, the Chicago Canal became an international issue affecting not only the lakes but Canada's St. Lawrence River, as well as the St. Clair and Niagara rivers.[212] The Canadian Department of Marine and Fisheries became concerned because "the water levels of the Great Lakes are very delicate. Storms, barometric changes, rainfall, even tidal changes, are felt…. The water is constantly pouring in from not only one but several inlets. The overflow, however, is now always out of the one inlet provided for that purpose; the second one formerly at Chicago has been plugged up."[213]

In 1895, Canada was quoting a report submitted by Brigadier-General O. M. Poe of the U.S. Army Corps of Engineers and signed by two majors. Again, the USACE was critical of the Chicago Canal project only, this time, their words were being heeded by another country. Construction of the Chicago Canal was still underway but the Corps would not relent.

By 1896, a number of entities were measuring pollution levels in the various Illinois River communities. One suggestion was simply for everyone to drink distilled water. This was immediately dismissed as impractical since not everyone had access to distilled water or the resources to buy it.[214]

[212] Canada, & O'Hanly, J. L. P. (1896). *Report on the effect of the Chicago drainage canal on the levels of the Great Lakes*. Ottawa: S.E. Dawson.

[213] *Ibid.*

[214] Illinois. (1896). *Annual report of the Illinois State Board of Health*. Springfield, Illinois.

Work dragged on. It was not until just before Christmas 1898 that the Sanitary District of Chicago put out a bid to contractors for a railroad bridge across the Chicago River near Taylor Street.

There were nearly 100 bridges spanning the Chicago River. Prior to construction of the Chicago Canal, there were only half a dozen major bridge construction companies in Chicago.[215]

There were other unexpected issues. An array of legal matters, permits, bonding issues and the like cropped up even during construction. The Secretary of War also approved the "Establishment of Harbor Lines" on March 3, 1899. The War Department declared official harbors all around the country, including the North Branch of Chicago River at Chicago, Ill.[216]

The Sanitary District of Chicago had to apply for a special conditional permit. On May 8, 1899, the Secretary of War granted a conditional permit, "Rules and Regulations Governing the Floating of Loose Logs, the Navigation of Canals, Etc., And The Opening of Drawbridges." The city drawbridges were a significant issue. Numerous bridges criss-crossed the Chicago River. In fact, there were 89 bridges affected by these permits and requirements under the legislation governing "Bridge of the Sanitary District of Chicago over South Branch of Chicago River at Loomis Street, Chicago, Ill." The canal builders were required to submit, to the Secretary of War, their plans for replacing bridges that reached across the now-wider Chicago River channel.

"Lift bridges" across the Chicago River were built by companies like Scherzer and their patented Scherzer Rolling Lift Bridge.[217] A history of the Scherzer Company explains, "The Scherzer Rolling Lift Bridge has the shortest possible length of movable span to bridge any required because, in opening, the movable leaves move back and away from the channel." The Scherzer bridge was added to construction plans and approved by the Secretary of War on Nov. 16, 1893. Among its other advantages, the Scherzer safety record was unblemished.

Bridge construction was ongoing. In 1903, eight bridges were replaced or built across the Chicago River.[218]

The canal was unofficially and unceremoniously—and perhaps illegally—water first entered the new canal. It was Jan. 2, 1900, and Chief Engineer Isham Randolph met with the board of trustees at Kedzie Avenue and shortly after 11 a.m. water began to flow. But managing the project was not flowing well at all. Lyman Cooley was replaced by William Worthen. Four months later, Worthen was replaced by Samuel G. Artingstall. He was replaced by Benezette Williams who stayed less than two months. Isham Randolph came onboard in 1893 and had stayed the course.

But, on Jan. 2, Randolph and the board were hoping to avoid the possibility of work being stopped by an injunction.[219] It seems the drainage board trustees and a special commission

[215] Cope, G. W. (1890). *The iron and steel interests of Chicago: Compiled and published for the information of the Iron and Steel Institute and Verein Deutscher Eisenhüttenleute, on the occasion of their visit to Chicago, October 13 and 14, 1890.* Chicago: Rand McNally Co.

[216] United States. (1800). *Annual report of the Secretary of War.* Washington: U.S. Govt. Print. Off.

[217] Scherzer Rolling Lift Bridge Co. (1897). *Scherzer rolling lift bridges.* Chicago: Scherzer Rolling Lift Bridge Co.

[218] Chicago Sanitary District. (1800). *Proceedings of the Board of Trustees of the Sanitary District of Chicago.* Chicago, Ill: The Board.

[219] *Engineering news.* (1902). New York: McGraw-Hill Pub. Co.

appointed by Gov. Tanner disagreed about some matters. It also just happened that Randolph attended the Western Society of Engineers banquet that night where he announced that morning's epic event saying, "That stream which has smelled to heaven for so many years is about to be cleansed and pure waters flow where vile streams have festered for so long."

Isham, and the trustees, were aware of an impending lawsuit and they wanted to do everything they could to make sure the canal began functioning. On Jan. 17, 1900, a little more than two weeks after Isham released the first flow of water, the State of Missouri filed a joint U.S. Supreme Court lawsuit against both the Sanitary District of Chicago and the State of Illinois. That original bill was an attempt to discharge Chicago sewage through a man-made channel into the Des Plaines River. That river is miles and miles from Missouri, but the fear was that sewage would eventually flow down the Des Plaines until it reached the Mississippi and the shores of Missouri. The charge was overruled.[220]

But that issue was far from over. Missouri devoted the next six years and a monumental amount of expense in preparing the case. In the end, on Feb. 19, 1906, the complaint was dismissed once and for all.

In the midst of all the legal issues and other details, the Sanitary District sought, and then received, permission from the state legislature to construct dams, water wheels and "other works appropriate to render available the power arising from the water passing through the main channel...." Their request was approved on May 14, 1903.[221] In 1908, the Illinois legislature approved a constitutional amendment declaring that power from the water-plant operating the Sanitary District of Chicago could release electricity, produced with water from the Chicago River, for the benefit of the state treasury. Today, the privately-owned electric utility Commonwealth Edison uses river barges to supply coal to its power generators. ComEd also uses water from the Chicago River to cool them.

Also in 1903, the district sought permission to straighten the Chicago River. It wasn't enough that engineers had elevated the river, had widened it and had made it deeper. Throughout the history of the canal, portions of the Chicago River have, at times, been straightened in order to improve navigation, in addition to being carved deeper and the direction of the water reversed.

This was another effort by Isham Randolph. It meant that the sanitary district could generate its own power—and it could begin to sell electrical power to Chicago industries. By generating and selling energy, the sanitary district was self-sustaining and self-supporting.

The impact of the reversal of the Chicago River was a serious concern to farmers who relied on the river for transportation and as a water source, waterway managers and commercial interests. Speculation abounded. But some of the same experts who worked on the lock at Sault Ste. Marie were making unrealistic predictions about the Chicago Canal. The same Gen. O. M. Poe, with the USACE, insisted that the Sault Ste. Marie lock must absolutely be 24 feet deep. Yet, when it

---

[220] Internal Improvement Commission of Illinois. (1907). *The Lakes and Gulf Waterway: Message of Governor Deneen and report.* Springfield, Ill: Phillips Bros., State Printers.

[221] Witmer, T. R., & United States. (1957). *Documents on the use and control of the waters of interstate and international streams: Compacts, treaties, and adjudications.* Washington, D.C: United States Department of the Interior.

opened in 1895, Poe could still not name a single vessel that needed more than 18 feet.

A private group, the "Gaylord Syndicate," briefly caused some grief. There were rumors afloat that a powerful syndicate was quietly buying up land along the Des Plaines River. It turned out to be one man, Robert Gaylord, and a few of his friends of moderate means.[222] The syndicate proved not to be a concern.

Gov. Deneen was determined to protect the canal. "That Chicago and Illinois should attempt something that looks to the future—that will not be obsolete before it can be completed—is made the subject of prejudice. The authorities seem to be more concerned in framing an indictment than in finding remedies...."[223] After the destruction of several devastating fires, the city was now far more interested in water.

Federal regulations controlling traffic on the Chicago River were quickly developed. Simply building the canal was not enough. The city needed to implement a complicated schedule for raising and lowering bridges so that ships could pass when they needed to, without a train having to wait for the bridge to be lowered.[224] And those scheduled needed to be easily available to international traffic passing through the Chicago Canal.

In 1895, during the creation of the Chicago Canal, the Illinois State Water Survey (known as the Survey), was established at the University of Illinois Department of Chemistry with Dr. Arthur W. Palmer as the head of the survey from inception until 1904. Palmer earned a bachelor's degree in chemistry in 1883 and a ScD in chemistry from Harvard in 1886. When work started on the Chicago Canal, Palmer was studying in Germany.

---

[222] "Gaylord Alone in Canal Fight: Drainage trustees discredit stories of wealthy backing to syndicate." *Chicago Tribune* 31 Oct. 1902. Print.

[223] Internal Improvement Commission of Illinois. (1907). *The Lakes and Gulf Waterway: Message of Governor Deneen and report.* Springfield, Ill: Phillips Bros., State Printers.

[224] United States, United States, & United States. (1938). *The Code of Federal regulations of the United States of America.* Washington: U.S. G.P.O.

The Chicago River

Under Palmer, testing began on waterways across the state of Illinois. A year later, on August 15, 1896, Palmer's chemistry lab was struck by lightning and burned. It took another four years to convince the Illinois State Legislature to fund a new chemistry lab. Eventually, the lab was built and water testing became a common practice with Palmer testifying about the results, when called upon. In 1900, Palmer's tests results were used to squash the lawsuit filed against the Chicago Canal by the State of Missouri.

Palmer's water quality reports set the standard for national water quality studies. His data has been used to establish century-long trends of pollution in the Mississippi River basin and in the Gulf of Mexico.

Today, the Water Survey is housed in three locations. The Water Survey Research Center is on the University of Illinois Camps, and regional offices are located in Peoria and Carbondale.[225]

An ongoing issue with repercussions today is the amount of water that can safely be diverted from Lake Michigan without impacting the entire Great Lakes region, in both Canada and the United States. Following a Federal Supreme Court decision in 1930, limitations were designated. Three decades later, the Supreme Court was called on again and, again; the Survey's results were used to determine safe levels.

Dr. Palmer was one of the first to propose that interdisciplinary research was necessary to solve complex environmental problems. He worked closely with Professor Stephen A. Forbes, who served as a curator of the Illinois State Natural History Society Museum, in 1872. Forbes, for whom Stephen Forbes State Recreation Area, near Kinmundy, is named, was known as the true "Father of Ecology."

Eventually, William C. Ackermann, Chief of the U.S. Department of Agriculture's

---

[225] Illinois State Water Survey. (1957). *History and activities of the Illinois State Water Survey*. Urbana, Ill.

Agricultural Research, and John C. Frye, Chief of the Illinois State Geological Survey, attempted groundwater studies in the Chicago Metropolitan Area. Ackerman became the "first technical assistant for water resources in the Office of the President." He created the first federal agency coordinating a water resources plan.

Out of this grew research by engineers. In the early 1980s, the Survey began conducting routine evaluation of the Mississippi, Illinois and Ohio Rivers. That research became the basis for planning potential navigation improvements and ecosystem-based management of the upper Mississippi and Illinois rivers.

Yet, flooding continued to be an issue just beyond the Chicago Canal, in the Illinois and Kankakee Rivers. Even as recently as 1993, Pres. Bill Clinton appointed a task force to study the impact of wetlands during floods.

As an outgrowth of the Survey and in response to the waters coming down from the Chicago Canal to the Illinois River, the U.S. Army Corps of Engineers began using hydrology and hydraulics to study silting in the Illinois River. In 2002, the USACE began another amazing feat, removing silt by building man-made islands in the Illinois River near Peoria.[226] The Survey is also involved with an ongoing multi-year project studying water resources in the Chicago Metropolitan Area.[227] The In-Stream Dissolved Oxygen Study of the Illinois River above Joliet (the section that connects directly with the Chicago Canal) became part of the Illinois Rivers Decision Support System's Water Quality Database.

As a result of all this research, it is possible to calculate how much water the State of Illinois must supply to the Great Lakes, in exchange for water moving "the wrong way." This creates water debt. In 2002, the Chicago Canal was drawing 2,919 cubic feet per second from Lake Michigan. In the late 1990s, Illinois' water debt to the Great Lake was 3725 cubic feet per second. The state's goal is to eliminate the water debit by 2019.

Today, the canal is operated by the Metropolitan Water Reclamation District of Greater Chicago. It is an independent government and taxing body. It is responsible for 883.5 square miles of Cook County, IL.

But, the relationship between the canal and the Great Lakes continues. On Feb. 6, 2016, the MWRDG announced they would deliver drinking water to residents of Flint, MI, "in light of the ongoing water infrastructure crisis plaguing the residents." [228]

The Chicago city flag commemorates the canal project. The flag is a white background with stars placed in between two blue stripes. "The top blue stripe represents Lake Michigan and the North Branch of the Chicago River. The bottom blue stripe represents the South Branch of the Chicago River and the Great Canal."[229]

---

[226] *Ibid.*
[227] *Ibid.*
[228] *Metropolitan Water Reclamation District of Greater Chicago.* (1889).Web. 2 Feb. 2016.
[229] "Municipal Flag." *Chicago Public Library*. Web. 2 Feb. 2016.

The Flag of Chicago

The Chicago River project is internationally known for its innovative solutions to public safety and transportation. In 1955, the American Society of Civil Engineers developed a list of Seven Modern Wonders.[230] They were:

- Empire State Building
- Panama Canal
- Hoover Dam
- San Francisco-Oakland Bay Bridge
- Chicago Sewage Disposal System
- Colorado River Aqueduct
- Grand Coulee Dam/Columbia Basin Project

Many people immediately think of the Chicago River as the waterway Chicagoans dye green every year. It is a tradition that Mayor Richard J. Daley started, in honor of St. Patrick's Day. He revived the St. Patrick's Day Parade in 1956, but the idea of dyeing the river green came later.

In 1962, the mayor thought of a novel way to celebrate, with the color green. He wanted to dye part of Lake Michigan green.

A childhood friend of the mayor, Stephen M. Bailey, Chicago Plumbers Union business manager, suggested dyeing the river green instead. Since then it has become a well-known tradition.[231]

---

[230] Russell, J. S., & American Society of Civil Engineers. (2003). *Perspectives in civil engineering: Commemorating the 150th anniversary of the American Society of Civil Engineers*. Reston, Va: American Society of Civil Engineers.

[231] McGuire, Jack. "The Greening of Chicago." *Chicago Tribune* 16 Mar. 1980. Print.

Anyone can see the city from the Chicago River. Narrated tours and cruises are available. The Wendella Boat Tours have been catering to sightseers since 1935. There are water taxi services available for commuters and tourists alike.[232]

Tourism and outings have been popular since the early years of the canal, but not all ventures created happy memories. On July 24, 1915, while tied to a dock, the S.S. Eastland rolled over on its side, blocking river traffic. Onboard were Western Electric employees, families and friends about to set sail for a company-sponsored day on the water. The disaster took the lives of 844 passengers and crew.[233]

Chicago has come a long way since the days of "Stinky River." The shores of the Chicago River are currently being watched over by eleven focus groups. There are five habitat surveys underway. There are 629 distinct vegetative units along the river today.

There are nine passive and active recreation habitat sites. They are located in forests, parks, lagoons and city open space along the shoulders of the river.[234]

In 1990, the City of Chicago drew up Design Guidelines and Standards, applying to all new development within 100 feet of the Chicago River. The responsibility for development along the river falls under the oversight of:

- U.S. Army Corps of Engineers
- Illinois Department Natural Resources / Office of Water Resources
- Illinois Environmental Protection Agency
- City of Chicago Department of Transportation Division of Engineering
- Metropolitan Water Reclamation District of Greater Chicago
- U.S. Coast Guard
- Illinois Environmental Protection Agency

Since 1979, the city has been assisted by Friends of the Chicago River. An ambition group, "Friends works in partnership with municipalities, businesses, community groups, schools, peer organizations, government agencies and individuals on projects that benefit the river."[235]

Significant improvements in the Chicago River's comeback from its polluted condition can be attributed to the Clean Water Act and the Friends of the Chicago River. Today, the shores of the river are home to great blue herons, beavers and some 70 fish species. Barges share the waterway with kayaks, sailboats and tour boats. An annual New Year's Day canoe trip has become a tradition for some Chicagoans.

Founded in 2006, the McCormick Bridgehouse & Chicago River Museum keeps alive the story of the Chicago River and its movable bridges.[236] In spring and fall, the museum gives live demonstrations of the Michigan Avenue bridge opening to allow boat traffic to sail through the

---

[232] In Not for Tourists, Inc., (2015). *NFT: Not for tourists guide to Chicago.*

[233] "Grad student finds long-sought footage of 1915 Eastland disaster." *UIC News (University of Illinois- Chicago).* 10 Feb. 2015. Web.

[234] Nilon, Charles and Huckstep, Scott. "Analysis of Chicago River Recreation Habitats." (2003) *Rivers for life: Managing water for people and nature.* Washington: Island Press.

[235] "Friends of the Chicago River." Web. 2.5.2016. chicagoriver.org

[236] "McCormick Bridgehouse & Chicago River Museum." Web. 2 Feb. 2016.

heart of Chicago.

According to the Friends of the Chicago River, "When Robert Cassidy published 'Our Friendless River' in a Chicago magazine in 1979, the Chicago River was truly a lost resource, rarely used for recreation and inhospitable for wildlife. In his piece, Cassidy defined the problems facing the Chicago River and suggested strategies or an 'action plan' that he felt would improve it. This helped lay the foundation for Friends of the Chicago River and through our efforts, the Chicago River has been truly transformed." In response, the Friends of the Chicago River have published, "Action Plan for the Chicago River: Getting Specific."[237]

It may come as a surprise to some that the Chicago River is used on Yom Kippur for *tashlik*, the cleansing of sins. Mediterranean cooks gather wild grape leaves for making *dolmas,* stuffed grape leaves.[238]

The Chicago River is embedded in American culture. In the historic scene from the movie *The Blues Brothers*, Jake and Elwood jump their car across the Chicago River just as the LaSalle Avenue bridge opens. They make it; the police following them do not.[239]

When a character from *The Fugitive* found himself near the Chicago River on St. Patrick's Day, he asks a memorable question. Biggs asks on St. Patrick's Day, observing the Chicago River, "If they can dye this river green today, then why can't they dye it blue the other 364 days of the year?"

When the Tea Party formed, supporters advocated dumping securities into the Chicago River in protest against government mortgage bailout policies.[240] Regardless, officials have since reversed the Chicago River's natural water flow in an attempt to curtail pollution and increase transportation by building the Chicago Canal. Today, environmental efforts continue, as does Chicago River transportation, and the land is gradually being returned to nature.

The Progressive Era

The Progressive Era strove to change America for the better. In some ways, it succeeded, but it left much work undone as matters beyond the nation forced a change of priorities. As much as America desired to remain removed from Old World politics, the country would find itself dragged onto the world stage in the 20th century, and the nation would never be the same.

In many ways, the Progressive Era resulted from the influx of immigration during that time. Prior to this influx, the bulk of American immigration consisted of Germans, English, Irish, and Scotch-Irish fleeing the turmoil of the German Empire, the Corn Laws, and the Potato Famine. As the new century dawned, new ethnic groups entered the nation in quantities never seen before. As one historian summarized it, "The new immigration, however, brought millions of immigrants to the United States from southern and eastern Europe. The chief peoples in this wave of immigration were Poles, Italians, Bohemians, and Russian Jews. Unlike the Irish, these

[237] "Action Plan for the Chicago River: Getting Specific." *Friends of the Chicago River.* Web. 2 Feb. 2016.

[238] Cordell, H. K., Bergstrom, J. C., & Conference on Integrating Social Sciences and Ecosystem Management. (1999). *Integrating social sciences with ecosystem management: Human dimensions in assessment, policy, and management.* Champaign, IL: Sagamore Pub.

[239] "Blues Brothers Central." 2 Feb. 2016. Web.

[240] Torlina, J. (2011). *Working class: Challenging myths about blue-collar labor.* Boulder, CO: Lynne Rienner Publishers.

immigrants spoke no English, and most were penniless and uneducated. They rarely possessed a trade that could translate to a skilled job. The new immigrants were often scorned by both native Anglo-Americans and the older, more established immigrants. Some immigrant groups (such as the Poles) created tightly knit ethnic communities and clung together for support. Other immigrant groups (such as Italians) were often made up of men who arrived without their families, worked for several years, saved their wages, and returned to Europe."[i]

In the first decade of the 1900s, roughly 783,000 immigrants entered Chicago, most of them Russians, Austrians, Poles, Italians, and Hungarians.[ii] In 1910 alone, over 800,000 immigrants came to Chicago, most of them Italians, Poles, and Czechs. By the end of the Progressive Era in the 1920s, almost 860,000 immigrants arrived, including large groups of Lithuanians, Poles, and Mexicans who were fleeing yet another civil war.[iii]

Blacks also migrated en masse to Chicago and other Northern cities during the Progressive Era, seeking work and hoping to start better lives away from the rampant racism of the South.[iv] They grouped along the Black Belt, a small strip along Chicago's South Side.[v] Already a sizeable population in 1910, more African-Americans moved into the city, and by 1930, over 230,000 blacks resided in the Black Belt. Segregated, as elsewhere in the nation, they were forced to expand south, west, and to a lesser extent, east.[vi]

The massive influx of immigrants revealed numerous cracks in America's cities in terms of health and politics. Corruption and party machines operated like organized criminals, making it difficult to distinguish them from actual criminal organizations seeping their way into American cities as never before. Facing overcrowded, filthy cities and corrupt politics, many groups started to work toward a better America. They succeeded better in some cities than others, as one historian lamented: "Crime and the reign of the captains of crime have entered the field of otherwise legitimate business. The "racketeer" is merely a captain of gunmen and a man who undertakes by force to accomplish and guarantee the trade regulations and the freedom from competition in the lesser industries, which in the higher and wealthier callings are accomplished by means of the trade association and by the "gentlemen's agreement." He is a captain of the gunmen whom organized vice and organized gambling and liquor selling have brought among us and have maintained."[vii]

Reformers in Chicago, like many of the nation's cities during the Progressive Era, had their work cut out for them. One historian noted that unlike other cities, "Chicago in the Progressive [E]ra never experienced the reforms that consolidated overlapping wasteful governmental bodies, encouraged by government experts, and diminished influence of local party politics."[viii] Indeed, Chicago would become notorious for its corruption throughout the 20th century.

Although the reputation remains, people still strove to fight that corruption. Groups such as the Citizen's Association, Civic Federation, and Union League Club struggled during Reconstruction to work for reform as industrial strife rose, but despite their efforts, by the dawn of the Progressive Era, many had given up hope of meaningful reform.[ix] As if to mock the reformers, two infamously corrupt politicians - Bathhouse" John Coughlin and Michael "Hinky Dink" Kenna - rose to prominence at that time.

"BATH-HOUSE JOHN" COUGHLIN

Former Turkish bath rubber; now alderman, poet,
financier, and active manager of Ward One

Coughlin

Kenna

Both men exemplified the sort of corruption detested by Reconstruction and Progressive Era reformers.[x] Corrupt and vain, the men typified the party machine politics of Reconstruction. Though they subverted the system, their support of the working classes endeared them to voters. As one man put it at the time, "To be recognized and represented by a crook is better than not to be recognized or represented at all."[xi]

Progressive Era reformers disagreed, and they galvanized with renewed resolve, regrouped and prepared for a fresh wave of reform work. The early leaders of this renewal were William Stead, Walter L. Fisher, Henry Demarest Lloyd, and Melville Stone.[xii] Sons of Protestant ministers all, they believed in the social gospel which advocated "that individuals should dedicate themselves to the redemption of others from societal as well as supernatural sins."[xiii] Such a belief became the official creed of the Progressive Era by 1908, when the American Methodist Episcopal Church formally adopted it. The early reform movement also received a boost from Populists who bolted from the Democratic Party after William Jennings Bryan's poignant but controversial "Cross of Gold" speech.[xiv] Though moved for reform, the reformers often butted heads, as ethnic and religious groups often distrusted each other until much later in the 20th century.

Predominantly middle-class, these reformers looked to politics with a newfound appreciation. Once seen as something of an undesirable career akin to undertakers or used car salesmen, those who entered the field did so out obligation, willingly dirtying their hands to serve their country. Conversely, Progressive Era reformers saw, in politics, the chance to reform the system from within.[xv]

By the first decade of Progressive Era, the reformers had achieved much, failed in other respects, and still had much to do. One historian explained, "Overall, though, Progressives accomplished tremendous things in the first decade of the 20th century. Many features of public life taken for granted today, such as civil service, city planning and zoning, primary elections, and secret ballots are their handiwork. In Chicago they particularly improved the police, city budgeting, planning, and the courts. So-called justice shops run by justices of the peace, bail bondsmen, and police were legislated out of existence by the creation of the municipal court in 1907."[xvi]

Though they had succeeded in many fields, they also failed to achieve reforms in others, and public ownership of mass transit and city charter reforms were two such failures. The failure of the charter reform especially stung, as the earlier charters left much to be desired regarding the balance of power between city alderman and rural state legislatures in the railroad companies' pockets. Such a song and dance of reform had occurred before in Chicago's history, and the Progressives believed they could improve it yet. [xvii]

Reformers also lamented the failure of transit reform. Where a mayoral candidate stood on the issue of municipal ownership decided elections, and railroad companies were notoriously corrupt.[xviii]

Throughout this time, there were other efforts to reform various aspects of the city, such as Chicago's police force. As one 1904 report noted, "Civilians behind the desk smoking. Sergeant in shirt sleeves. At roll-call men stood in slouchy positions and talked to each other while orders were being read…Not sufficient number of men to properly care for the precinct. Cellar in disgraceful condition, partly due to the taking care of tramps who used old paper for bedding which is a menace to the safety of the house on account of fire, and to the health of the men in the station."[xix]

Clearly, plenty of work remained for Progressive Era reformers. The police force was under the thumb of two gambling bosses, Mont Tennes and "Hot Stove" Jimmy Quinn, whose activities led to 60 indictments once the dust had settled.[xx] The gambling bosses used the police force to rig elections in their favor, and they distributed campaign literature and removed Republican voters from the polls. Despite such efforts, the Democratic candidate lost, so reformers redoubled their efforts to fix police corruption, once and for all.[xxi]

Bolstered by the election of President Theodore Roosevelt, who, as president, had earlier come to the aid of Chicago Police Commissioner Edward McCann, the Progressives continued the cause of reform.[xxii] Their next target was the city's budget, which reformer Charles Merriam considered a joke, thanks to having the lowest tax rate of any city in America. That was combined with, as he put it, "the lowest revenue per capita, the lowest revenues per capita…The local revenue system is decentralized, unsystematic, necessarily expensive, and irresponsible."[xxiii] The same issues plaguing the city's budget reflected the overall goals of Progressive reformers, which included consolidating government agencies, reducing redundancy, and removing corruption.

Their early efforts in these regards met with little initial success, as one historian explained. "For the next ninety years, Chicago suffered public employees whose duties were 'few and far between.' In 1911 reformers believed that Chicago was ready to elect Merriam as mayor. He ran and lost to Harrison, in part because a playboy named William Hale Thompson and the corruption he represented were ascending as Progressivism receded."[xxiv]

Increased Diversity

While the Progressives fought for reform and the naturalization of the immigrants, the immigrants lived their lives as best they could. One such group of immigrants, the Poles, started to arrive during the 19th century, but their numbers remained small until the Progressive Era.[xxv] By 1910, 210,000 Poles resided in Chicago, and that number nearly doubled by 1930. Arriving from the rural lands of Eastern Germany and Western Russia, they lacked trade skills and money. Moreover, many were illiterate in Polish and could not speak English.[xxvi]

The Poles clustered in specific neighborhoods for protection. Their largest grouping was the appropriately named Polish Downtown on the Near Northwest Side, and another neighborhood housed many Poles in South Chicago near the steel mills.[xxvii] The other major centers of Polish settlers were the Lower West Side and a cluster of lands near the Union Stock Yards.[xxviii] Like many immigrants, the Poles built their institutions and churches in their neighborhoods, and the Near Northwest Side housed two massive Polish Catholic parishes at St. Stanislaw Kostka and Holy Trinity.[xxix]

In addition to churches, the Poles also formed death-benefit societies and loan associations.[xxx] Thanks to such efforts, more Poles than any other ethnic group managed to become Chicago homeowners.

The largest and most significant institution for the Poles remained, as in Europe, the Catholic Church. Along with churches, they also built parochial schools. In time, they would build more of those schools than their fellow Catholic immigrants, the Italians.[xxxi]

The Italians followed the Poles in the 1850s when they arrived in number for the first time in Chicago, and by 1910, 45,000 Italians resided in the city.[xxxii] Most of them came from rural central and southern Italy, where instead of the wealth of the Old Italian city-states, they mostly traded in tomatoes and organized crime.[xxxiii] Italian immigration patterns differed from other ethnic groups in several ways, as they tended to migrate in three distinct ways. Many Italian men came to America, saved their wages over several years, and returned to Italy. As many as half of the Italian immigrants migrated with the goal of eventually returning to the Old World.[xxxiv]

Others found work through a local Italian labor broker, an established migrant who likely spoke English and served as guide and translator for new arrivals, as well as getting them work.[xxxv] This system, familiar to Italian men used to the tit-for-tat nature of southern and central Italy, favored the many single men seeking temporary, unskilled employment. The guide, a labor broker known as a *padrone,* naturally took a percentage of his client's wages.[xxxvi]

The third form of Italian immigration was known as *campanilismo*. As explained by one historian, "The men from entire villages in southern Italy would often immigrate en masse to America; these men took up residence with friends, neighbors, and relatives from the Old

Country. Chicago reformer Jane Addams observed that often an entire tenement house would be filled with Italian tenants hailing from the same village. In effect, whole villages (minus many wives and children) immigrated intact. For example, men from Naples and Messini lived in Chicago's Near West Side community, immigrants from Palermo and Catania lived on the Near North Side, and men from Genoa lived in the south end of the Loop (near the present-day Merchandise Mart). Settlement patterns such as this enabled first-generation Italian immigrants to preserve much of their ethnic heritage and many of their customs."[xxxvii]

Being single men, the bulk of Chicago's Italians often settled in slum areas, massed into large groups, and worked outdoors as railroad, in construction, or as market vendors.[xxxviii] Reformers looked at these temporary workers seeking funds in America before returning to their families with despair. Progressive Jane Addams once remarked, "[t]he South Italians more than any other immigrants represent the pathetic stupidity of agricultural people crowded into city tenements."[xxxix]

Unlike their Polish counterparts, southern and central Italians had grown dissatisfied with the Roman Catholic Church, which often sided with wealthy landowners at the expense of the peasants residing in Chicago.[xl] Compounding the issue, local churches were often run by the Irish, who did not welcome Italians into their congregations. When Italian priests reached Chicago in the early 20th century, they managed to reverse the immigrants' discontent with the Church.[xli] Bolstered with newspapers in their native language and supportive societies, Italians returned to the flock, though as the years went on, they more often stayed in the United States.[xlii]

Another religious minority moved to Chicago in numbers during the early 20th century. Besides Catholics, Jews also immigrated to the predominantly Protestant United States. Fleeing Russian pogroms and rising German anti-Semitism, if not acceptance, they at least found a life free of persecution in America. The first few thousand Jews to reside in Chicago hailed from Germany and acclimated to the city well, just as they had in the German Empire in the 19th century. Whereas only about 10,000 Jews resided in Chicago in the late 1800s, the number rose to 80,000 by 1900. By 1930, thanks to the Bolshevik Revolution and Russian Civil War, their population numbered nearly 300,000.[xliii] This made Chicago the third-largest Jewish population center, with New York City in second and Warsaw, Poland in first.

The bulk of these immigrants came from Russia and acclimated to America very differently from their German brethren.[xliv] Hailing largely from Russia, Poland, and Austria-Hungary, they settled in Chicago's southwest area near the downtown. This area became the Jewish neighborhood, a cramped, crowded, dangerous area with cheap housing and a good view of Canal Street.[xlv] Peddlers and vendors crowded the area, hawking their wares in Yiddish. One Chicago native who visited the neighborhood had a vivid recollection of the area: "The smell of garlic and of cheeses, the aroma of onions, apples, and oranges, and the shouts and curses of sellers and buyers fill the air. Anything can be bought and sold on Maxwell Street. On one stand, piled high, are odd sizes of shoes long out of style; on another are copper kettles for brewing beer; on a third are second-hands [sic] pants; and one merchant even sells knives and household tools salvaged from the collections of junk peddlers. Everything has value on Maxwell Street, but the price is not fixed. It is the fixing of the price around which turns the whole plot of the drama enacted daily at the perpetual bazaar of Maxwell Street…The sellers know how to ask ten times the amount that their wares will eventually sell for, and the buyers know how to offer a 20th."[xlvi]

It took capital to sell goods, and most Jews arrived in America lacking such capital, or even a penny to their name. Lacking any trade, many first arrivals started their entrepreneurial skills as door-to-door salesmen. Those with the skills and acumen to survive the difficult life of peddling door to door found upward mobility much easier to achieve.[xlvii] Those who first came to America faced hard times, but their children, building on the hard work of their parents, often did quite well and moved on to financial and political success.

While still in Chicago, however, they faced conflict with their fellow immigrants, including their fellow Jews.[xlviii] German Jews, having easily assimilated into Chicago city life thanks to an urban background better integrated than in their homeland, considered their Eastern counterparts an embarrassment. While the German Jews were accepted by their fellow Chicagoans, the Easterners tended to stick to their neighborhoods while clinging to the Old World customs of the provincial peasantry.[xlix] This included their attire - German Jews wore American clothing while the Easterners stuck to the long coats, long beards, and oversized peasant dresses. Religiously, Easterners stuck to an orthodox interpretation of the faith, while their more urban counterparts practiced what is today considered Reformed Judaism. When it came to the class struggle, the German Jews more often than not sided with capital, while their Eastern counterparts often led the fight for labor.[l] One Chicago rabbi summed the issue up by stating the two groups were "divided by pecuniary, intellectual, and social distinctions, provincial jealousies, and even religious distinctions and differences."[li]

Despite this, or perhaps because of it, the German Jews heavily invested in institutions to better integrate their eastern counterparts into American society. Chicagoans like Sears & Roebuck President Julius Rosenwald aided in the funding of the Chicago Hebrew Institute.[lii] The easterners tended to reject such patronizing efforts, instead forming their societies and institutions, just as their Catholic immigrant counterparts. Thanks to such efforts, eastern Jews could afford to leave their corner of Chicago by 1910. With the railroads crowding Maxwell Street, Jews expanded westward.

Rosenwald

African-Americans from the South replaced them.[liii] Crowded, divided, subdivided, and re-divided into cramped, crowded tenements, the rapidly growing black neighborhoods began to attract tourists. Reformers, reporters, and thrill seekers with skewed ideas traveled to the Black Belt's Stroll.[liv] Bustling with music clubs and movie theaters, the Stroll proved the most profitable and respectable aspect of the Black Belt, similar to Paradise Valley in Detroit. Referred to as "the Bohemia of Colored Folk," all who visited acknowledged the area's respectability, charm, and culture. Several visitors noted, rather ironically, that whites seeking to "slum it" or achieve cheap thrills beyond the borders of "proper" white society marred the otherwise honest and proper businesses and their regular patrons.[lv]

Unlike other ethnic groups in Chicago, blacks were singled out as the antithesis to Progressive Era values. Considered uneducated vagrants and sharecroppers, ignorant and incapable of integrating into urban life - completely ignoring that their European counterparts could and did - reformers considered the black community one in need of containment and discipline.[lvi] Still, the tourists came, sensationalizing the Stroll, and adding to the stigma blacks faced in Northern cities. One such report on the famous Pekin Theater called it a den of "lawless liquor, sensuous shimmy, solicitous sirens, wrangling waiters, all tints of the racial rainbow…A brown girl sang…Black men with white girls, white men with yellow girls, old, young, all filled with the abandon brought about by illicit whisky and liquor music."[lvii]

Thus, the black community was deliberately contained and prevented from integrating during the Progressive Era. Efforts were made to aide them, as was the case with other Chicagoan groups, but with limited success.

Another religious minority was making its way into Chicago, one with a long history as a small but important facet of the city. The number of Greeks in Chicago was a small but prominent aspect of the city's immigrant population, forming one of the oldest Greek communities in the United States.[lviii] Settling on the Near West Side, the Greek neighborhood earned the monikers of Greek Town and the Delta.[lix] One writer at the time described the community: "Practically all stores bear signs in both Greek and English, coffee houses flourish on every corner, in the dark little grocery stores one sees black olives, dried ink-fish, tomato paste, and all the queer, nameless roots and condiments which are so familiar in Greece. On every hand one hears the Greek language, and the boys in the streets and on the vacant lots play, with equal zest, Greek games and baseball. It is a self-sufficient colony, and provision is made to supply all the wants of the Greek immigrant in as near as possible the Greek way. Restaurants, coffee-houses, barber-shops, grocery stores, and saloons are patterned after the Greek type, and Greek doctors, lawyers, editors, and every variety of agent are to be found in abundance."[lx]

Considered individualistic and ambitious by their contemporaries, the Greeks tended to rub people the wrong way, particularly the Italians whose jobs they took. Rather than manual labor, however, Greeks tended toward mercantile and artisan endeavors, opening small shops and swarming the area with fruit stands.[lxi] By 1919, as many as 10,000 of the 18,000 Greeks in Chicago owned their businesses, though their efforts in the fruit market only exacerbated the enmity between them and the other Mediterranean groups.[lxii]

While Greeks worked to own their own business and strike out as hard workers, other ethnic groups strived for the American dream of homeownership. Hailing from the Balkans, Chicago's Czech population would become one of the largest urban populations in the world.

The Czechs, or Bohemians, first reached Chicago in 1850 and by 1870, numbered around 10,000. By 1895, they numbered 60,000, having created their community, known as Pilsen. Within the next 15 years, Chicago's population of 110,000 Czechs made it the second largest urban population of Czechs after Prague.[lxiii]

Unlike other immigrant groups, the Czechs usually arrived with an education and some money to their names. Like the Poles, they desired a home to call their own and thus started loan associations to bolster their efforts. A study written in 1895 noted Czech frugality in their dream of homeownership: "Often good artisans were compelled to work for low wages, even $1.25 a day; still, out of this meager remuneration they managed to lay a little aside for that longed-for possession-a house and lot that they could call their own. When that was paid for, then the house received an additional story, and that was rented so that it began earning money. When more was saved, the house was pushed in the rear, the garden sacrificed, and in its place an imposing brick or stone building was erected, containing frequently [sic] a store, or more rooms for tenants. The landlord, who had till then lived in some unpleasant rear rooms, moved into the best part of the house."[lxiv]

Thanks to such efforts, many Czechs moved out of Pilsen into a stretch of Chicago cut through by California Avenue, which earned it the moniker of Czech California. Whether a home, a social hall, or a brewery, Czech structures never failed to impress those who looked upon them. Such was their prominence in the neighborhood that their language was taught in local high schools.[lxv] Though living amongst themselves, the Czechs, hailing from the last multi-ethnic empire in Europe, had no trouble mingling with the rest of Chicago. Though they lacked the numbers of other prominent ethnic groups, the Czechs formed pluralities with other blocs to have their voices heard.[lxvi]

Scandinavian immigrants also left a lasting mark on Chicago during this early period of the 20th century, and like the Greeks, they arrived at an already established neighborhood. Swedes soon proved the dominant group of this bloc, numbering 121,000 by 1920.[lxvii] As early as 1880, three small but distinct Swedish neighborhoods had existed within Chicago. Swede Town, the largest, resided on the Near North Side, not far from the Chicago River. The two smaller communities settled on the Near West Side and Near South Side.[lxviii] Thanks to these early immigrant communities, Swedes arriving in the early Progressive Era managed to avoid inner-city slums by settling in the outer areas of the city, where their pioneering ilk had settled decades before. Thanks to such a dispersal, the Swedes managed to integrate into Chicago's melting pot much easier than other ethnic groups.[lxix]

Together, immigrants from all the various places faced the trials and tribulations of the Progressive Era, especially the reform efforts focused on urban living. Out of such reform efforts, one would turn out to be far more trouble than it was worth, for with it came organized crime the likes of which Chicago had never seen before.

Prohibition in Chicago

Though Prohibition was ultimately a poorly conceived and poorly implemented disaster, it is not as simple a story as it might first appear to be. The Temperance Movement, as it was first known, dated all the way back to the 1840s, when drinking was an undeniable problem in American life. Historians estimate that per capita consumption of booze was as high as 7 gallons of pure alcohol a year, well over three times the current rate, and the equivalent of 90 bottles of 80-proof liquor a year. In response to this very real problem, groups like the Daughters of Temperance began cropping up, and later the Women's Christian Temperance Union. The Prohibition Party was founded in 1872, but it was the Anti-Saloon League, founded in 1893, that made prohibition a viable political force.

Temperance was connected in unexpected ways to a variety of other causes. The WCTU was at the center of the women's suffrage movement: it provided a training ground for women in political activism, and women concerned about moral issues like drinking realized they would have greater impact if given the right to vote. Most prominent abolitionists were in favor of temperance, as were prominent black leaders like Frederick Douglass and Booker T. Washington. Prohibition also attracted activists of a very different sort: beer and saloons were very much associated with the new wave of immigration, and the ASL in particular had a strongly anti-immigrant bent. Thus, the politics of the temperance movement was all over the map, and made for strange and contradictory alliances.

Prohibition also came to be connected with the campaign for a federal income tax. The alcohol excise tax accounted for a substantial amount of the government's budget, forcing supporters of Prohibition to answer the question of how to replace that income, and thus creating additional momentum for the 16th Amendment approved in 1913. And conversely, the need to bolster the federal budget in the early days of the Depression became one of many reasons cited for Prohibition's repeal.

Passing Prohibition was one thing, but enforcing it was another, and in many ways Prohibition seemed doomed from the start. The new Prohibition Bureau was a part of the Treasury Department, whose head, Andrew Mellon, never fully supported the law. The Bureau was given only 1500 field agents to start with, and much of the hiring of agents was influenced by the Anti-Saloon League, which used the positions to pay back political favors from the Prohibition campaign. In a fascinating historical footnote, it turns out Capone's eldest brother, who had earlier moved out West and disappeared from sight, reinvented himself under a new name and became a well-known and highly regarded Prohibition Agent. He eventually reconnected with his family, visiting them yearly in Chicago and largely managing to keep his two lives separate.

The ways of circumventing Prohibition were many and varied. Whiskey and gin and rum were smuggled in through Canada and the Bahamas, among other places. A line of ships along the East Coast permanently docked just beyond the three-mile border, and essentially serving as liquor warehouses, was known as Rum Row. Doctors were allowed to write prescriptions for "medicinal" alcohol, and exemptions for wine designated for Communion were available. In addition to all the money to be made from outright bootlegging, apparently legitimate businesses thrived as well: for example, the number of Walgreens pharmacies shot up from 20 to 525 over the course of the 1920s. Foreign travel shot up, and ship lines developed "cruises to nowhere" or "booze cruises."

Disenchantment with Prohibition grew steadily as the decade progressed. So-called "dry" crusaders didn't help their cause with overly zealous measures like the Jones Law, which aimed to make all violations of Prohibition a felony. But it was the stock market crash and the Depression that was the nail in the coffin for Prohibition. Voters were disillusioned with the Republican Party, and in the 1932 election FDR argued that the government desperately needed the income from alcohol taxes. To a large extent that was accurate; during the first year of Repeal, such taxes accounted for 9% of all federal revenue. In February 1933, the 21st Amendment (repealing the 18th) was introduced, and when in December the necessary number of states had ratified it, Prohibition's 14 year history was over.

Among Prohibition's long-term (and unintended) consequences was the nationalization of organized crime. The complex transportation schemes required to move liquor like Canadian whiskey across the border, then to New York, and then on to Chicago also fostered the creation of regional and national networks among racketeers and bootleggers. Organized crime became organized and bureaucratized as never before. As historian Selwyn Raab wrote in *The Five Families,* "Prohibition had been the catalyst for transforming the neighborhood gangs of the 1920s into smoothly run regional and national criminal corporations… Bootlegging gave them on-the-job executive training."[241]

By 1920, Chicago's population was nearly 3 million, the second largest in the country, and it was the undisputed capital of mid-America. Dominated economically by industries like meatpacking, lumber and the railroads, Chicago was a richly diverse and heavily segregated city. Lacking the established elite and long-standing cultural traditions of eastern cities like New York and Boston, Chicago was notable for its loose and open nature. It was a city in which an ambitious businessman (or gangster) could make an almost immediate impact. In the eyes of many, its looseness extended to matters of morality as well. In his 1904 book *The Shame of the Cities,* muckraking journalist Lincoln Steffens summed the city up this way: "First in violence, deepest in dirt; loud, lawless, unlovely, ill-smelling, irreverent… the 'tough' among cities, a spectacle for the nation."[242]

Johnny Torrio was summoned to Chicago to be the right-hand man for James "Big Jim" Colosimo, who had emerged from the post-war years as the leader of the city's most prominent organized crime syndicate. Colosimo lived large and extravagantly, and he saw the business-like and unassuming Torrio as a perfect match. The cornerstone of Colosimo's expanding empire was a large network of brothels, and the new Prohibition laws provided yet another possibility for growth. Even before this expansion, Colosimo came into frequent conflict with the Black Hand, which had prompted his association with Torrio in the first place. When Torrio first introduced Capone to Chicago, Capone worked as a bouncer and bartender at one of Colosimo's brothels, the Four Deuces.

However, Torrio's arrival on the scene happened to coincide with Colosimo's rapid and unexpected demise. Big Jim fell fast and hard for a young actress and singer, and rashly divorced his wife and former business partner, leaving the day-to-day operations almost entirely to Torrio. Because of this, as well as his reluctance to engage in liquor smuggling, Colosimo was increasingly perceived as vulnerable, a situation that was quickly taken advantage of by Torrio. When Big Jim returned to Chicago after his recent second marriage, Torrio called him to let him know that a shipment was arriving at his café. When Colosimo showed up at the café to get the package, he was shot and killed.

Though nobody was ever convicted, it has long been assumed that Colosimo's assassin was none other than Frankie Yale, Torrio's and Al Capone's old associate back in New York. By this time Yale had established himself as one of the most prominent gangsters in New York City, but perhaps jealous of Torrio's new success in Chicago and wishing to make his own mark, Yale travelled to Chicago and on May 11, 1920 he allegedly took out Colosimo in the first of many notorious gangland hits to come. Yale was picked up after an eyewitness identified him, but he was later released when the witness claimed his memory had failed him. Capone himself also continues to be a suspected assassin of Big Jim.

---

[241] quoted in Okrent, *Last Call,* p. 345
[242] Bergreen, p. 77

Big Jim Colosimo

Big Jim may have been going soft, but he had done a credible job of organizing a criminal syndicate, and regardless of who murdered Big Jim, the political climate in Chicago was a perfect setting for Torrio to establish himself in the wake of Colosimo's killing. New mayor "Big Bill" Thompson openly promised to turn a blind eye to the Prohibition laws—declaring that Chicago was "wet," and so was he. Torrio quickly ingratiated himself with the Thompson administration and began expanding the network he inherited from Colosimo, as well as establishing peace with a number of the many other crime syndicates in the city. It wasn't long before his operation included thousands of speakeasies, brothels, and gambling joints. Torrio needed some men he could trust to help him run his new empire, and it was at that point that he turned to his 22 year old protégé Al Capone.

Mayor "Big Bill" Thompson

After eight scandal-ridden years in office, the permissive "Big Bill" Thompson was finally forced to withdraw from the 1923 mayoral election, and his successor, William Dever, vowed to make a radical change in direction—not only enforcing Prohibition, but cracking down on organized crime. The new policy heightened tension between the various gangs competing for a share of all the illegal profits to be had in Chicago, and it brought about the early stages of a long series of turf wars in the city.

Mayor William Dever

Torrio's response was to keep a low profile in Chicago itself and shift the focus of operations to the suburbs. Thus, Torrio and Capone chose Cicero, a sleepy working-class suburb whose residents loved their beer but were more conservative when it came to vices like prostitution. In late 1923, Torrio set up the first two of many brothels to come, established a profit-sharing arrangement with rival gangs, and then left Capone in charge while he took some time off to move his aging mother back to Italy. In an effort spearheaded by older brother Frank—who with his tall good looks was the most publicly visible of the Capone brothers—the Capones began a systematic effort to take control of Cicero's political establishment. They put up their own candidates, intimidated the opposition, and stole ballot boxes, whatever it took: and sure enough, the Capone-backed candidates were swept into office by wide margins.

With Cicero's City Hall in his back pocket, Capone and his brothers engaged in aggressive expansion, establishing a large new brothel in the neighboring suburb of Forest View (which came to be called "Caponeville"), a major new gambling hall, and taking over the local racetrack. The only opposition the brothers encountered came from the local paper, the *Cicero Tribune,* run by a high-minded journalist named Robert St. John.

Although Torrio tried to maintain the peace among Chicago's many racketeers and organized crime syndicates, turf battles in what the press called the "Beer Wars" began breaking out and escalating. So-called "gangland-style" murders rose from 29 in 1922 to 52 in 1923. One of the major players in the war—the Irish gangster Dion O'Banion, the most prominent organized crime figure on the North Side—made a small fortune through the flower shop he ran as his front business: it became accepted practice, even for rival gangs, to order flowers for the constant stream of gang funerals through his shop.

O'Banion

The other major players in the Beer Wars were the six Genna brothers, a tough and volatile group of Sicilian bootleggers. Torrio and Capone maintained an uneasy peace with them, but tension ran high between the Genna brothers and O'Banion and ultimately full-scale war broke out. O'Banion hijacked one of the Genna trucks, and then in an ambitious double-crossing scheme leaked a tip to the police that set up Torrio and Capone to be arrested at a brewery the three of them jointly owned. Capone escaped, but Torrio did not. Though he was soon out on bail, even Torrio gave up on keeping the peace, and in November of 1924 he and Capone teamed up with the Genna brothers and arranged a dramatic slaying of O'Banion in his own flower shop. For the hit, Torrio and Capone relied on an old acquaintance: none other than Frankie Yale. When Yale entered O'Banion's flower shop with gunmen John Scalise and Albert Anselmi, O'Banion recognized him and greeted him with a handshake. Yale then held onto O'Banion's hand while Scalise and Anselmi fired bullets into O'Banion's chest, cheeks, and throat, killing him on the spot.

The murder of O'Banion only heightened the now burgeoning gang war between the hoods on the North Side and the Torrio/Capone syndicate on the South Side. The violence continued unabated as O'Banion's allies—including "Hymie" Weiss and "Bugs" Moran—fought to hold onto O'Banion's North Side turf and exact revenge for his murder. Still facing charges and an inevitable trial, Torrio exited the scene for Hot Springs, Arkansas, again leaving Capone in charge. Knowing he was a target, Al took heightened security measures, but even still he just narrowly escaped an assassination attempt by Weiss, Moran, and Vincent "The Schemer" Drucci on January 25, 1925, who riddled Capone's car. The failed attack featured a new weapon on the Chicago gang scene: the Thompson submachine gun, or "tommy gun" as it would popularly be known. Capone quickly acquired his own arsenal, and the Beer Wars took on a new savagery.

Hymie Weiss

Bugs Moran

Two days later, Torrio was himself the object of an assassination attempt. As Torrio was heading toward his apartment after shopping with his wife, Weiss, Moran and Vincent Drucci poured gunfire into Torrio's car, hitting him in the jaw, lungs, groin, legs, and abdomen. Moran walked up to finish Torrio off with a shot to the head but had run out of ammunition, and the three assailants fled before making sure Torrio was dead. Somehow, the severely wounded Torrio managed to survive, spending weeks recovering in the hospital, with Capone providing protection around the clock. He healed only to have to finally face the federal charges that came out of the brewery raid. Though convicted and sentenced to serve nine months, the wounded Torrio pulled the necessary strings and had an easy time of it in jail in a well-furnished private cell. Upon being released, he announced his retirement and was spirited away to New York. Happy to make it out alive, Torrio told Capone, "It's all yours Al. Me? I'm quitting. It's Europe for me."

Capone

Capone was now fully in charge of the Chicago Outfit, but despite his rapid rise to power, he had until now largely stayed out of the public eye. A number of media stories following Frank's murder failed, in fact, to even get his name right. But upon assuming control of Torrio's organization in the spring of 1925, Capone relocated the center of his operations to a high-profile hotel, the Metropole, and made a new effort to enter and remain in the limelight. He carefully fashioned a public image, not as a gangster, but as a well-dressed, charismatic businessman. He became close friends with the journalist Harry Read, who helped school Capone on his public image, and Capone began appearing at public events like baseball games. He even made almost daily visits to City Hall, and though he had no interest in public office, he carried himself like an elected official.

Capone undeniably struck an impressive public figure. Already very wealthy, Capone traveled in style, frequently wearing custom suits, chomping on cigars, enjoying good food and drink, and frequently accompanied by women. Clearly a celebrity, he and the media relished each other, and it was through the media that Capone delivered the classic quotes he was known for: "I am just a businessman, giving the people what they want," and "All I do is satisfy a public demand."

Of course, nobody was more aware than Capone what kind of danger he was actually in. Hand-in-hand with his new public visibility, Capone implemented a series of extravagant security measures. His new headquarters at the Metropole included a network of tunnels originally built for hauling coal but now refurbished as alternate exits. He traveled in a customized armored

Cadillac sedan that weighed seven tons and was always accompanied by a convoy of bodyguards. "Hymie" Weiss and "Bugs" Moran were still bitter over O'Banion's murder and had one by one picked off several of the Genna brothers. Capone figured sooner or later they would come after him again.

Chicago had seen its share of notorious murders over the course of the 1920s, but the killing of an assistant state attorney in the spring of 1926 truly shocked a city that wasn't easily shocked, and it triggered a crisis that would ultimately discredit city and state officials alike.

In a bizarre night that would take months for authorities to unravel, William McSwiggin, the attorney who had tried to indict Capone for murder back in 1924, got caught up in a Cicero turf war between Capone and two rival bootleggers, the O'Donnell brothers. While maintaining a tough-on-crime public image, privately McSwiggin had made accommodations with a number of gangsters, including Capone. With a penchant for vice as a card player, gambler, and drinker, McSwiggin naturally came into contact with and even befriended Al Capone.

On this night in 1926, however, McSwiggin chanced into meeting up with the O'Donnells after he had been out drinking and his car broke down. That same night, the brothers made a fateful decision to go cruising in Cicero, and the group made their way to the Pony Inn, a Capone-run speakeasy near Capone's headquarters in Cicero. Capone got word that the O'Donnells' Lincoln had been spotted cruising his territory, interpreted this as a provocation, and had the group (which also included the sons of two cops) gunned down as they exited a local bar.

As fate would have it, the O'Donnells escaped, but McSwiggin and the two young men were killed. While Capone went into hiding, the city was in an uproar over the killing of a well-known prosecutor whose seedy connections were a mystery known only amongst his associates. The newspapers were full of speculation, and McSwiggin's boss, state attorney Robert Crowe, publicly declared his belief that Capone was behind the murder. He deputized 300 detectives who scoured Cicero and Chicago, looking for clues. Over the course of six months, six separate grand juries were convened, but no indictment was ever handed down. Powerless to find or indict him, public officials began a campaign of harassment targeting various Capone businesses, all of which simply underscored the futility of the high-profile investigation.

Remarkably, Capone remained at large for nearly four months, initially hiding out with friends in the outlying community of Chicago Heights. He then put even more distance between himself and Chicago, retreating 200 miles away to Lansing, Michigan, home to a vibrant Italian-American community, a number of whom had relocated from Chicago. At first keeping a very low profile near a lake outside of Lansing, Capone over the months came out of the shadows and became a visible if discreet presence in Lansing, well-known in the Italian community, and even among public officials and police. Those who knew him during this period invariably describe him as well-dressed, polite, and generous with the community. It appears he took stock of his life at this point, and made a decision to try to reinvent himself as a respectable businessman.

Knowing he couldn't run forever, Capone began a series of unofficial long-distance negotiations with Chicago law enforcement, and in late July of 1926 returned to Chicago and turned himself in. It was a risky move, and Capone casually asserted his innocence to anyone who would listen, describing the murdered McSwiggin as a friend, and even bragging that he was on the Capone payroll. The gamble paid off when the judge quickly dismissed the case for lack of evidence.

Discredited by the fiasco of the McSwiggin investigation, William Dever was ousted from the mayor's office and replaced in early 1927 by his old foe "Big Bill" Thompson. With the amiable and lax Thompson back in office, Capone emerged from his unofficial retirement and assumed a more visible public role than ever. His headquarters at the Metropole expanded to fifty rooms, nearly the entire hotel, and was the site of non-stop drinking and gambling and prostitution. Capone was seen prominently at a wide range of sporting events, especially Cubs games, and was a member of the official delegation greeting Charles Lindbergh after his successful transatlantic flight. He hosted a huge public party following the much-anticipated heavyweight rematch between Jack Dempsey and Gene Tunney, and he even conducted the band he had hired as it played Gershwin's "Rhapsody in Blue."

The year 1927 saw the Capone organization's income hit new highs—over $100 million by some estimates. A brief stretch of violence broke out as Capone skirmished with an up-and-coming rival, Joseph Aiello, trying to move in on the always hotly contested North Side territory. But a few months later, fearing for his life, Aiello and his two brothers fled town. Capone held a press conference and brazenly announced, "I'm the boss. I'm going to continue to run things."[243]

Though Al Capone appeared to be on top of the world at the close of 1927, the elements of his downfall were starting to fall into place. While Chicago Mayor "Big Bill" Thompson was content to look the other way, a new breed of law enforcement officials had no such patience for business as usual. Among these was a new chief of police, Mike Hughes, who promised a crackdown on gangs and hundreds of new cops on the street. Angered by this new policy, and not trusting or respecting Thompson, Capone impulsively announced he was retiring from the Chicago scene—and this time seemed to really mean it. In a long, rambling, self-pitying monologue to the press, Capone declared he was heading to Florida at the end of the year. "Let the worthy citizens of Chicago get their liquor the best they can. I'm sick of the job. It's a thankless one and full of grief."[244]

Though the new Chicago chief of police succeeded at times in making life difficult for Capone, it was three other officials who were ultimately instrumental in bringing him down. The most famous was Eliot Ness, a Treasury agent later hired to work for the Chicago Prohibition Bureau. Ness conducted a series of dramatic raids targeting Capone's bootlegging operation—a story he captured with considerable embellishment in his book *The Untouchables,* later made into both a TV series and a movie.

[243] Bergreen, p. 239
[244] Bergreen, p. 262

Elliot Ness

Ness is best remembered as the man most responsible for bringing Capone down, but in fact it was U.S. Attorney George Johnson, the man who hired Ness for the Chicago office, who played a more substantial role in Capone's demise. He saw to it that, for the first time, various agencies coordinated their efforts against Capone at a high level. Perhaps just as important, and working almost entirely out of the limelight, was Treasury Department investigator Frank Wilson, who worked tirelessly for years to compile a case against Capone for tax evasion. More worried about the various murder raps he was associated with, Capone never took the tax evasion charges seriously until it was too late. They would ultimately bring him down in the early 1930s.

Thanks to the efforts of Capone and his ilk, a stiff drink was easy to find in Chicago. As one historian explained, "Prohibition was defied openly and on a large scale, and many Chicagoans were involved in the illegal liquor business either as suppliers or as consumers. Federal law notwithstanding, fifteen city breweries operated at capacity in 1924 and supplied beer to the city's twenty thousand speakeasies, or undercover saloons. Chicagoan Stanley Kell later recalled that bootleggers hid their liquid gold in his church. "The man that used to distill the booze and beer used to hide it in the basement of the church. Revenue officers would never believe that the church was the sanctity for the beer. I remember going down in the basement of the church, the beer smell was there. I'd say: what are all those barrels of beer doing here? And good Father Healy, he used to be quite a little devil with all that beer down there."[lxx]

It's been estimated that 60% of the Chicago police force participated in bootlegging activities, their silence bought with sums ranging from $15-$500 a month.[lxxi]

Chicago and the Great Depression

The Great Depression was the most significant economic catastrophe to strike the world in the 20th century, and from the Stock Market Crash of 1929 until World War II, the nation faced unemployment on a massive scale. Poverty and vagrancy ran rampant as the nation wallowed in misery and an uncertain future.

Despite this, people continued to live their lives, and the people of Chicago were no exception. One historian noted, "Homelessness reached epidemic proportions. Many Chicagoans lost their homes to banks, as foreclosures in the city jumped from 1,300 in 1929 to 15,200 in 1933. Evictions provoked riots."[lxxii]

A contemporary account of the times related how people "couldn't walk three doors without walking into people's furniture…They evicted a lady, she was sick and she had ten or twelve children. They s[a]t her out in the middle of the street. White, colored, they came from everywhere, they had a meeting in front of the house. What I saw was thousands of people gather there and put these people back in their home. They turned the gas and light on and took up a collection. The police wagon drove into a crowd and turned into a riot. I heard the shots. Four people were killed."[lxxiii]

Shantytowns of cardboard and scrap lumber littered the city, forming perfect breeding grounds for fires and disease. By the end of 1931, 1,500 Chicagoans crowded under the Michigan Avenue bridge to sleep,[lxxiv] while unemployment reached as high as 40%. Those with work often labored for half their pre-Depression earnings.[lxxv]

The city's black population especially suffered. Over 60% of working blacks did so in unskilled jobs during the height of the Depression, compared to only 17% of whites.[lxxvi] A third of the city's population received relief aid between 1934 and 1937.[lxxvii] Housing construction languished, industrial production slowed to a crawl, and even as the nation started on the road to recovery, it trailed behind the rest of the country in terms of recovery.[lxxviii]

Government employees were no better off. "By 1933, fourteen thousand public schoolteachers, denied paychecks for several months, picketed the Loop financial district. Tear gas tossed by police broke up the crowd, but teachers and city workers both continued to demand their pay. Besides the schools, city hall was $280 million in debt, with unpaid employees numbering 40,123. Unlike Mayor Ogden in 1837, Mayor Edward Joseph Kelly could not personally bail out the city. Unlike Mayor Heath in 1876, he could not call on the Citizens' Association to tide things over with a mere million-dollar loan. Not only were the city's debts too huge but civic groups themselves were going broke."[lxxix]

Kelly

Between New Deal relief and funds siphoned from organized crime, the mayor managed to generate a revenue stream regular enough to keep the city functioning. Thus, Chicago's solvency, in part, relied on the city being seen as a political hotspot for President Franklin D. Roosevelt in the 1936 reelection. Thanks to Kelly's political success, President Roosevelt placed him in charge of Chicago's federal patronage.

The influx of New Deal funding allowed for public works that managed to keep things chugging along through hard times.[lxxx] As one historian explained, "The New Deal was extraordinarily valuable to Chicago. One of the government's anti-depression programs, the Works Progress Administration, brought forty thousand jobs to the city. The machine controlled all those jobs. The WPA and a second New Deal program, the Public Works Administration, embarked on myriad construction projects around the city. For examples [sic], during the 1930's [sic] the WPA and PWA constructed the seventeen-mile-long Outer Drive (later renamed Lake Shore Drive) along Lake Michigan, landscaped Lincoln Park, built the State Street subway, erected thirty new public schools, introduced the first three public housing projects to the city, enlarged Midway Airport, and built several new parks. For Chicago's unemployed legions, such projects provided much-needed jobs and paychecks. Grateful Chicagoans thanked Mayor Kelly and the machine."[lxxxi]

Some grew so desperate to revitalize Chicago that they planned something drastic to boost the city's economy: another World's Fair. The fair they planned for was the Century of Progress Exposition of 1933.[lxxxii] The organizer avoided public funding and involving the city's corrupt municipalities, determined that the Exposition stand on its own legs. As the fair advertised, "A Century of Progress was conceived and created to meet your tastes, however varied they may be. On the one hand, science beckons to serious interest, and, on the other, fun and carnival crook inviting fingers. From May 27 to November 1, 1933, the interest of a considerable part of the civilized world is focused upon 424 acres of land that lie along the shore of Lake Michigan, edging Chicago. A little while ago this site was [P]lacid [L]ake. Now, shimmering beside the water, a dream city is risen. It lights the sky with splendor, yet soon will disappear and be merely memory."[lxxxiii]

Extended into 1934, the fair's success was arguable, though at the time it proved incredibly popular.[lxxxiv] Still, it would take more than a fair to end the Depression. As the 1930s wore on, the nation slowly recovered, with employment on the rise and industrial output recovering to pre-Depression levels.

World War II

Like the rest of the United States, Chicago readied itself for the Second World War in ways not seen since the Civil War. Unlike the Great War, Chicago fully mobilized itself for the most destructive conflict in modern history.

One historian described Chicago's war footing, pointing out that "full mobilization began with preparation for enemy air attacks. When air raid sirens sounded, Chicagoans extinguished all lights and sought cover under beds or in air raid shelter[s]. Sixteen thousand volunteer air raid wardens policed the city, searching for the careless who endangered the city's safety by leaving a lamp burning. Chicago journalist Mike Royko was nine years old when the war started. He recalled the air raids from a child's perspective."[lxxxv]

As the young journalist remembered, "The siren would go off and everybody would turn off the lights." The air raid warden would then "go around the neighborhood banging on doors and yelling, 'Your lights are on.' He'd write down people's names if they had a little light on in their apartments. I didn't like this. My parents were downstairs running the tavern, so I'd have to turn out those damned lights."[lxxxvi] Older Chicagoans remembered how the air raid drills brought the war home, making it seem much closer than Europe or the Pacific.[lxxxvii]

With war production in full swing, Chicago's industry finally recovered from the Depression. Factories like Stewart-Warner switched from automobile parts to fuses, instrument panels, ammunition boxes, and practice bombs. The Pressed Steel Car Company joined with Pullman-Standard to build tanks.[lxxxviii] International Harvester built torpedoes, artillery shells, and military tractors. Elgin National Watch built detonation fuses. Thanks to war contracts, $9 billion in industrial revenue poured into Chicago.[lxxxix] The massive increase in production required workers, and to fill the need, 300,000 women joined men in the factory workforce.

Along with government war production contracts, the military and the federal government also funded projects directly. Military facilities required building, refurbishing, and maintaining, and

Chicago was no exception. Indeed, over $100 million in federal funds went toward just that in Chicago alone.[xc] The Great Lakes Naval Training Center was one such facility, and a third of all war-time navy personnel visited the Center at one point during their service. Locals volunteering or drafted for the war mustered at Fort Sheridan, and 10,000 pilots earned their wings at the Glenview Naval Air Station.[xci]

Thanks to increased war production, more blacks migrated north in search of work. One such man recalled his experience in Chicago during the war: "I used to be afraid, too, when my children were smaller. I used to say, "Oh, I would like to do something. I would like to vote differently, but maybe I better not. Maybe this will be changed and it'll be good. I stopped being afraid when I got my first good job. When I got my first big, good—I don't say a big one—the best I ever had, when I got in the defense plant in World War II. I got a good salary. And I didn't even realize how wonderful it was not to be afraid. I didn't even realize it until…later days. But all of a sudden I was just automatically doing what I wanted to do, for the first time since I had children. But it was money. It was a good, fat paycheck, taking it home every week…every week. And it made me feel, well, I was free."[xcii]

Unfortunately, things were not all going well for Chicago's black population during the war. As one historian noted, "During the war, African Americans remained confined to a South Side Black Belt called Bronzeville. It developed jazz, invented urban blues, and generally created a high, uniquely American culture. Reform groups convened a conference on 'The Negro and the War,' urging tolerance. As always, though, the subterranean Chicago history was written by vice. Cook County had impaneled a grand jury in 1941 to investigate gambling. What did it find? 'Shocking conditions.' Negroes gambled even if they were on relief, the panel was appalled to note. Blacks would place bets of a nickel, dime, or quarter on a 'policy wheel,' a canister from which lottery numbers were draw[n]. Policy had been the target of a Citizen's Association anti[-]vice campaign forty years earlier. Blacks did not totally control this racket, although that myth was propagated. Annual revenues were estimated at $7 million. Neither the mob nor the political machine disregarded the attraction of $7 million."[xciii]

Even amidst the devastating war, the city of Chicago could not escape the deep roots of vice etched into its fabric. White or black, overt or covert, throughout the war, vice in the city continued more or less as it had before. With the revenue from Prohibition gone, gambling formed the bulk of organized crime's income.[xciv] The police force, corrupted as usual by easy money, turned a blind eye to such crimes. Even in a time of war, they did little to stop the rampant gambling, though they did make sure to perform plenty of arrests to maintain appearances.[xcv]

By the time of D-Day in June 1944, the civil service commission finally found the nerve to attempt actual reform by firing the corrupt police chief and seven captains for their permissive attitude toward illegal gambling.[xcvi] Such earnest efforts of reform and progress caused some to reminisce on the struggle for change: "Our tax system which was crumbling in 1906 is crumbling still more in 1943. Our difficulties with the general property tax, which were bad enough then, are far worse now…Many efforts have been made to bring about [an urban revenue amendment to the Illinois Constitution of 1870] and thus far have failed…There were in 1933 some 1,642 governmental agencies in the region and there is still something like that. You must get the services of an expert if you are going to count them all."[xcvii]

Indeed, reform efforts reminiscent of the Progressive Era resumed during the war, with efforts such as the Chicago Committee on Racial Equality, formed to document the issue of racism and discrimination faced by Chicago's black population.[xcviii] Such efforts were likely sparked by the large increase in the black population due to southerners traveling north in search of work. While the Black Migration continued, a new ethnic group entered Chicago in numbers for the first time. That their arrival coincided with the war was no coincidence, for it involved a black stain on America's history, well remembered by those who experienced it.

Japanese Americans arrived in Chicago in the worst way, interned as prisoners in their own country. One historian mentioned Chicago's ties to the controversial internment of Japanese Americans on the West Coast in the wake of the attack on Pearl Harbor: "In early 1942, the federal government rounded up 110,000 Japanese Americans from the western states and interned them in guarded detention camps, fearing there were still loyal to Japan and therefore posed a threat to the security of the United States. Later, many of these imprisoned Japanese Americans were allowed to relocate to cities far from the West Coast. Nearly thirty thousand moved to Chicago and became the city's Japanese American pioneers. Most were settled in 'buffer zones; between white and black neighborhoods in the South Side's Kenwood community or along North Clark Street, which dived the North Side's affluent Gold Coast from slums to its west. Local newspapers supported the Japanese resettlement, local employers eagerly hired the new arrivals, and overt discrimination against the hardworking Japanese was rare."[xcix]

Other immigrants from enemy countries also fared poorly. German Americans, used to being discriminated against during the Great War and well-enough established to be able to stay low, managed as they had during the last world war. Italian Americans, however, became new targets, thanks to Mussolini's fascist regime siding with the Third Reich.[c] Facing questions about their loyalty, just as the Germans had during the Great War, Chicago's Italian population assimilated as quickly as possible to avoid suspicions. Fortunately, the discrimination of the Great War by Americans against their fellow Americans was not repeated as much against the Italians and Germans. Local newspapers lauded both the Italian and German ethnic groups for their loyalty.[ci]

The arrival of women's baseball in Chicago was another byproduct of the war. Many baseball players had been drafted, and those who remained formed a hodgepodge of men unfit for military duty. With Major League Baseball's survival in doubt, Chicago Cubs owner Philip K. Wrigley created the All-American Girls Baseball League.[cii] Though Wrigley would withdraw from the All-American Girls Baseball League after the war, the stopgap measure kept baseball alive and ensured a new form of the sport would enter Chicago's sights.[ciii]

Wrigley

World War II eventually ended, and that brought new challenges to Chicago. "World War II soldiers came home and created the biggest, most consistent and expansive prosperity the world has ever seen. At the time, though, Americans feared that the end of wartime production would bring back another depression. The ruling classes, returning soldiers, and their Rosie the Riveter wives and girlfriends were afraid. Whatever President Harry Truman's achievements in postwar geopolitics, his immediate domestic problem was avoiding another peacetime depression amid bitter national labor strikes. Housing and jobs were scarce. Veterans were abandoning their native cities for hastily erected suburbs. Chicagoans faced a difficult transition to a peacetime economy, just as after World War I. traditional reformers valiantly continued trying to improve education, secure clean elections, and put men in jobs through public works."[civ]

The Civil Rights Era

Since before the Civil War, America's black community had been treated as second-class citizens when they were free. After the Civil War, many fought to quash the rights they had received after five brutal years of bloodshed on their behalf. After World War II, new voices rose up to end the discrimination and grant blacks the rights they deserved. Reformers spoke out against racism in every major city, and Chicago was no exception. At the same time, reformers once more fought to straighten out Chicago's infamous crookedness.

Like other cities throughout the nation during the Civil Rights Movement, Chicago saw its fair share of riots. Though it would be some time before Chicago had to face such a riot, Cicero,

Illinois erupted in racial violence in 1951. The result of 4,000 whites rising up to prevent a black war veteran from moving his family to a better apartment, the incident forced Governor Adlai Stevenson to declare martial law in the city.[cv] Following the riot, Chicago carefully worked its housing so that blacks were sequestered in a ghetto on the city's South Side and Near West Side.[cvi] As one historian observed, such efforts commenced at a national level as well: "The federal government's new post-World War II urban redevelopment programs provided the means for keeping blacks in the ghettos. Federal money assisted major cities in demolishing blighted neighborhoods an in replacing substandard housing with low-income public housing. In Chicago, that meant leveling dilapidated homes on the South and West Sides and replacing them with towering high-rise housing complexes. The city council, the Metropolitan Sanitary District, and the Illinois Commerce Commission all possess[ed] veto power over proposed public housing sites; the CHA extended virtual veto power to alderm[e]n in whose wards…housing complex[es were] being considered before suggesting sites to the city council. This system resulted in forty-nine of fifty-one approved public housing sites between 1955 and 1966 being located in all-black areas. The CHA, the one institution that might have challenged the city's formidable de facto housing segregation, catered to white desires."[cvii]

The 1950s was a grim time for Chicago's black population. Unlike his predecessor, Chicago's new governor actively discriminated against the city's black population.[cviii] Blacks remained in the ghetto, unable to escape it without repercussion, and the few blacks with power in the city mostly accepted the status quo rather than risk an incident like the Cicero riot.[cix]

In 1948, the U.S. Supreme Court banned racially restrictive housing deeds.[cx] Slowly but surely, blacks were able to leave the ghetto, and whites fled, in turn, to the suburbs. "White Flight" came to Chicago, just as it had come to other major cities across the United States.

As population movements took place, reformers continued their efforts to clean up Chicago's dirty politics. The greatest block to reform during the Civil Rights Era was the fact that little happened without Chicago's mayor, as reform required his support.[cxi] As the decades passed, Chicago's mayors increasingly centralized their power to get things done, limiting, in the process, efforts at genuine reform.[cxii] When reform came from higher up, the city's mayors had little recourse.

In 1958, the U.S. Senate began an investigation into Chicago's hotel and bartender unions in a high-placed effort at reform in direct opposition to the mayor's office. Led by two of the Kennedy brothers, the committee learned of mayoral protection money rackets and other such unsavory tactics committed within Chicago's government.[cxiii] In 1959, the committee investigated further corruption. Though far away in the nation's capital, the corruption of the city's police brought the charges home.

At the time, Chicago citizens maintained the practice of bribing police when asked for their licenses, handing cash over along with their identification. Eventually, the police upped the ante by joining criminals in robbing retail stores. Such blatant criminal activity roused even the infamously corrupt Chicago to action.[cxiv]

While reformers at home and in the nation's capital struggled to clean Chicago up, the city's black population readied itself to fight for the rights they believed were over a century overdue, and the culmination of their efforts resulted in a race riot. One historian vividly described the riot: "Chicago's predominantly black West Side erupted in violence on Tuesday, July 12, 1966, over a fire hydrant being turned off by police in ninety[-]degree heat. Because of de facto segregation, black children had access to only one public swimming pool; therefore, they sought to cool themselves by using the city's fire hydrants. Turning on fire hydrants for cooling purposes probably started in Chicago when the city first introduced them. In any case, it had become a tradition established by countless generations prior to 1966. As soon as the police departed, residents again opened the hydrant. Apparently determined to show their authority, police returned and turned the illegally opened hydrant off again. Shortly thereafter, the neighborhood erupted into violence. By Friday of that week, two people had been killed, about eighty injured, two policemen shot, and over four hundred arrested, mostly young black teenagers. The damage to West Side businesses and property exceeded two and one half million dollars. Mayor Richard J. Daley requested mobilization of the National Guard from Governor Otto Kerner in order to quell the riot. The fact that such a minor incident involving a fire hydrant sparked such violence revealed the existence of underlying problems in the city of Chicago."[cxv]

40 days later, Mayor Richard J. Daley met with a representative of the Chicago Freedom Movement. Dr. Martin Luther King, Jr. represented the black community following the Chicago Riot.[cxvi] The two sides talked extensively over 10 hours of the segregation affecting Chicago with sit-ins and other non-violent demonstrations as active in Chicago as they were across the nation. The meeting rocked the mayor's office. Daley ruled Chicago as thoroughly as the likes of Huey Long, and as word of the meeting got out, the mayor watched as picketers protested outside his office.[cxvii]

Daley

As the Civil Rights movement continued, the mayor tightened his grip on Chicago, perpetrating violence and corruption the likes of which Chicago had grown all too used to over the years. Between the Civil Rights Movement, Vietnam, and corrupt presidential elections, Mayor Daley had his hands full, even as his health declined.[cxviii]

The culmination of the latest batch of reform occurred when Mayor Daley signed a decree in 1972 forbidding the firing of public workers on political grounds. Though it did little to quell the power of political machines, it provided the foundation for later reform efforts.

This was not, however, the end of Mayor Daley's troubles. As one historian noted, "When he accepted the Shakman decree, Daley had a bigger problem. The new US attorney was taking reform, when [he] considered a branch of law enforcement, into a dimension never contemplated by the Citizens' Association, the Secret Six, Kefauver, the Big Nineteen, or Alinksy, Scala, and Shakman. This dimension established reform as a permanent campaign against public officials and as a fixture inside government itself. The fixture was viewed as necessary because public officials presumably were always vulnerable to corruption. Reform was not the province of goo[-]goos, street demonstrators, labor agitators, religious revivalists, or neighborhood activists so much as it was a program of three-piece-suited lawyers in the US Department of Justice. President Nixon appointed as US attorney for the northern district of Illinois a Chicago lawyer named James R. Thompson."[cxix]

Thompson set his sights quickly and thoroughly on cleaning Chicago up, and it did not take long for him to form a comprehensive list of targets, including corrupt War Sanitation Superintendent Joseph Jambrone, Republican Senator Edward T. Scholl, Alderman Casimir Staszcuk, Cook County Commissioner Floyd Fulle, Alderman Fred Hubbard, Cook County Clerk Edward J. Barrett, State Senator Donald Swinarski, Alderman Joseph Potempa, Alderman Frank Kuta, and Daley's pet private investigator, John J. Clarke.[cxx] Thompson would see all of them arrested for their crimes and corruption, but through it all, Mayor Daley remained in office. Never defeated at the polls, Daley died of a heart attack in 1976, shortly after winning the 1975 election.[cxxi]

The End of the 20th Century

The loss of a major political boss like Daley created a massive power vacuum in Chicago, and the city's response to that vacuum helped shaped it as it moved ahead. A historian summed up just how much turbulence resulted in Daley's wake, writing, "During the Daley years of the late 1950s, the 1960s, and the early 1970s, many Chicagoans had grown accustomed to stability as well as to building projects and landslide Democratic victories. Local politician William Singer observed in 1975 that people voted for Richard J. Daley and the Cook County Democratic Party machine, "not because the precinct captain forced or cajoled them, but because they made a decision that they were for Daley. They felt a great sense of stability in [the] knowledge of what they had…It was an incredible thing. There was an enormous stability factor." That stability came to an end with Daley's death in 1976. As the supremely powerful figure in the CCDP, Daley had been able to control the ambitions of his assistants. They were more or less content with their secondary status, because unseating Daley was unthinkable. With the boss gone, however, local politicians began to war with one another. Daley had controlled the mayor's office for more than twenty years, between 1955 and 1976; over the next fifteen years, five different mayors ascended to city hall. Transition replace continuity; uncertainty replaced stability."[cxxii]

Thus, the reliability and stability of the corrupt gave way to the transitional and slightly less corrupt. The transition of the last years of the 20th century prevented the Democratic Party machine from recovering after Daley's death. With no major head to run the machine, it collapsed less than a decade after his death.[cxxiii]

As the 1980s started, Chicago, like the rest of the nation, faced a recession, one that left the mayor's office looking worse for wear. Labor unrest in both the private and public sectors wracked Chicago during the early 1980s.[cxxiv] Not only did the mayoral office suffer from a lack of solid leadership, but so did the mayoral government staff. One historian remarked of the mayor in the early 1980s, "Few politicians in Chicago's history could match Byrne for her zaniness, madcap, and daring acts that were to mar the solid and substantive acts of her administration. Unfortunately for her, too many Chicagoans mistook her style for her substance."[cxxv]

The fragility of Chicago's government coincided with the rise of a politically active black population in the city. Having fought for the rights they deserved, they gathered their strength and entered the political scene in their own right.[cxxvi] After a rocky start, the effort paid off with the election of a black mayor in 1983.[cxxvii] One historian noted the irony of the iconic victory, pointing out, "Almost all black political leaders in Chicago knew that Washington was their only viable mayoral candidate. Two problems emerged. First, Washington did not want to run. He remembered his crushing 1977 mayoral defeat and the low voter turnout among blacks. It was only after much cajoling and pleading that Washington agreed to consider running, but in return for his concession he requested that one condition be met: he wanted to see fifty thousand new black registered voters. This was a problem that could be resolved with relative ease. An enormous and enormously successful voter registration campaign ultimately registered 140,000 new black voters before the 1983 Democratic mayoral primary."[cxxviii]

Harold Washington

Amid a racially and politically charged election, Washington won by a 46,000 vote margin.[cxxix] With its first black mayor, Chicago's city council turned its back on the mayoral office, preventing cooperation between the seats of city power. Loaded with a corrupt alderman, for the first time since Daley's arrival the council held real power, and they were determined to use it.[cxxx] Washington managed to win reelection, fighting the city council and what remained of the party machine. He was the first mayor after Daley's death to do so.[cxxxi]

The next mayor to take office was none other than Daley's son, Richard M. Daley, at the end of the 1980s. Winning reelection in 1991 and 1995, he was an efficient mayor, unlike his father.[cxxxii] Both he and those who came before him faced the problems of figuring out how to modernize Chicago's economy, especially as it started to weaken.[cxxxiii] Job losses, education issues, and rising crime plagued Chicago and other major cities, and people increasingly fled to the suburbs to escape the urban troubles affecting their cities.[cxxxiv]

As the 1990s drew to a close, the city looked ahead to ending its poverty, crime, and education woes with another bout of reform and development.[cxxxv] One historian observed that at the end of the 20th century, some people believed Chicago was "a dying city with a bleak future. Such pessimistic prognosis [sic] often stem from comparing today's city with an idealized version of the city, perhaps the Chicago of the 1950's [sic]. The city will never return to its glory days, these critics claim. This claim overlooks how the Chicago of 1960 differed significantly from the Chicago of 1925. If history teaches us anything, it is that the Chicago of 2030 will look little like the Chicago of 1990. The only constant throughout the city's history has been chance. Chicago has successfully adapted to new situations and responded to new challenges."[cxxxvi]

Put simply, Chicago was always and still is Chicago. A local song may have said it best of all:

"Chicago, Chicago, that toddlin' town
Chicago, Chicago, I will show you around
I love it
Bet your bottom dollar you'll lose the blues
In Chicago, Chicago
The town that Billy Sunday couldn't shut down
On State Street that great street I just want to say
They do things they don't do on Broadway
They have a time, the time of their life
I saw a man, he danced with his wife
In Chicago, Chicago my hometown
Chicago, Chicago, that toddlin' town
Chicago, Chicago, I'll show you around
I love it
Bet your bottom dollar you'll lose the blues
In Chicago, Chicago
The town that Billy Sunday couldn't shut down
On State Street that great street I just want to say
They do things that they don't do on Broadway
They have the time the time of their life
I saw a man and he danced with his wife
In Chicago
Chicago
Chicago, that's my hometown"[cxxxvii]

Online Resources

Other 19th century history titles by Charles River Editors

Other Chicago history titles by Charles River Editors

Other titles about Chicago on Amazon

Bibliography

Bach, Ira J. (1980), Chicago's Famous Buildings, The University of Chicago Press, ISBN 0-226-03396-1, LCCN 79023365

Buisseret, David (1990), Historic Illinois From The Air, The University of Chicago Press, ISBN 0-226-07989-9, LCCN 89020648

Clymer, Floyd (1950), Treasury of Early American Automobiles, 1877–1925, New York:

Bonanza Books, OCLC 1966986

Condit, Carl W. (1973), Chicago 1910–29: Building, Planning, and Urban Technology, The University of Chicago Press, ISBN 0-226-11456-2, LCCN 72094791

Cronon, William (1992) [1991], Nature's Metropolis: Chicago and the Great West, New York: W.W. Norton, ISBN 0-393-30873-1, OCLC 26609682

Genzen, Jonathan (2007), The Chicago River: A History in Photographs, Westcliffe Publishers, Inc., ISBN 978-1-56579-553-2, LCCN 2006022119

Granacki, Victoria (2004), Chicago's Polish Downtown, Arcadia Pub, ISBN 978-0-7385-3286-8, LCCN 2004103888

Grossman, James R.; Keating, Ann Durkin; Reiff, Janice L. (2004), The Encyclopedia of Chicago, University of Chicago Press, ISBN 0-226-31015-9, OCLC 54454572

Jirasek, Rita Arias; Tortolero, Carlos (2001), Mexican Chicago, Arcadia Pub, ISBN 978-0-7385-0756-9, LCCN 2001088175

Lowe, David Garrard (2000), Lost Chicago, New York: Watson-Guptill Publications, ISBN 0-8230-2871-2, LCCN 00107305

Madigan, Charles (2004), Madigan, Charles, ed., Global Chicago, Urbana: University of Illinois Press, ISBN 0-252-02941-0, OCLC 54400307

Miller, Donald L. (1996), City of the Century: The Epic of Chicago and the Making of America, New York: Simon and Schuster, ISBN 0-684-80194-9, OCLC 493430274

Montejano, David (1999), Montejano, David, ed., Chicano Politics and Society in the Late Twentieth Century, Austin: University of Texas Press, ISBN 0-292-75215-6, OCLC 38879251

Norcliffe, Glen (2001), The Ride to Modernity: The Bicycle in Canada, 1869–1900, Toronto: University of Toronto Press, ISBN 0-8020-4398-4, OCLC 46625313

Pacyga, Dominic A. (2009), Chicago: A Biography, Chicago: University of Chicago Press, ISBN 0-226-64431-6, OCLC 298670853

Pridmore, Jay (2003), The Merchandise Mart, Pomegranate Communications, ISBN 0-7649-2497-4, LCCN 2003051164

Pogorzelski, Daniel; Maloof, John (2008), Portage Park, Arcadia Publishing, ISBN 9780738552293

Sampson, Robert J. (2012), Great American City: Chicago and the Enduring Neighborhood Effect, Chicago: University of Chicago Press, ISBN 978-0-226-73456-9

Sawyer, R. Keith (2002), Improvised dialogue: emergence and creativity in conversation, Westport, Conn.: Ablex Pub., ISBN 1-56750-677-1, OCLC 59373382

Schneirov, Richard (1998), Labor and urban politics: class conflict and the origins of modern liberalism in Chicago, 1864–97, Urbana: University of Illinois Press, ISBN 0-252-06676-6, OCLC 37246254

Slaton, Deborah, ed. (1997), Wild Onions: A Brief Guide to Landmarks and Lesser-Known Structures in Chicago's Loop (2nd ed.), Champaign, Ill: Association for Preservation Technology International, OCLC 42362348

Smith, Carl S. (2006), The Plan of Chicago: Daniel Burnham and the Remaking of the

American City, Chicago visions + revisions, Chicago: University of Chicago Press, ISBN 0-226-76471-0, OCLC 261199152

Spears, Timothy B. (2005), Chicago dreaming: Midwesterners and the city, 1871–1919, Chicago: University of Chicago Press, ISBN 0-226-76874-0, OCLC 56086689

Swanson, Stevenson (1997), Chicago Days: 150 Defining Moments in the Life of a Great City, Chicago Tribune (Firm), Chicago: Cantigny First Division Foundation, ISBN 1-890093-03-3, OCLC 36066057

Zurawski, Joseph W. (2007), Polish Chicago: Our History-Our Recipes, G. Bradley Pub, Inc., ISBN 978-0-9774512-2-7

Free Books by Charles River Editors

We have brand new titles available for free most days of the week. To see which of our titles are currently free, <u>click on this link</u>.

Discounted Books by Charles River Editors

We have titles at a discount price of just 99 cents everyday. To see which of our titles are currently 99 cents, click on this link.

Works Cited

[i] Spinney, Robert G, *City of big shoulders: a history of Chicago*, Northern Illinois University Press (2000), pg. 123-124.

[ii] Ibid, pg. 125.

[iii] Ibid, pg. 125.

[iv] Not that the north was much better.

[v] Baldwin, Davarian L, *Chicago's new Negroes: modernity, the great migration, & Black urban life* (2007), pg. 23.

[vi] Ibid, pg. 23.

[vii] Landesco, John, *Organized Crime in Chicago*, Illinois Association for Criminal Justice (1929), pg. 816.

[viii] Merriner, James L., *Grafters and Goo Goos: Corruption and Reform in Chicago, 1833-2003*, Southern Illinois University (2004), pg. 61.

[ix] Ibid, pg. 66.

[x] Ibid, pg. 67.

[xi] Ibid, pg. 69.

[xii] Ibid, pg. 73.

[xiii] Ibid, pg. 73.

[xiv] Ibid, pg. 74.

[xv] Ibid, pg. 75.

[xvi] Ibid, pg. 81-82.

[xvii] Ibid, pg. 82.

[xviii] Ibid, pg. 83.

[xix] Ibid, pg. 84.

[xx] Ibid, pg. 84.

[xxi] Ibid, pg. 85.

[xxii] Ibid, pg. 85.

[xxiii] Ibid, pg. 86.

[xxiv] Ibid, pg. 88.

[xxv] Spinney, *City of big shoulders*, pg. 124.

[xxvi] Ibid, pg. 124.

[xxvii] Ibid, pg. 124.

[xxviii] Ibid, pg. 125.

[xxix] Ibid, pg. 124.

[xxx] Ibid, pg. 125-126.

[xxxi] Ibid, pg. 128.

[xxxii] Ibid, pg. 130.

[xxxiii] Ibid, pg. 130.

xxxiv Ibid, pg. 130.
xxxv Ibid, pg. 130-131.
xxxvi Ibid, pg. 130-131.
xxxvii Ibid, pg. 131.
xxxviii Ibid, pg. 131-132.
xxxix Ibid, pg. 132.
xl Ibid, pg. 132.
xli Ibid, pg. 133.
xlii Ibid, pg. 133.
xliii Ibid, pg. 133.
xliv Ibid, pg. 133.
xlv Ibid, pg. 133.
xlvi Ibid, pg. 135.
xlvii Ibid, pg. 135-136.
xlviii Ibid, pg. 136.
xlix Ibid, pg. 136.
l Ibid, pg. 136. A rather fascinating subject tin its own right, actually.
li Ibid, pg. 136.
lii Ibid, pg. 137.
liii Ibid, pg. 137. More accurately, southern blacks moved into Maxwell Street, and to this day the region is predominantly African American.
liv Baldwin, Davarian L, *Chicago's new Negroes*, pg. 25.
lv Ibid, pg. 25.
lvi Ibid, pg. 25.
lvii Ibid, pg. 26.
lviii Spinney, *City of big shoulders*, pg. 137.
lix Ibid, pg. 137.
lx Ibid, pg. 138.
lxi Ibid, pg. 138.
lxii Ibid, pg. 138.
lxiii Ibid, pg. 138-139.
lxiv Ibid, pg. 139. Gotta love loose zoning laws.
lxv Ibid, pg. 139.
lxvi Ibid, pg. 140.
lxvii Ibid, pg. 140.
lxviii Ibid, pg. 140.
lxix Ibid, pg. 141.
lxx Ibid, pg. 176.
lxxi Ibid, pg. 177.
lxxii Ibid, pg. 192.
lxxiii Ibid, pg. 192.
lxxiv Ibid, pg. 192.
lxxv Ibid, pg. 193.
lxxvi Ibid, pg. 193.
lxxvii Ibid, pg. 193.

lxxviii Ibid, pg. 193.

lxxix Merriner, *Grafters and Goo Goos,* pg. 132-133.

lxxx Ibid, pg. 133.

lxxxi Spinney, *City of big shoulders*, pg. 197.

lxxxii Merriner, *Grafters and Goo Goos,* pg. 136.

lxxxiii "1933/1934 Chicago World's Fair website", http://www.cityclicker.net/chicfair/index.html.

lxxxiv Merriner, *Grafters and Goo Goos,* pg. 136.

lxxxv Spinney, *City of big shoulders*, pg. 198.

lxxxvi Ibid, pg. 198.

lxxxvii Ibid, pg. 198.

lxxxviii Ibid, pg. 199.

lxxxix Ibid, pg. 199.

xc Ibid, pg. 200.

xci Ibid, pg. 200.

xcii Ibid, pg. 201.

xciii Merriner, *Grafters and Goo Goos,* pg. 147.

xciv Ibid, pg. 148.

xcv Ibid, pg. 147-148.

xcvi Ibid, pg. 148.

xcvii Ibid, pg. 148-149.

xcviii Spinney, *City of big shoulders*, pg. 202.

xcix Ibid, pg. 202. The contrast between the stereotype of hardworking Asians versus lazy blacks is another fascinating subject that is alas beyond the scope of this article.

c Ibid, pg. 202.

ci Ibid, pg. 202.

cii Ibid, pg. 202-203.

ciii Ibid, pg. 203.

civ Merriner, *Grafters and Goo Goos,* pg. 149.

cv Abrams, Charles, "Forbidden Neighbors; a study of prejudice in housing," Harper & Brothers (1955). pp. 103.

cvi Spinney, *City of big shoulders*, pg. 206.

cvii Ibid, pg. 206. Such practices were committee din other cities as well, such as Detroit.

cviii Ibid, pg. 207.

cix Ibid, pg. 207.

cx Merriner, *Grafters and Goo Goos,* pg. 165.

cxi Ibid, pg. 172.

cxii Ibid, pg. 173.

cxiii Ibid, pg. 173.

cxiv Ibid, pg. 173-174.

cxv Shaw, Ronald E. "A Final Push for National Legislation: The Chicago Freedom Movement." *Journal of the Illinois State Historical Society (1998-)* 94, no. 3 (2001): 304.

cxvi Ibid, pg. 304.

cxvii Ibid, pg. 304-305.

cxviii Merriner, *Grafters and Goo Goos,* pg. 188.

cxix Ibid, pg. 189.

[cxx] Ibid, pg. 197-198. Chicago's notoriously corrupt alderman had been an issue since the Progressive Era.

[cxxi] Spinney, *City of big shoulders*, pg. 239.

[cxxii] Ibid, pg. 242.

[cxxiii] Ibid, pg. 242.

[cxxiv] Ibid, pg. 243.

[cxxv] Ibid, pg. 244.

[cxxvi] Ibid, pg. 244.

[cxxvii] Ibid, pg. 245.

[cxxviii] Ibid, pg. 246.

[cxxix] Ibid, pg. 249.

[cxxx] Ibid, pg. 250.

[cxxxi] Ibid, pg. 251.

[cxxxii] Ibid, pg. 253.

[cxxxiii] Ibid, pg. 257.

[cxxxiv] Ibid, pg. 258.

[cxxxv] Ibid, pg. 261.

[cxxxvi] Ibid, pg. 267.

[cxxxvii] Che Smith / Marc D. Shemer, "Chicago", Universal Music Publishing Group, Sony/ATV Music Publishing LLC.

Made in the USA
Las Vegas, NV
30 November 2021